ISBN 978-1-330-96384-5
PIBN 10127085

Similar Books Are Available from
www.forgottenbooks.com

Travels in the Interior of Africa
by Mungo Park

Via Rhodesia
A Journey Through Southern Africa, by Charlotte Mansfield

A Visit to India, China, and Japan in the Year 1853
by Bayard Taylor

Italian Castles and Country Seats
by Tryphosa Bates Batcheller

Captain Cook's Third and Last Voyage to the Pacific Ocean, Vol. 1 of 4
In the Years 1776, 1777, 1778, 1779 and 1780, by James Cook

Travels in Peru and Mexico
by S. S. Hill

A Handbook for Travellers in Southern Italy
Comprising the Description, by John Murray

The Handbook for Travellers in Spain, Vol. 1
by Richard Ford

A New Collection of Voyages, Discoveries and Travels
by John Adams

The Sacred City of the Ethiopians
Being a Record of Travel and Research in Abyssinia in 1893, by J. Theodore Bent

The Outgoing Turk
Impressions of a Journey Through the Western Balkans, by H. C. Thomson

Travels in the Old World
Illustrated, by J. M. Rowland

The Travels of Marco Polo, the Venetian
The Translation of Marsden Revised, by Marco Polo

Travels in Arabia
by Bayard Taylor

From the Gulf to Ararat, an Expedition Through Mesopotamia and Kurdistan
by G. E. Hubbard

From Occident to Orient and Around the World
by Charlton B. Perkins

The Periplus of the Erythræan Sea
Travel and Trade in the Indian Ocean By a Merchant of the First Century, by Wilfred H. Schoff

Five Years in a Persian Town
by Napier Malcolm

Central Asia, Travels in Cashmere, Little Tibet, and Central Asia
by Bayard Taylor

The Bondage and Travels of Johann Schiltberger
A Native, by Johannes Schiltberger

Morning Advertiser.—"In the book under notice we feel the heavy hand of the adept manipulator of matter for purposes of 'copy.' Mr Fraser's words flow calmly along like the current of some broad peaceful river. He deals with two great battles...... and in neither does he quicken the blood by his description of those sanguinary conflicts.......The way is dry, and it is a long time before we feel we can take any particular interest......for the average reader this general survey of an extended field of operations will produce a sense of monotony against which it will be hopeless for him to fight.......A third of the book passes gravely away before we arrive at a point of actual interest.......It may be that Mr Fraser is such an old war-horse that the sight of men dying in their thousands is a subject for calm analysis."

Morning Post.—"Mr Fraser has done eminently well in a field of journalism which boasts such brilliant names as Russell, Forbes,......and his book gives evidence of all the qualities which the war correspondent must possess as his stock-in-trade—cheeriness, readiness and resource, a sense of humour, and a facility for clear and rapid composition."

Northern Chronicle.—"We like Mr Fraser's volume because of the spontaneity and picturesqueness of style, the journalistic instinct displayed in just telling the reader what he wants to know, and the fine grasp he has of the art of effective generalisation."

Outlook.—"The first authentic narrative of Kuroki's campaign which it is possible for a soldier to appreciate......the work of a modest, efficient, and *bonâ fide* war correspondent."

Oxford Magazine.—"The book includes accounts of fighting on land which are in no way remarkable as history or as fine writing. Includes a valuable chapter on the artillery lessons of the war......as a critic of strategy the author is less convincing ......he relies probably on the short memory of his readers to cloak any disclosures which time may make to prove him to have been in the wrong."

Pall Mall Gazette.—"Mr Fraser's book contains some haunting pictures of this vast and bitter struggle. He has, moreover, a sense of humour which lightens up many of his pages, a keen gift of observation, and a happy faculty of setting down his impressions in vivid language."

Saturday Review.—"Gives vivid accounts of the battles of the Yalu, of Towan, and of Manja Yama, and of the fighting generally under General Kuroki."

Scotsman.—"There are many delightful passages in the book......there is a fund of quiet and rich humour in the narrative which is always pleasing. The work is altogether one of singular interest."

The Speaker.—"Mr Fraser's is a workman-like narrative of the progress of the war as far as it concerned Kuroki's division. It contains much interesting matter about the troops engaged, the people of the country, and the conditions of campaigning, written with a rather laborious lightness. His account of the fortunes of the despatch-boat *Haimun* is exceedingly lively reading."

Spectator.—"Mr Fraser has a roving eye for the comedies of life—his narrative of the battles of the Yalu, the Motien Pass, and Laoyung is the work of a man who understands military operations."

Sphere.—"Mr Fraser's book is valuable not merely as a war record but as a scientific essay."

Standard.—"In Mr Fraser's book will be read a clear account, told in easy, breezy language, of how the Far East looks in time of war. Mr Fraser makes many pertinent observations, and his book is throughout instructive and entertaining."

The Times.—"Mr Fraser possesses in no small degree the sovereign virtue of a war correspondent—the capacity to tell a plain story plainly. His criticism of the military operations are often shrewd and to the point, and what he has to say about the preponderating part played by artillery in this war deserves the notice of experts."

Week's Survey.—"Written with much verve and abundant humour."

Western Mercury.—"When the narrative has fairly begun the reader will find that it is difficult to leave it until it is finished."

Westminster Gazette.—"Mr Fraser has a fund of genuine humour which he draws upon as occasion requires with excellent results. Altogether his book is one of great interest."

Yorkshire Observer.—"Mr Fraser is equipped with an alert and impressionable mind, and with a humorous and pithy style of narration—his descriptions of the battles are exceedingly good, and a real contribution to the study of strategics."

Yorkshire Post.—"Mr Fraser writes so brightly of the trials and tribulations which were the common lot of correspondents at the opening of the land campaign that we are sorry when it becomes needful to superimpose tragedy on the comedy of war. This is a book worth reading."

The Short Cut to India

A little Baghdadi.

ort Cut to India

The Record of a Journey
along the Route of the
hdad

FRASER

TIONS, MAPS, AND SKETCHES

Blackwood and Sons

The Short Cut to India

The Record of a Journey
along the Route of the
Baghdad ·Railway

BY

DAVID FRASER

AUTHOR OF
'A MODERN CAMPAIGN' AND 'THE MARCHES OF HINDUSTAN'

WITH 90 ILLUSTRATIONS, MAPS, AND SKETCHES

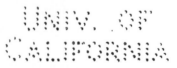

William Blackwood and Sons
Edinburgh and London
1909

DR428
F7

PREFACE.

THE journey recorded in this volume was undertaken with the object of seeing the regions through which the Baghdad Railway is projected to run. Turkey in Asia is in itself interesting country, and offers abundant material to the traveller who contemplates the perpetration of a book; while the fact that a railway to the Persian Gulf affords a short cut to India gives him something to write about of more than local interest.

Owing to an accident on the road which delayed me for some months, publication occurs much later than was intended, with the consequence that events have overtaken me with disconcerting rapidity. My journey was completed at the moment the Young Turk seized the reins of government. The book deals, therefore, with things as they were under the old conditions. As general politics are but slightly touched upon, however, the situation, so far as it concerns my narrative, remains unaltered, and it is only necessary to remind the reader that I had crossed the Taurus Mountains, and written the chapter upon sections one and two of the Baghdad Railway, before the announcement that guarantees for another four sections had been allocated to the Germans by the Turkish Government. Final chapters deal with that announcement, and generally bring the subject of the Baghdad Railway up to date. What I hope may prove of service to students of the question are the appendices, which include the *Convention*, the *Cahier des Charges*, the *Statuts*, and the *Convention Additionnelle*, documents relating to the Baghdad Railway which, so far as I am aware, have not before been available to the public.

I have to express my indebtedness to the editor of 'The Times of India' for permission to make free use of a series of letters which appeared in that paper under the heading of "The Diary of a Traveller."

D. F.

January 1909.

CONTENTS.

CHAP.   PAGE

    I. CONSTANTINOPLE .   .   .   1

   II. RAILWAYS IN ANATOLIA   13

  III. THE BAGHDAD RAILWAY CONVENTION   .   .   .   31

  IV. SECTIONS ONE AND TWO   .   .   .   47

   V. THE TAURUS MOUNTAINS   63

  VI. THE CILICIAN PLAIN   74

 VII. THE ROAD BY CARAVAN   .   .   .   86

VIII. AMONG THE KURDS   102

  IX. ALEPPO .   112

   X. THE EUPHRATES   .   .   .   124

  XI. AN ADVENTURE .   .   .   138

  XII. A CITY OF TERROR   155

 XIII. LOCAL POLITICS   168

 XIV. DIARBEKIR   176

  XV. AFLOAT ON A RAFT   186

 XVI. RISKS OF THE VOYAGE   196

XVII. MOSUL .   212

XVIII. LOCUSTS, SHARKS, AND ROBBERS .   .   .   222

 XIX. BAGHDAD AND IRRIGATION   234

  XX. ON A LYNCH STEAMER .   247

 XXI. BUSSORAH AND THE BAR   258

XXII. ROUTE OF THE BAGHDAD RAILWAY   277

XXIII. THE POPULATION QUESTION   296

XXIV. MAIL CONTRACT AND GULF SHIPPING   308

XXV. THE BAGHDAD RAILWAY QUESTION   318

APPENDICES—

    CONVENTION DE LA SOCIÉTÉ IMPÉRIALE OTTOMANE DU
        CHEMIN DE FER DE BAGDAD   335

    CAHIER DES CHARGES   354

    STATUTS   370

    CONVENTION ADDITIONNELLE   .   .   .   379

LIST OF ILLUSTRATIONS.

FACING P.

A LITTLE BAGHDADI   *Frontispiece*

THE SWEET WATERS OF EUROPE, WHICH FLOW DOWN INTO THE
    GOLDEN HORN   .   .   .   2

SCENE ON THE BOSPHORUS   .

A KEEPER OF THE GATES OF FELICITY   .   .   .

A POOR ARAB WOMAN

MOSQUE ON THE BOSPHORUS   .

COUNTRY-BOAT IN THE GOLDEN HORN

PALACE OF THE SULTAN'S MOTHER ON THE BOSPHORUS .   10

THE SULTAN'S OLD PALACE, WITH YILDIZ KIOSK ON THE HILL
    BEHIND   .   10

BRIDGE OVER THE GOLDEN HORN   10

A BIT OF THE ASIATIC SIDE OF THE BOSPHORUS   12

A NEGRO SYBARITE   .   .   .   30

THE LAST STATION ON THE EXISTING SECTION OF THE BAGHDAD
    RAILWAY   50

"   THE ASPIRING BAGHDAD RAILWAY PURSUES ITS WAY INTO
    THE LONELY WILDERNESS . . ."   50

EREGLI, TYPICAL OF THE STATIONS ON THE BAGHDAD RAILWAY   52

THE MARKET-PLACE OF EREGLI   52

SCENES IN THE GORGE OF THE TAURUS THROUGH WHICH THE
    BAGHDAD RAILWAY WILL PASS   .   54

WHERE THE BAGHDAD RAILWAY WILL PASS   .   70

JUSTINIAN'S BRIDGE OVER THE SIHUN (ANCIENT SARUS) AT ADANA   78

A BIT OF ADANA   80

JUSTINIAN'S BRIDGE OVER THE JIHÛN (PYRAMUS) AT MISSIS
    (MOPSOUESTIA) 80

A MESOPOTAMIAN WELL 104

A KURD WOMAN 108

ALEPPO CASTLE 114

GATE OF THE CASTLE AT ALEPPO 116

A CORNER OF THE OLD BRITISH CONSULATE, AND A HOUSE BUILT
    IN THE ALEPPO STYLE OF ARCHITECTURE, BOTH FLOODED
    BY THE KOWEIK 122

OLD CRUSADING CASTLE AT BIREJIK 130

A TURKISH YAILIEH 130

FERRY-BOAT ON THE EUPHRATES 132

EMBARKING A YAILIEH AT BIREJIK 132

THE MAN WHO DID THE DEED 140

        AND

THE MAN WHO CAUGHT HIM, BIMBASHI MUSLIM BEY, A.D.C. TO
    H.M. THE SULTAN 140

ANCIENT VIADUCT AT URFA (EDESSA) 158

ARMENIAN NURSES 158

THE POOL OF ABRAHAM AT URFA 162

A SWIMMING-POND AT URFA 162

A FAMOUS HITTITE INSCRIPTION AT ALEPPO, WHICH NOBODY CAN
    DECIPHER 176

THE GOOD SAMARITAN WHO TOOK ME IN — THE REV. W. M.
    CHRISTIE OF ALEPPO 176

"BRINGING HOME THE SHEAVES" OF MULBERRY LEAVES 180

OLD CARVINGS AND INSCRIPTIONS ON THE WALL OF DIARBEKIR . 180

". . . RICHLY CARVED PILLARS AND CAPITALS AND FRIEZES OF
    MARBLE AND PORPHYRY . . ." 182

A STREET IN DIARBEKIR 182

DIARBEKIR—THE MARDIN GATE 184

THE KHARPUT GATE 184

READY FOR SEA 186

A FLEET OF KELEKS ON THE TIGRIS 186

A LITTLE KURD GIRL 192

IN THE GORGES OF THE TIGRIS 196

FACE OF A PRECIPICE HONEYCOMBED WITH CAVE-DWELLINGS 198

REMAINS OF A MAGNIFICENT ROMAN BRIDGE . 200

KELEKS ENTERING THE GORGES BELOW HASSAN-KEIF 200

A KURDISH VILLAGE ON THE TIGRIS 204

THE MURDERED YEZIDI . 204

THE WALLS OF MOSUL, OVERLOOKING THE TIGRIS 212

WINNOWING CORN UNDER THE SHADOW OF JONAH'S TOMB AT
    NINEVEH . . . 212

THE BRIDGE OF BOATS AT MOSUL 214

A FUTURE WINNER OF THE ARAB DERBY 214

CHALDEAN WOMEN AT MOSUL . 218

A CHEERFUL GIVER . 218

IRRIGATION WORKS IN MESOPOTAMIA 232

"   THE CREAKING AND SKIRLING AND WAILING WHEELS ." 232

BAGHDAD, SHOWING THE FLOODS BEYOND THE WESTERN BANK . 238

A DEVIL'S ELBOW, AND OTHER SCENES IN THE LOWER REACHES
    OF THE TIGRIS 248

"   WE SAIL IN CONSTANT PERIL OF ATTACK" 250

"   THIS SPORTING OLD BOY AGREED TO LOAD FOR ME" 250

COUNTRY-BOATS ON THE TIGRIS . 252

TURKISH GUARD ON A LYNCH STEAMER . 254

SOME OF THE PASSENGERS 254

EZRA'S TOMB—A PLACE OF PILGRIMAGE FOR JEWS 256

A BAZAAR IN BUSSORAH 256

BITS OF THE BUSSORAH CREEK 266

BUSSORAH—THE KOWEIT GATE 272

THE BUSSORAH CREEK 274

BRIDGE OVER THE CREEK AT BUSSORAH 274

A TURKISH COFFEE-SHOP . . 306

MAP . . *At end*

THE SHORT CUT TO INDIA.

CHAPTER I.

CONSTANTINOPLE.

WHEN the steamer that brought me to Turkey reached the wharf at Constantinople, I put myself into the hands of a hotel tout. Usually I scorn such gentry, but there are moments when even a lord may associate himself with a crossing-sweeper. I had been warned against the Turkish Customs, and against Turkish officialdom in general. Never himself to kick against the pricks is one of the first lessons learnt by the traveller, and in pursuance of this principle I selected a buffer. He knew me to be British long before I opened my mouth; indeed the whole fraternity had marked me down as the one pigeon on board while the vessel was yet far off. Early in the proceedings I had hoped that a kavass would have been sent to meet me, but the official channel through which I had hoped for this assistance happened to be temporarily closed, so that I was thrown upon my own resources. When I fixed upon one gentleman there was much gnashing of teeth among his *confrères.* A

A

big cloth cap, brown boots, and a fresh complexion mark the great prize of the Constantinople hotel-porter. He knows they belong to the simple Englishman, who must have the best hotel, who can never speak a word of any language but his own, who never knows the difference between nickel and silver, who is incapable of understanding foreign currency, and who always pays what is asked for fear of his dignity. Each tout who failed to capture me regarded me as a swindler who had jockeyed him out of a sovereign. This is a feeling that I love to inspire.

A full Major stopped me as I proceeded down the gangway. He read my passport through, blew out his stomach, and waved me past. By degrees very untrustworthy-looking ruffians accumulated my luggage on the quay under the direction of my tout, and when all was collected we proceeded to the Douane. We entered a big room crowded with people and baggage, whereof my ten pieces formed no inconsiderable part. By degrees my things were piled on the counter, and when the tale was complete my gentleman took me to various places where I signed my name, paid for stamps, and said *Bon jour*. This expression is habitual with Turkish officials, its meaning being known to all, and its use implying a complete acquaintance with the French language, where usually none exists. Examination was an important function, to be avoided, whispered my mentor, by payment of a piastre per piece. I got out my money and passed a handful over to my escort, glancing at the Customs officer just in time to observe his eyelids flapping downward. I then said to him in French that I had nothing dutiable, and would be obliged if he would pass my things. My fellow corroborated in Turkish, bowed persuasively, and put forth his fist in that deprecating manner which sug-

The Sweet Waters of Europe, which flow down into the Golden Horn.

gests on the part of the right hand an action of which the left knows nothing. The little blue labels were quickly dabbed on, and the hamals ordered in a deed-is-accomplished-righteously manner to remove those baubles. The tout's right fist gathered courage, the officer lost interest in the proceedings, and without ostentation the money was transferred. My private opinion is that the gentleman in uniform had expected a ten-franc piece, and that he was disappointed to receive only ten piastres, or two francs. But we both *bon joured* with cordiality, and the ordeal was over. From ship to hotel the whole business cost me exactly 8s. 4d., and I imagine not many of my countrymen can claim to have done so much at so discreet a price. "Thank your stars," said a new-made acquaintance at Constantinople, "that you escaped the clutches of the kavass. He would have let you in for a couple of sovereigns at the least."

Constantinople lies on the European side of the Bosphorus, and is cut in two by the Golden Horn. This estuary of the sea has been formed by two small rivers which join together and flow into the Bosphorus near its entry into the Sea of Marmora. The last mile or so of its course is curved like the horn of an ibex, hence the name. The Golden Horn divides Stamboul, the native city, from the European quarters of Galata and Pera, and adds greatly to the beauty of Constantinople as well as to its wealth. Spanned by a rickety old bridge, which opens to let shipping through, the Golden Horn is yet crowded with hundreds of caïques, the picturesque owners of which make a good living by ferrying passengers. People crossing the bridge on foot have to pay each a toll of a halfpenny, while a vehicle is mulcted fivepence. The æsthetic Turk— the Turk has taste—frequently prefers to pay a penny for a caïque, and to enjoy from the blue water a few minutes' peaceful contemplation of his beautiful city, rather than pay half the money to cross on foot and be jostled by beggars and unbelievers.

The Turkish capital has the reputation of being beautiful from the outside, and filthy from within. The streets are certainly not over-clean, but they are paradise compared with the dirt of Peking, or Teheran, or Chicago. The people who besmirch Constantinople's good name are of the kind who travel by *train de luxe* and live in palatial hotels. The homely voyageur who wants to be quit of the European aspect of Oriental towns, can easily forgive somewhat muddy and uneven streets, for he thinks, perhaps, that they are lesser evils than the municipal maladministration or corruption which are so often responsible for scientific scavengy. For practical purposes Constantinople is quite clean enough; it would cease to be Constantinople if it were any more sophisticated than it is.

From the point of view of the traveller life at the Turkish capital has several drawbacks. He will probably find himself domiciled at one of the leading hotels at a minimum cost of twenty francs per day. The price would not be unreasonable if the fare and service were good and extras restricted, but where the waiters are the worst-mannered and the greediest it would be possible to encounter, and the food extremely ordinary, one quickly longs for a change. Having been heavily charged for a room with a blank outlook, with an extra two francs per day for my morning tub, I decided to try a more modest hostelry, where I was given a fine room overlooking the beautiful Bosphorus, and where the cost was exactly half. The Khedivial Palace Hotel is not so fine a place as its name suggests, but for ten francs a day its polyglot owners and attendants do one wonderfully well.

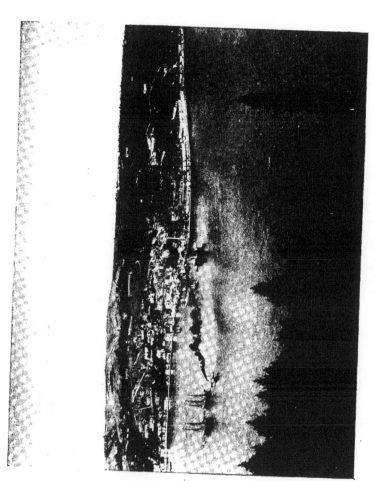

Scene on the Bosphorus.

Settled in the town, almost the first thing with which one becomes acquainted is the coffee, and there being in my memory a recollection of the execrable concoction usually served under its name in free and enlightened England, it may be that lovers of it will be glad to know how the real article may be made. The process is perfectly simple and within the reach of the humblest kitchen. Needless to say, the bean itself should be freshly ground, for ·coffee soon loses flavour. If shut up in a tin, coffee keeps fairly well, but the connoisseur likes it new ground every day. Then as to the grinding, the little handmills used in England are not very effective, for it is imperative that coffee to be made in Turkish fashion shall be ground absolutely to flour. A hole in a stone and a heavy iron pestle are the usual instruments of manufacture, and the poorest household boasts this equipment.

The Turkish cup is very tiny, and contains no more than a small mouthful. For each cup to be served a big teaspoonful of coffee should be used, and the measure of water should be about a tablespoonful. The Turks use a little metal pot with a long handle, tall-shaped so as to permit boiling up. When the water in this utensil boils the coffee is put in and stirred. The pot is then replaced on the fire. In less than a minute the water boils again and brown froth rises to the top. The coffee is then ready, and should be poured into the cup. Connoisseurs demand that the pot shall be brought to the boil three separate times. Usually several small cups are made at once, and the one poured out first is regarded by Turks as the cream of the brew. This, however, is always floury to the taste, and not preferred by Europeans, who like the after cups, in which the sediment settles if allowed to stand. At the top there will then be a strong black liquor, and, below, about a

third of the cup will be grounds. The Turks shake the
cup and drink all of the sediment they can, but the
European taste is for the liquor alone. Arabs never use
sugar, but in Turkey you always order without, with
little, or with much sugar. The medium kind is preferred by Europeans, and consists of half the quantity
of sugar to coffee, put into the water to boil with the
coffee. This may be supposed to be very sweet, but
the brew is so strong that the sweetness proves ac-
ceptable. The Turk usually drinks a mouthful of
cold water before taking his coffee, and a tumbler
ful is always presented with the cup. He drinks up
at once, but the European generally likes to sip.
Strength is the aim of the Turkish coffee-maker, and
the effect on the heavy drinker is sometimes disastrous,
but this need not prevent the visitor to Constantinople
from having all he wants. The coffee vice is not to be
acquired in a day.

The streets and bazaars have been described many
a time, and it is not for me to touch what has been
beautified by the fancy of poets and poetasters. They
are unique to those who visit the East for the first
time, but ordinary enough to the Asiatic wanderer.
One type of passer-by, however, was new to me, and I
observed it with interest. Tall the individual always
was, dressed as well as any duke's valet in melton and
broadcloth, very floppy in the feet, knocked in the
knees, sloping in the shoulder, and generally of the
kind to be thrown down by a puff of wind. His pace
was a laboured saunter, his eye contemptuous of surroundings, his face a perpetual criticism on the vanities
of this world. His colour varied between pure black
and coffee-brown, with a physiognomy that seemed a
blend of Negro and Arab. Think of the face of
Rameses II., whose mummy lies in the museum at

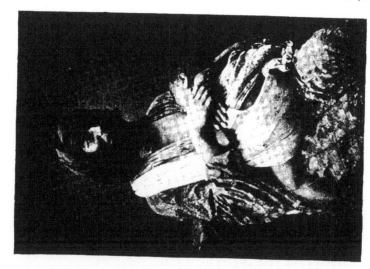

A poor Arab Woman.

A Keeper of the Gates of Felicity.

Cairo, and you have the style of thing. Only there is no eagle in the eye of these loafers of the streets of Constantinople. I wondered who and what they could be, until hearing behind me a strange language in a sweet feminine voice, I looked round to note the speaker. And then I knew, for the voice came from one of these tall individuals with the knock-knees. Keepers of the Gates of Felicity is their official title in the Sultan's household, and a poor job is theirs, for with the cup ever at their lips they cannot drink.

But everything in Constantinople is eclipsed by one of its attractions. Here, between Europe and Asia there lies a narrow strip of water. Nowhere more than a mile in breadth, sometimes only a bare thousand yards, this ribbon of blue wanders to and fro with the aimless perseverance of a river. The current strikes one shore and is headed off to the other in a gentle turmoil of bubbles and whirlpools. The stream placidly follows the direction given it and crosses its narrow channel, until the opposite shore is reached. Here the land suffers its soft embrace for a little time, and the water flows peaceably onward. Then a rocky point intercepts its course, there is a hurrying round the obstacle, and a troubled departure for the other side. And so throughout their path between the Seas the waters are the sport of two continents, hustled from one to the other, bundled backward and forward, worried and buffeted, until they find rest and happiness in the laughing expanse of Marmora.

A prevailing northern breeze banks up the waters of the Black Sea in its southern inlets. Where the Bosphorus offers an opening they tumble through in tumultuous waves and press southward until caged by the shores of the fast narrowing strait. The waves subside, but there is ever the pressure in rear to impel them onward. From side to side the current races, rebounding angrily from the projections that change its course. Peace comes in Marmora. Or perhaps a new wind is met that will hurl it back whence it came, for the southern breeze drives the waters north, despite an everlasting under-current from the Black Sea. So here, where there is no tide, there is yet eternal ebb and flow, ceaseless eddying, perpetual exchange between the great inland seas that are joined by this slender thread dividing East from West.

Though narrow, the passage scoured by the water is deep. The fleets of all the nations might here find safe anchorage together, and yet leave room for ten times as many. On either hand projecting hills rise almost straight from the water's edge, guarding the lane of sea below from storm and gale. The Asiatic side is bluff and precipitous, the European soft and rolling. Everywhere the slopes are dark with forest, or brilliant with lesser vegetation now faintly tinged with the hues of autumn. Every shade of colour from the deep leaden velvet of the cypress to the pale evanescent green of the willow lies steeping in the sunlight. Between its variegated banks flows the Bosphorus, blue as the core of a turquoise, scored with lines of sparkling water where the current runs swift, lying mirror-like in broad bays, ever shimmering, ever moving, caressing its shores with little lapping waves, reflecting every fleecy cloud in the sky, and duplicating its banks upon its own smooth bosom.

Man indeed has been worthy of this triumph of Nature. In every direction the rippling water is cleft by the prow of tiny shallop, stately sail-driven ship, or mysteriously moving steamboat. Brightly painted liners, ugly lumbering tramps, white steam yachts, noisy paddle-boats, graceful Levantine schoon-

Country-boat in the Golden Horn.

Mosque on the Bosphorus.

ers, country sailing-boats, and hundreds of darting
caïques spin a perpetual network of wakes upon
the shining expanse. There is the deep beat of
paddles, the puffing of engines, and the calling of
the mariners ever echoing between the hills. Rolling
over the waters comes the hoarse thunder of a great
steamer's warning to smaller craft, the quick fierce
scream of the steam-whistle eternally cuts the air, and
at each half-hour there floats by in the breeze the
unspeakable melody of a thousand ship-bells.

But most wonderful among the beauties of the Bosphorus are the dwellings that line its banks. To say
there are ten miles of palaces would hardly be untrue.
From the mouth of the Golden Horn to Therapia there
stretches one long line of heavy masonry embankment
against which the water never ceases lapping. Throughout those many miles of shore human artifice has pushed
out into the water a platform of stone upon which
stands one continuous line of palaces, mansions,
villas, and bungalows. Occasionally a narrow road
occupies the frontage, but the bulk of the houses look
directly down upon the blue floor from which they rise.
Each house has its tiny landing-stage, each its river-
door, and each a low dark canal running underneath.
To have a river in the scullery must simplify house-
keeping, but what opportunity it offers for dark deeds!
Many of these water entrances are fitted with heavy
iron gates that prevent ingress or egress, and give
medieval and ominous appearance to places otherwise
bright and cheerful.

The Bosphorus is well served with passenger steamers
plying on either bank. At the bridge which crosses
the Golden Horn is the starting-point, and from here
one morning I commenced the little voyage that I shall
believe to my dying day is the most fascinating the

wide world can offer. The steamers are big paddle-
boats with an upper deck covered with a canvas
awning. They do not compare with the wonderful
castles on the Mississippi, or with the river - boats
of Burma, for they are old and worm-eaten. But the
engines, which mostly date back to Crimea days, are
still full of life, and perform their daily task with a
regularity that says much for the quality of English
machinery of fifty years ago. The lower deck is
thickly crowded with several hundreds of the extraordinary mixture that composes the lower classes of
Constantinople; above there is a well - dressed and
cosmopolitan throng, speaking nearly every language
under the sun. Many of the first-class passengers are
bent on sight-seeing like myself, and among them is
no less than Sherlock Holmes in the very flesh.

We shoot out from the bridge and steer northward.
We are soon in the Bosphorus itself and spinning past
the piled-up terraces of the European quarter of the
town. The tall houses of Pera on the hill behind
glisten brightly in the morning sun, and a few minutes
later we pass a long shining palace, once the permanent
residence of the Sultan. On the ridge above stands
the huge edifice of Yildiz Kiosk, where the Sultan now
dwells, and where has been hatched so much devilry.
Beyond, there are the palaces of the Sultan's mother
and his many relations, all patrolled by sentries who
keep the water - front free of intruders. For miles
there is nothing but the palaces of princes and pashas,
each with its white landing-stage and its terrace of
garden behind. Every now and then we halt, sometimes before a great mosque, sometimes at a little
section of bazaar that has crept in between the
palaces.

Not far north of the city stand the giant remains

Palace of the Sultan's Mother on the Bosphorus.

The Sultan's old Palace, with Yildiz Kiosk on the hill behind.

Bridge over the Golden Horn.

of the Roumeli Hissar, a fortress erected by Moham-
med II. in 1453 to menace Constantinople and dominate
the northern approaches. Stone balls said to weigh six
hundredweight were thrown by the artillery mounted
on its walls. Now an American college occupies a
commanding position above the ancient fort, and bom-
bards Turkey with semi-educated young Greeks and
Armenians, speaking English with a twang like a
banjo. Two more palaces, those of the Khedive of
Egypt and his mother, are the next landmarks, and
then the palaces are succeeded by less pretentious but
altogether charming chalets and bungalows. All Constantinople flits to the upper Bosphorus in summer,
for bathing, fishing, and fresh air. A swimmer takes
his morning dip straight out of his bedroom, while
children fish from the windows all day long. Life
is exquisite in these shady, painted houses, with their
verandahs looking out over the waters and the green
jalousies breaking the glare. It is only when a dead
camel becomes entangled in the wooden piles of the
landing-stages that the delightful monotony is marred.
Then it is as if all the tanneries in the world had
come to pay a visit.

At Therapia are the summer quarters of the various
embassies, and the little inlet that holds the yellow-
funnelled, white yachts of the Ambassadors. From
Therapia a clear view is obtained of the entrance to
the Black Sea, whence a never-failing wind blows
in summer. Beyond Therapia the heavy stone embankment, which runs along the European shore for
about ten miles, ceases and gives way to nature, except
where picturesque little hamlets occur. The northern-
most point touched at by the regular steamers is within
three miles of the Black Sea, and here my boat crossed
over to the other side and commenced the return

journey. The Asiatic shore is not so fashionable, and the stone embanking is much broken, while the houses are often tumble-down. Still for mile after mile they fringe the water, sometimes standing one behind the other in terraces, sometimes throwing up the hillside, while in rear are beautiful gardens bright with flowers and shady with overhanging trees.

Who lives in all these wonderful places and in the densely-inhabited streets and lanes of old Stamboul? The Turk is much in the minority. Every nationality in Europe is represented, from the Finn to the Greek, from the Portuguese to the Hungarian. Easterns of every race swarm in the city. Egyptians, Arabs, Abyssinians, Syrians, Chaldeans, Persians, Armenians, Afghans, Hindus, Jews, Zanzibaris, Japanese, Tartars, Siamese, Malayans, Burmese, Turcomans, Philippinos, negroes of every shape and shade of colour. What do they all believe, what do they eat, wherewithal do they live? Every possible degree of diversity of thought and custom is here gathered together on the shores of the beautiful, magnificent, fascinating Bosphorus. Its hills have looked down for thousands of years upon the changing phases of human existence, have seen fleets and armies, civilisations and religions, come and go like gusts of wind. Common to every age and every period must have been at least one feeling—the feeling that the blue Bosphorus has no rival in the world; that man might wish for no more than to live and to die upon its lovely shores.

A bit of the Asiatic side of the Bosphorus.

CHAPTER II.

RAILWAYS IN ANATOLIA.

MUCH as I should have liked to linger in Constantinople, it was always necessary to remember that the whole length of the Turkish Empire lay before me, and that I must travel several thousand weary miles ere I could return to the shores of the Bosphorus and sit me down in Paradise. For the poor scrivener there is little rest in this world, little reward in lucre, little meed of human sympathy. He is hustled from pillar to post, from Dan to Beersheba, with a heartlessness seldom accorded even to the commonest criminal. Regarded by the established as a mossless rolling stone, by his publisher as a mere machine for the concoction of false literature, he becomes a cynic whose only recreation lies in the telling of traveller's tales, and in the drawing of innocent legs. A woful profession.

From Constantinople my road lay along the Anatolian Railway to Konia, thence to Eregli by the first section of that world-famous scheme, the Baghdad Railway. The train leaves Haidar Pasha—a station, not an old gentleman, as sometimes supposed in political circles— on the Asiatic side of the Bosphorus, at some unearthly hour in the morning, which suggested the advisability of leaving Constantinople the evening before and spending the night in a hostelry adjacent to the railway terminus. Once committed to this plan, I found that

no boats were allowed upon the Bosphorus after sunset,
and that I must catch the last ferryboat at six, or get
up at three the next morning to make connection with
the train. Upon inquiring the reason for restriction
of the water traffic, I was informed that the Sultan
objected to his subjects moving about after sunset,
when he could not keep his eye upon them. Because
of this the Bosphorus is deserted at night, and for the
same reason trains are not allowed to run after dark.
The Sultan lives in continual terror of assassination,
and of revolt against his rule. One of his precautions
against the latter is restriction of travel throughout
the country. To this end has been invented the
teskeré system, whereby travellers of all nationalities
must carry from town to town a document requiring
visa by the police. A teskeré is easily procured by all
Europeans except Russians, but a Turkish subject does
not get one lightly. The price of a teskeré, and its
continual *visa*, is a source of considerable income to
the Government, while the system affords a magnificent
opportunity to the official, who usually makes his unfortunate countryman, who wishes to travel on business
or pleasure, pay sweetly for the precious privilege. A
realisation of this obstacle to free circulation of the
population is essential to an understanding of the conditions of life in Turkey. The restriction shows the
fear that is in the mind of the ruler, and the despotic
power that he wields.

Having reached the quay whence the steamer started,
I had a brief encounter with the Turkish official. A
brass-buttoned individual came up and intimated to
my servant—a Greek youth yclept Socrate—that he
was going to examine my luggage, but that he was
prepared to desist for four piastres — eightpence.
Socrate has great respect for the Turk, and advised

immediate payment. But the irritability engendered
by civilised travel—it is only upon the real road that
one's disposition warms into geniality—made me stub-
born, and I argued that having been through the
Customs on my entrance into Turkey they had no
right to examine my baggage thereafter. The man
showed me his gold buttons and declared himself of
the Douane. But I hardened my heart, and ordered
Socrate to tell him to go away, as I would neither give
backshish nor allow my baggage to be touched. With
tears in his eyes Socrate begged me to pay and avoid
trouble. So then I addressed myself to the Turk
direct, and told him to GO. To emphasise my meaning I shouldered myself between him and my baggage, and turned my back upon him. He hung about
sheepishly for a while and then departed. At the
time I thought it a try-on, but I afterwards heard
that baggage was really subject to examination at the
quay. Anyhow Socrate's respect for his master went
up several degrees, and when a few minutes later I
gave two porters exactly a quarter of what they demanded he began to realise that he served a citizen
of no mean country. He had never dreamed of such
cavalier treatment of the Turk, and, ever since, his
ambition has been to become a British subject.

At the other side we were taken by porters to a low
haunt which the proprietor described as the first hotel
in the place. I was shown the best room in the house,
one with three beds, and told the price was a franc per
bed. I asked for a smaller room, and was shown one
with two beds, which I said I would take at two francs.
When all my baggage was bestowed, the man said to
Socrate that a mistake had been made, and that the
price was two francs per bed, or four for exclusive use
of the room. One gets very tired of Greeks. I found,

however, that one gets much more tired of Greek beds, for during the night I was literally devoured. Never have I welcomed daylight so heartily, and the necessity to be up and off.

At the station the Customs people tried me again. This time I utterly declined to take any notice of them, and warned them off my baggage in an unmistakable manner. A great commotion ensued, and business-like gendarmes surrounded us. Then the station-master appeared and respectfully enough—he was Armenian —asked me why I objected to the examination of my baggage. I declared myself British, and that having been examined when I landed in Turkey I would not submit to it again. He pleaded that it was the regulation of the railway and a mere formality. Finally, we came to a compromise by my allowing them to open a small handbag. Then all my things were tumbled into the train, British prestige having been vindicated and the Turkish face saved.

One hears much of German commercial enterprise in Turkey, and particularly in connection with the Anatolian Railway, which is a purely German concern, though bearing a Turkish name. But on the railway itself there is little to indicate Teutonic surroundings. All the police are Turkish, all the minor officials Turks, Greeks, and Armenians, while the only languages used are French and Turkish. Throughout the whole of three days' journey I saw only a single German, the engineer for the Baghdad section. The system is Prussian as regards the permanent way, and most of the rolling-stock comes from Germany. But the fact is that the people who run the line, though German, care first for their own pockets and next for Germany. They buy or employ what is cheapest or most suitable, and do not care a finger-snap for the origin of an article or a servant. True, much material must be of German manufacture in order that they may retain the political and diplomatic support essential to their welfare in the future. But that support secured, in the case of most German enterprises in Turkey, and schemes fairly afloat, patriotism occupies a small place in the calculations of promoters. The tendency to deal with the Fatherland must always be strong, but it is founded chiefly upon the fact that the German knows the goods available in his own country better than the goods of other countries, that his manufacturers are induced to make according to sample more readily than according to standard, and that credit and banking facilities are more easily obtained at home. But it remains that the majority of German commission agents in Turkey do as much business in English goods as in German, and that they are perfectly indiscriminate in importing into the country what they can sell, regardless of its origin. It does not do to under-estimate the political importance of commercial enterprise on the part of Germany in Turkey, but at the same time it is easy to over-estimate its significance. The master impulse in every German engaged in business in Turkey, as in business men of every other nationality, is to make money for himself as quickly as possible. We have only to look at the defunct Transvaal, or the flourishing United States of America, where naturalisation was, and is, an aid to business, to see how many Englishmen and Germans are prepared to exchange their nationality for another which shall afford them the opportunity to attain greater personal prosperity. Patriotism is a great and overwhelming sentiment in moments of crisis, but in the everyday affairs of life it is frequently forgotten.

Hardly is Haidar Pasha left behind than the rail-

road swings south-east towards the shores of the Sea of
Marmora. Sometimes the train runs along the top of
a cliff which affords an extensive view of the lovely
islands dotting the blue water, and again it descends
to the very edge of the clear tideless sea whose tiny
waves lap the embankment within a few feet of the
grinding wheels. Little bays curve the coast-line,
in each a miniature Naples, with its white houses
and green background reflected in the placid mirror-
like water. Small fishing-villages appear every now
and then, each with its little fleet of boats suspended
in the transparent depths. The small stone piers are
picturesque affairs, busy in a somnolent sort of fashion,
occasionally given up to red-fezzed and baggily-trousered
urchins who play with the shrill abandonment of irresponsible childhood. For half the day we skirted these
idyllic shores; then the scenery changed.

At Ismid we entered a great level plain, thickly
populated and widely cultivated. This broad stretch
of alluvium presaged the neighbourhood of mountains,
and soon we found ourselves in a maze of foothills
amidst which the train wound in and out with much
heavy labour. Consultation of the map showed a distant snow-capped peak to be the Mysian Olympus of
old, and it came home to one that the train rolled over
classic ground. Two hours out of Ismid we began to
rise in earnest, and at a station called Biledjik the
altitude was recorded as 900 feet. This, however,
proved to be but the beginning of the climb to the
central plateau of Asia Minor. From Biledjik the
railroad makes a most remarkable ascent. In exactly
ten miles we rose just 1024 feet, which amounts to the
heavy grade of 1 in 50. Speed fell off to six and seven
miles per hour, and in places it seemed as if we must
stick altogether. Meanwhile the view was most im-

pressive, for we curled in and around and through the
spurs of a great wall of rock that dominated a narrow
valley far below. After one wide curve the little town
of Biledjik seemed to lie at our feet, the people to be
no bigger than flies, the foaming river a mere thread
of silver. Up and up climbed the train, through a
dozen tunnels, over innumerable bridges, along magnificent gorges, until darkness came and I could see no
more. For varied scenery, exquisite on the shores of
Marmora, dark and forbidding in the gorges that give
approach to Guiveh, grand and impressive on the
mountain side above Biledjik, there are few railways
in the world that can equal the first day's journey on
the Anatolian line. At Eski-Shehr we halted for the
night, having taken thirteen hours to cover the moderate distance of 194 miles. Deducting stoppages our
average speed came to no more than eighteen miles per
hour, while inclusive of halts we progressed at the rate
of only fifteen miles in the hour, showing that if it were
not for the scenery travelling on the German railway
would not be an exciting pastime.

Eski-Shehr stands at a height of 2400 feet above the
sea, and is worthy of notice on account of the remarkable development it has undergone since the advent of
the railway in 1892. From here diverge the lines to
Angora, Konia, and Constantinople, constituting Eski-
Shehr the centre of a system totalling 1033 kilometres
in length. A mere village in pre-railway days, German
enterprise has changed it into a flourishing town. Being
selected as the principal depot of the railway, it quickly
sprang into prominence, and now it is one of the busiest
places in Anatolia. The railway alone represents a population of 600 families, the adults of whom are drivers
or guards for the trains, engineers for the workshops,
or porters to deal with the heavy traffic. The total

rolling-stock of the system, said to number 50 locomotives and 2000 carriages and trucks, is housed and repaired at Eski-Shehr. The workshops are large and finely equipped, all the plant, said to be worth several hundred thousands sterling, coming from Germany. Over 400 men are employed, of whom very few are Germans, the great majority being Turks, who seem to show much aptitude for engineering, with a sprinkling of Greeks, Armenians, Italians, Austrians, &c. Out of 700 men connected with the railway at Eski-Shehr, I was told that less than twenty were German. Two doctors maintained by the company for the benefit of the employees are Greek. A school, established by the company for the education of the children of employees, is conducted on purely German lines, instruction being given in the German language, the subjects including German, Armenian, and Greek, Turkish and French being obligatory. The school has an attendance of 100 altogether, of which 60 are Greeks, and of the others only a few are Germans, or German-speaking Austrians or Swiss. From all of which may be deducted the conclusion, already indicated, that the Germans are much more concerned to run their line economically, than to bring swarms of their countrymen from home at high expense.

The chief export from Eski-Shehr is grain, but a less bulky and much more valuable commodity found in the neighbourhood runs it close. Of meerschaum Eski-Shehr is the largest producer in the whole world, three separate mines situated within a few hours' journey of the town being the only important ones known. Native miners rent a claim from the Government and do their own digging. The raw product is sold to agents for Austrian firms, who clean and polish it, and export it to Vienna in a half-finished condition. The Government makes £8000 per annum out of the mining rights and royalties. In our school-days we were given to understand that meerschaum was petrified sea-foam, but I understand that it is nothing but clay of a fine and peculiar quality, with a chemical name of no profit to know. How one's illusions drop away with increasing years! Eski-Shehr is celebrated for one other thing, and that is the hotel of Madame Tadia. Madame's nationality I know not, nor do I know whence sprang Monsieur, long deceased. But I do know that Madame provided me with a sweet, clean, and comfortable bed for one franc, and that her ability to manufacture Scotch broth and *café au lait* is descended upon her straight from heaven.

From Eski-Shehr the original line of the Anatolian Railway runs due east to Angora, known to the ancients as Ancyra of the Phrygians, and to Europe as the home of a scarce breed of goat. This is the route by which the Germans originally planned to proceed towards Mesopotamia and Baghdad, but from which circumstances diverted them. The branch line to Konia leaves the old main line to continue its course along the northern half of Asia Minor, and makes a long southern detour until at Afium-Kara-Hissar it enters the territory of the rival railways from Smyrna. Of the Smyrna-Aidin it is sufficient here to say that it is a British concern, costs the country nothing, and gives a dividend to its share-holders. It is to the Turk a standing illustration of what honest enterprise can do for all concerned. Curious that, in spite of the object-lesson afforded by this railway, the Turkish Government has deliberately permitted another concern, at great expense to Turkey, to encroach upon the hinterland marked out by nature for extension of the British line. The Anatolian Railway from Constantinople costs the Government untold francs per annum for every kilometre of its length, and it has crossed the path of the Smyrna-Aidin concern so as completely to check further development. Nearly all that the German line has done the British line might have done for Turkey, at no expense to Turkey. Not only has this British railway been disappointed of its reasonable hopes, but it is denied the right to connect its line with its German rival, which would give the opportunity of quoting through rates to its patrons. In this respect the other Smyrna line has had more success, for it has effected a junction while the Smyrna-Aidin has never got within fifty miles of the German line.

The Smyrna-Kassaba Railway owes its existence to British enterprise, and in 1873 had reached Ala-Shehr, the old and original Philadelphia, a distance of some 170 miles from Smyrna. After the lapse of a certain period, under the terms of the concession the Turkish Government possessed the right to take over the railway, and this they exercised. So far the railway had done very well commercially, but the Turks were heavily backshished by a French syndicate, and exercised their right only to transfer the line from British to French control. Heretofore this railway had enjoyed no guarantee from the Turkish Government, but as a French company was to furnish the funds to buy out the British company, the new capitalists stipulated for a guarantee. This was provided at the rate of 2,310,000 francs per annum, for the whole distance of 266 kilometres. For extension of the line to Afium-Kara-Hissar, another 18,881 francs of annual guarantee per kilometre was to be found by the Turkish Government.

The original portion of the line has cost Turkey alto-

gether no more than £160,000 in guarantees, for by
the terms of the agreement the guarantee declines as
the takings increase. During the last few years there
has been steady improvement in traffic, and hereafter
it may be assumed that the original portion of the line
will constitute no charge on the revenues of the country. In regard to the extension, however, the position
is very different. Commenced in 1897, the line was completed during the following year, since when Turkey
has paid an average guarantee of £140,000 annually.
There is little perceptible improvement in traffic, and
I believe it is a fact that the company are making
small efforts to effect improvement, being content to
rest on their oars and draw the guarantee. This
guarantee, as already mentioned, amounts to 18,881
francs per annum per kilometre. Allowing for an
expenditure on construction of £8000 per mile — I
am assured by a railway expert who knows the line
and the country that this is an ample estimate—we
find that the guarantee is equivalent to 15 per cent
per annum on the capital sum involved—viz., 251 kilometres = 157 miles × £8000 = £1,256,000. The company
of course is bound to maintain a service of trains, which
runs away with a good deal of their income from the
Turkish Government; but it remains that after deduction of working expenses, calculated on the same scale
as paid by the Baghdad Railway to the Anatolian
Railway for management of their line (*vide* page 53),
there is still enough left to pay the dividend of 12 per
cent to shareholders. The Company's accounts, however, show only dividends of a most modest character,
and one wonders where the discrepancy lies. But
when it is discovered that debentures for 70,000,000
francs, or £2,800,000, were issued in connection with
the prolongation, and it is recollected that the pro-

longation must have cost less than half this sum to
build, we realise that upon construction were made
enormous profits, which it has been thought discreet
to conceal.

Here we have an excellent illustration of the utter
perniciousness of the guarantee system as imposed
upon the Turks by greedy foreign financiers. The
company exploiting this section of railway have found
for them annually a sum of money which pays working expenses and a dividend. Every penny earned
by the railway, up to the limit of the guarantee,
goes, not into the pockets of the shareholders, but
towards diminution of the guarantee provided by the
Turkish Government. Obviously, while traffic receipts
remain far below the figure of the guarantee, it is a
matter of indifference to the company how much the
railway earns. In fact, the company have only one
real anxiety, and that is to comply with conditions
as regards maintenance of a train service at the
least possible expense to themselves. Every penny
they save in working goes into their own pockets.
The trifle they make in earnings does not enrich
them, but merely reduces the Turkish liability for
guarantee. Under these conditions it pays a railway
company positively to discourage traffic. Certainly
we cannot conceive of the purchase of new rolling-
stock, or the lowering of rates, or of any other steps
which will add to working expenses. The company
being run on commercial and not on altruistic lines,
we cannot expect from them anything but a policy
of *laisser faire*, a situation extremely unfortunate for
Turkey.

This ill-used country seems to have very bad
fortune in all that concerns railways. When the
Kassaba line was extended to Afium-Kara-Hissar,

junction was effected with the Anatolian line, which brought Smyrna into direct communication with Constantinople. From a western point of view nothing could be more desirable, or more propitious of advancement, than the establishment of railway connection between the two chief commercial centres. The distance between Smyrna and Constantinople by the railway route is about the same as that between London and Inverness, and capable of being traversed in twelve to sixteen hours. But instead of the joyful inauguration of an express service, which would carry mails and stimulate business in a variety of ways, something quite different happened.

Smyrna is the ancient outlet for the trade of Asia Minor, and most of the important caravan routes converge upon it. The tendency for commerce to gravitate towards the markets of the world along the lines of least resistance remains true whether transport is by railway or cart or camel. No sooner was the Smyrna line linked up with the Anatolian system than exports from the central plateau of Asia Minor began to show an inclination to desert the Constantinople route and to revert to the old one to Smyrna. For instance, grain from Konia could be passed along the Anatolian line to Afium-Kara-Hissar, transferred there to the Kassaba line, railed to Smyrna and shipped, more cheaply than if it were sent through Constantinople. The consequence was a raising of rates between Konia and Afium-Kara-Hissar which defeated this tendency. It now costs on the Anatolian Railway to send wheat from Konia to Constantinople (759 kilometres) £T20 per truck, as compared with £T13 to Afium-Kara-Hissar (272 kiloms.), a discrimination that entirely kills transport *viâ* the last-named place, whence there are still

to be incurred the rates to the coast at Smyrna, another 517 kilometres. There has been established at
Constantinople (Haidar Pasha station) in recent years
a quay company which charges heavy dues and other
expenses on goods arriving at the terminus. There is
identity of interest between the quay company and
the railway company, which results in co-operation in
the endeavour to bring as much traffic as possible to
Constantinople. Already stultified by the rivalry between the two companies, the junction next suffered
complete destruction, for the Sultan, in pursuance of
his futile and disastrous policy of restricting travel and
communication, ordered that the rails connecting the
two stations at Afium-Kara-Hissar should be torn up
altogether. This, be it noted, is the doing of a
Government who subsidise the railways concerned to
the extent of some £350,000 annually, money spent,
presumably, with the object of developing the economic
condition of the country. Turkey would seem to
have a monopoly of this preposterous variety of inconsistency.

My lonely journey along Asia Minor was to be
pleasantly interrupted at Afium-Kara-Hissar—Afium
is Turkish for opium, a commodity widely cultivated
in the neighbourhood—by a meeting with two British
officers, engaged upon the characteristic pursuit of
game. They had made an interesting trek in the
interior, and were making use of the railway to reach
a new base of operations at Konia. They were both
young, which did not prevent their possession of beards
worthy of Abraham. I gave a tea-party in my compartment and found my newly laid in butter, sardines,
jam, &c., greatly appreciated. My guests had been
without many of the frills to existence for some time,
and ate with a heartiness that did the Service credit.

Few things delight the British taxpayer so much as to see his hard-earned money spent in the manner chosen by my young friends. They knew nothing of Turkey or its language, but just launched themselves into the only big game country within reach of their limited leave. They had roughed it with a vengeance, and were keen on continuing until the last moment possible. What better training could there be for field work, and what finer expression of the soldierly spirit could there be than this deliberate choice of the hard and enterprising life entailed by a sporting expedition in a semi-civilised land? We are prone, some of us, to grudge our soldiers their frequent furlough, but when it is spent in this manner the soldier is keeping himself in condition and fitting himself for his profession to a degree possible in no other way except by active service. It has been my privilege in recent years to see a little of the Continental officer in contiguity to his British *confrère*, and if I may say so without the appearance of patronage, I would like to express the opinion that the British officer has nothing to fear from comparison. It is possible that the foreigner is a trifle more scientific, though even that is not sure in these days of strenuousness in our army. But for the practical man, with a knowledge of woodcraft, with an eye for country, with experience of camp life, with highly developed stamina and powers of endurance, for in fact much that makes the ideal regimental officer, give me the British officer to back against any other in the world. It seems a little unnecessary thus to paint the lily, but it has happened within the last year or two that I have frequently heard it regretted that the journalist should be so down on the soldier. I cannot answer for the whole of the profession, but I am glad to take the opportunity to speak for myself.

Konia reached, we all made for the local hostelry, which turned out to be a palatial building entitled the *Hôtel du Chemin de Fer de Baghdad*. At the station we were interested to find a beautiful *train de luxe*, with a saloon decorated with flowers and upholstered in crimson morocco, compartments luxuriously fitted with beds, toilet, &c. ˙ This we discovered to be the special train of the German Ambassador, who was engaged in his annual tour of inspection. While we were arguing about our luggage at the station, there came a rush of obsequious Turkish officers brushing everybody out of the way of a modest-looking but imposing gentleman in a top hat. I was facing the movement, and at once gave way before my betters. But one of the young officers had his back to the Ambassador, and when the Turks tried to hustle him out of the way he just turned mildly upon them and wanted to know what they meant by shoving him. Meanwhile the Ambassador walked round the obstacle without ado, but the Turks were completely flabbergasted to find the great man so treated — unintentionally of course — and the culprit showing no signs of guilt. At the hotel with the significant name there was a better dinner than usual, owing to the fact that the Ambassador was giving an entertainment to his compatriots. We each had two rounds of ice-cream, and I was rejoiced to think how unsophisticated my inside remained, after all these long years.

Konia, the ancient Iconium, is a very old city, and said to be the first place to emerge after the Deluge. St Paul visited it twice, once in company with Barnabas, and the other time with Timothy. It was here that the great apostle was taken for a heathen god, and had much ado to prevent the

priests of Jupiter doing sacrifice to him. There are
very few signs of the ancient civilisation visible, the
town being now entirely modern. The advent of the
Anatolian Railway has brought considerable prosperity,
many Greeks and Armenians, and a few Europeans,
doing a large trade. A branch of the Ottoman Bank,
managed by a Syrian Agent who speaks excellent
English, pays very well.

Konia is the scene of an endeavour on the part of
the Turkish Government to populate a wide region
that only needs inhabitants to blossom forth into great
productivity. Even the Sultan cannot augment the
population, either by natural or supernatural means,
so that the civilised device of immigration has been
employed. The Government keeps agents in the
Crimea, the Caucasus, Roumelia, and elsewhere to
invite Mahomedans to transfer their place of residence.
The great inducement is the change from Christian
countries to a Mahomedan country. Immigrants are
promised land, houses, seed - corn, &c., and all the
facilities for making a new start in life. The object
is plain enough, and would be entirely laudable if
effectively striven after. Increased cultivation will
bring increased revenue, the influx will provide further
population from which to recruit the army, while the
strengthening of the Mussulman, as compared with
the Christian element, will tend to ease the question
of Mussulman *versus* Christian, which is always to the
fore in Turkish politics. Unfortunately, however, this
excellent policy is not pursued in a manner likely to
have the desired result. An Emigration Commission
in Constantinople discusses with local authorities the
allocation of immigrants arriving in the country.
Numbers of unfortunate families are dumped upon
communities whose officials would rather not have

them.   When arrived they are given land, of which
there is plenty, but the houses and corn are quite
another matter.   The local authorities are already
harassed by demands for remittances to Constantinople, and the infliction of immigrants simply adds
to their difficulties.   The consequence is that the
unfortunate newcomers fall between two stools, their
sufferings usually being of the kind that only the
patient Oriental can endure.   Within the last ten
years some 2000 families have been brought into the
Konia district.   Terrible mortality occurs among the
children and old people, and when at last something
is done it is often after the sufferers are broken in
health and spirit.   I saw in Konia long rows of miserable huts in which were a remnant of people who had
arrived two years before, many of whom had died of
starvation, and some of whom were kept alive only by
charity.   Apparently most of the promises made to
them by the Turkish Government had been broken.

A Negro Sybarite.

CHAPTER III.

THE BAGHDAD RAILWAY CONVENTION.[1]

ONE of the biggest feats of legerdemain performed in recent times is that involved in the formation of a company to build a railway to Baghdad. Commercially such a railway would seem to be of great importance, while politically and strategically its construction might have far-reaching results. (The maker of the line is Germany; by its means Germany is to colonise Asia Minor, reduce Turkey to vassalage, absorb Mesopotamia, oust Great Britain from the Persian Gulf, and finally to extend the mailed fist towards India.) I am not aware that any pan-German has ever actually said that India is to be the ultimate reward of Teutonic enterprise, but I have no doubt that many have thought so. Anyhow, many sanguine Germans expect that construction of the railway will lead to some of the other consequences set forth, and it would seem, also, that some pessimistic Englishmen think that what Germans desire must come to pass if England stands by and permits Germany to proceed. To endeavour to discover what Germany has to gain by construction of the railway, and what England stands to lose, was the main object for which the

---

[1] The texts of the Convention and subsidiary documents appear in the Appendices.

journey recorded in this volume was undertaken. My
route followed closely along the proposed alignment of
the railway, and as the country traversed suggests
observations bearing upon the subject, they will be
interpolated in my narrative. Meanwhile a brief
review of the history of the scheme, and of the circumstances that led to its development, may not be
unwelcome to readers who have not studied the
question.

The idea of a railway to Baghdad is a very old one,
the first to push the matter, so far as I am aware,
being Mr, latterly Sir William, Andrew, an Indian
railway official of considerable renown. Sir John
Macneill and General Chesney in 1857 reported upon
the route between Alexandretta, in the north-east
corner of the Mediterranean, and Bussorah, the river
port near the head of the Persian Gulf. Their estimate was for 1000 miles of railway, at a cost of £7500
per mile, giving a total of about seven and a half
millions sterling. They apprehended no serious engineering difficulties, and were of opinion that the railway must soon pay its way. There was then, of course,
no question of a guarantee. For twenty years the
enthusiastic Andrew advocated his scheme, writing of
it that it "will bind the vast population of Hindoostan
by an iron link with the people of Europe," grandilo-
quent sentiment that did not sound sufficiently attractive to the financiers of those days. But in 1872 Andrew
triumphed to the extent of obtaining the appointment of a Select Committee of the House of Commons
to examine the question. The Committee went deeply
into the matter and finally approved of the idea, the
Government of India concurring. Nevertheless the
nimble financier was not to be drawn, and funds were
never forthcoming. The Egyptian trouble in the early

eighties gave the Euphrates Valley Railway scheme, as it was then known, a tremendous fillip, for it was feared that Arabi Pasha would damage the Suez Canal, and break our line of communication with India. Our occupation of Egypt immediately thereafter, and the assurance of the safety of the Canal thereby secured, put an end to all idea of the necessity of an alternative route to India, and Sir William Andrew's hopes were finally blasted.

Before proceeding to discuss the more modern history of the scheme, however, it will be instructive, in view of the present political situation in Turkey, to note the then relations between Turkey and ourselves as indicated in some of the papers placed before the Parliamentary Committee of 1872. The projectors of the scheme entered into correspondence with the Turkish Ambassador in London, and obtained from him the assurance that his Government gave it their full support. "You are well aware," wrote Musurus Pasha to Sir George Jenkinson, M.P., one of the projectors, "that I should like to see constructed a railway from Constantinople to Bussorah, and the Imperial Government would readily grant the same terms for making it; but as I fear this is more than can be accomplished at present, I content myself with the line from the Mediterranean for the Persian Gulf: whether the valley of the Euphrates or Tigris be preferred is immaterial for me; but it seems that by the former, which has been already surveyed, the railway would be the cheapest and easiest to be made, in consequence of the flatness of the country, and therefore the cheapest. So that you see it is not the conditions of the Turkish Government which are wanting to any other line, but rather because of the cheapness and natural advantages offered by the Euphrates Valley

C

route, especially to England, whose assistance is requisite."

This letter was written in 1871, when British influ ence was paramount in Constantinople, and when we had only to ask for concessions to receive them. One of the great advantages presumed for the railway was that it could be used for the transport of troops and military material to either India or Persia—the latter contingency always possible in view of Russian activity in Central Asia. Turkey had nothing to say against our plans, and indeed every aspect of the question was discussed in a manner that suggested that the territory in which the railway was to be built was British, and not Turkish at all. Contrast English influence of those days, as indicated by the tone of the Turkish Ambassador's letter, with our position in Turkey to-day! The reigning Sultan was then our special pro-tégé, England was the sworn protector of Turkey, and the Kaiser still in swaddling-clothes. Now we are the Sultan's deadliest enemy, to the fate of Turkey we would appear to be almost indifferent, and the Kaiser is the special guardian of the Sick Man.[1]

Mr Gladstone's return to power in 1880 marked a great change in our relations with Turkey. Hitherto we had regarded the Ottoman Empire as constituting a valuable defence against aggression upon our line of communication with the East, and to maintain its in-dependence we had intervened when the Russian army was at the gates of Constantinople during the Russo-Turkish war. It was the presence of our fleet in the Bosphorus that alone prevented Russia from obtaining possession of the waterway between the Black Sea and the Mediterranean. We saved Turkey then, not for

---

[1] This was the situation when the writer made his journey in Turkey. Recent events have resulted in a revolution in international relationships at Constantinople.

philanthropic reasons, but because we were compelled
for our own sake to keep Russia within bounds.   Our
action earned for us in Turkey great gratitude, which
exists among many Turks to this day.   But our occupation of Egypt followed very shortly, and the goodwill entertained for us by the Sultan disappeared.
With England in possession of Egypt, and with the
key of the door to the East in her pocket, Turkey's
strategic position as regards our eastern communications declined in importance, and our former policy of
bolstering up the Ottoman Empire was abandoned.
This desertion, combined with our occupation of the
territory of a Turkish vassal, our attitude towards
the Armenian question, and such pinpricks as Mr
Gladstone's denunciation of the Sultan as the "Great
Assassin," resulted in complete loss of the prestige we
had hitherto enjoyed in Constantinople.

This state of affairs gave Germany her opportunity,
and the Emperor William's steadfast friendship for
the Sultan, maintained even when all Christendom
was aghast at the Armenian atrocities, earned for
Germany the place we had wantonly vacated.   German
influence became paramount where formerly British
counsels were regarded as law. I Germany lost no time
in profiting by her opportunities, a course deemed
highly Machiavellian by many people in England, but
for which we, at least, ought to venture no condemna-
tion in view of our own strict adherence to business
in our dealings with Turkey.   The moment Turkey
ceased to be valuable to us we dropped her like a hot
coal, while we had no hesitation in ignoring Turkish
susceptibilities when the Egyptian opportunity offered.
No wonder the Sultan gave freely to his new friend,
nor must we forget that Germany has had to pay for
her privileges in various political ways.

An early expression of Germany's newly acquired

influence in Constantinople was the granting to a German syndicate of a concession for the construction of a railway to Angora, a town in the middle of Asia Minor, but considerably nearer the Black Sea coast than that of the Mediterranean. There already existed a short line to Ismid, on the sea of Marmora, and from this point the Germans commenced construction in 1889. In 1893 the line was completed to Angora, measuring, together with the section from Constantinople to Ismid, which was transferred to the new Anatolian Company, 578 kilometres altogether. The Turkish Government, in consideration of the capital expended, guaranteed a gross return of 15,000 francs per kilometre, with a reduced guarantee for the section taken over; that is to say, the Turkish Government agreed to supplement the annual earnings of the railway up to a total, per kilometre, of 15,000 francs. This appears to have been the beginning in Turkey of that pernicious system which enables a railway company to enjoy a guarantee to obtain funds for a dividend without making a real effort to earn one. I shall have much more to say on this subject hereafter, and in the meantime will content myself with remarking that between 1889 and 1907 Turkey has spent over nine millions sterling on this variety of extravagance, and that there presently exists upon her revenues an annual charge of £600,000 sterling, which cannot be materially diminished for very many years to come; indeed it would be trebled were the Baghdad Railway ever completed on the terms provided in the existing Convention.

The construction of the line to Angora was immediately followed by a resuscitation of the idea of a railway to Baghdad and the Persian Gulf. New schemes differed from the old in that they now included the realisation of the wish, expressed in the letter of Musurus Pasha quoted above, for a line to link Constantinople itself with Mesopotamia. Angora was well on the way, ideas in regard to communications had been greatly enlarged, and Turkey was awaking, not indeed to the desirability, but rather to the expediency, of development of the provinces upon European lines. Various applications for a concession were made, but the Germans held the field against all comers. They obtained permission to extend their railway from Angora right through Asia Minor to Diarbekir, a town situated on the upper reaches of the Tigris. From Diarbekir they were to have the right to extend to Baghdad, and ultimately to the Persian Gulf. The superiority of this scheme over the British one, which aimed to connect Baghdad only with the Mediterranean, and not with Constantinople, is obvious. The British plan secured little or no strategic advantage to Turkey, whereas the German proposal involved a tremendous increase of military power. It made available for war in the Balkans all the troops bottled up in the inaccessible regions of Asia Minor. It would enable Turkey, in the event of trouble with Russia, to throw troops upon her eastern border, an extremely difficult task under existing conditions. It simplified the Armenian and Kurd questions, and offered various other advantages that the British Euphrates Valley scheme could never afford.

But it was all too good to be true, as the Sultan speedily found out. Russia strongly objected to the prospect of her ancient enemy being put in possession of so excellent a weapon. Much diplomatic pressure resulted in there being thrust upon Turkey the Black Sea Basin Agreement, which reserved to Russia the right to undertake railway enterprise in the north of Asia Minor, to the exclusion of everybody else.

The Russian zone included a great portion of the
Anatolian Company's route to Diarbekir, and the
Agreement, which did not take documentary form
until 1900, effectually put an end to German and
Turkish ambition in this direction. Meanwhile, however, the Anatolian Company had not been idle, for
they had obtained an extension of their original concession which gave them the right to construct a long
branch to Konia, a new development of considerable
significance to British interests.

Hitherto it had appeared that German and British
railway enterprise might proceed through Asia Minor
upon parallel lines without interfering one with the
other. The natural sphere of the German line was in
the north, while the south would seem to have been
clearly ear-marked for the British Smyrna-Aidin concern. But the concession for the Konia extension of
the German line brought the Anatolian Company right
across the natural line of advance of the British
company, thereby putting an end to its legitimate
expectation of extension along the ancient trade-route
between Konia and Smyrna. For this unfortunate
result we have nobody to blame but ourselves. Our
diplomacy was quite unable to cope with German
influence at Constantinople, owing to the change of
policy in regard to Turkey already mentioned, while
the Smyrna - Aidin Company had been so far an
unprofitable concern owing to inefficient management,
and was utterly unable to help itself. The discovery
of an attempt to smuggle dynamite, the importation
of which into Turkey was forbidden by law, helped
to prejudice the Government against the company, to
whose appeals for recognition of their claims deaf ears
were turned.

The German company, being defeated in its intention to extend along the north of Asia Minor, now proceeded with its Konia branch, which was completed in 1897. The advance to Konia marked a step nearer Mesopotamia, and once more the Baghdad Railway project became the subject of discussion. Nobody now attempted to dispute the German claim to construct the long-talked-of line, and various schemes were formulated and laid aside. Finally the Emperor William, during one of his visits to Constantinople— neither of which, by the byè, has ever been returned by the Sultan—clinched the matter and earned for himself the title of Imperial Carpet-bagger. The direct outcome of his visit was the famous Baghdad Railway Convention óf 5th March 1903.

This Convention, by mutual arrangement, was substituted for the concession held by the Anatolian Railway, and provided for the constitution of a joint-stock company under the name of *Société Impériale Ottoman du Chemin de Fer de Baghdad*, which was to take the place of the Anatolian Railway Company in all that related to the extension of their line from Konia to the Persian Gulf. The parties concerned were practically the same, the chief interest behind both the Anatolian Company and the Baghdad Company being the Deutsche Bank. Salient features of the Convention were that the company was to be Turkish and not German, that a heavy kilometric guarantee was provided, that the concession was to last for ninety-nine years, that the terms on which the Turkish Government might take over the railway were prohibitive, and that construction might be delayed indefinitely owing to circumstances arising out of *force majeure*, such as a war between European Powers, or a radical change in the financial situation of England, Germany, or France.

No sooner had the Convention been signed than the world was made aware of the fact. The wildest rumours became current in England regarding the terms of the Convention, which was universally declared to be highly menacing to British interests. The point chosen for the terminus of the line was Koweit, the Sheikh of which was under British protection. The Germans admitted that the good offices of England were required to permit the carrying out of the final stage of the scheme, and they were prepared to admit the participation of British capital on equal terms, in exchange for the necessary facilities. They declared that the railway might easily be built as far as Baghdad without our assistance, but they were prepared to let us in, partly on account of the question of the terminus, and partly because there was in-volved a great deal of money which it was more con-venient to obtain by contributions from all the Powers than from Berlin alone. It was, indeed, far better to bring in England, France, Austria, and anybody else who was prepared to share in the enterprise. If Turkey defaulted, then the Powers would work together and add the railway guarantee liability to the obligations administered by the *Dette Publique*, and no one would suffer—except Turkey.

Nobody in England relished the idea of a German railway penetrating into our preserves in the Persian Gulf, and cutting into our monopoly of the trade of Baghdad. But Mr Balfour's Ministry admitted their inclination to participate in the scheme, on the ground that it was better to share in the railway than to see it constructed without us. We had learnt the unwisdom of refraining from participation in projects we could not prevent by our experience in connection with the Suez Canal. There would be in the present

instance no hard-up Khedive to sell us his shares, and
the Germans made it quite clear that if we did not
come in at the beginning we could not expect to be
allowed in afterwards.

While the British press was hammering away at the
scheme in ignorance of the actual terms of the Convention, Herr Gwinner of the Deutsche Bank, one of the
signatories to the Convention, sent to *The Times* the
text of the document itself, wherefrom it appeared that
all the anathema heaped upon it was abundantly justified. The Government was severely attacked for having
coquetted with a scheme that was obviously detri-
mental to our interests, and in which existed clauses
that seemed deliberately designed to undermine our
position in the Persian Gulf. It can only be said for
the Cabinet that nothing had actually been done, and
that perhaps nothing would have been done without
assurance that the equality promised should be actual
and operative. But suspicion of the Government in
its dealings with Germany was deeply rooted in the
country at the time, and in saying that "it seems
almost inconceivable that the British Government
should have entertained suggestions for the promotion
of the scheme, without having fully informed themselves as to the contents of the Convention which
determines the constitution of the company and the
control to be exercised over the undertaking," a
Times leader accurately voiced the general feeling.

Coming to the terms of the Convention which excited so much opprobrium, we find some which suggest
more greed upon the part of the Germans than sense,
and that we should have been expected to participate
in a scheme of which the following is a condition
argues nerve of a high quality. Article 29 forbids the
working of any section of the line between Bussorah

and Baghdad which may have been built before completion of the main line from Konia to Baghdad. It is well known that British and Indian trade virtually monopolise the commerce of Lower Mesopotamia. Our position at Baghdad is unique, and is the reward for much good work done in the Persian Gulf and its littoral. Given a railway between the Gulf and Baghdad, it is obvious that whatever impetus to trade might ensue British trade would be the principal gainer. If, on the other hand, the railway descended from its German base in the north, and broke ground by degrees in what may reasonably be termed British preserves, it is equally obvious that German trade would be the gainer.

An important feature of our position in the Gulf is the concession for the navigation of the waterway to Baghdad. The port of Bussorah, situated on the Shat-el-Arab, the great river formed by the junction of the Tigris and the Euphrates, and distant some sixty miles from the sea, is open to the shipping of all the world. But the remaining 500 miles of the water-route to Baghdad, *viâ* the Shat-el-Arab and the Tigris, is strictly closed to the outside world, and the only foreign steamers permitted to ply upon it are those of the Lynch Company. This privilege has been greatly sought after in the past, and Germany, in particular, would pay heavily to obtain a similar concession, or a transfer of the existing one. Fortunately, the latter contingency is highly improbable, for the firm of Lynch Brothers, though said to be a trifle querulous in their dealings with the Foreign Office, are patriotic to the last degree, and their custody of a privilege highly important to British commerce will never pass to Germany except over the dead bodies of the principal partners. But Article 9 of the Convention allows the company, during construction, to acquire and use steam and sailing vessels and other boats on the Shat-el-Arab, the Tigris, and the Euphrates for the transport of materials and other requirements. Will any sane person, knowing the ways of Turkey and Turkish officials, and realising the German faculty for magnifying an inch into an ell, maintain that this condition, together with the right to establish ports at Baghdad, Bussorah, and the terminus on the Persian Gulf, conferred by Article 23, would not effectually destroy the value of the navigation privileges in these waters now enjoyed by British shipping?

The manner in which the kilometric guarantee was to be provided is unusual, and there can be little doubt, in view of subsequent proceedings, that the object of the method adopted was the milking of the Turkish Government. The object of a guarantee all the world over—except, apparently, in Turkey—is to secure to providers of capital a minimum rate of interest until such time as the enterprise financed has developed into a paying concern. But there is to be no fierce striving after business in the case of the *Chemin de Fer de Baghdad;* an even, uneventful, Oriental repose is to be the keynote of its policy. Turkey is to pay this peaceful piper with a vengeance. The guarantee is not to last only until the railway earns a dividend, but is to continue for nine-and-ninety long years, at the end of which weary period the burden falls automatically from Turkey's worn-out shoulders, owing to the operation of a sinking fund, and the line becomes Turkish property.

A difficulty in Turkey is to make sure that, when a liability is incurred, the obligation to pay will be duly observed. Europe has mercifully invented one way which insures prompt settlement of debts, the way of the *Dette Publique*. This institution is an outcome of the Russo - Turkish War, after which European holders of Turkish bonds combined, at the time of the Turkish default, with the aid of their respective Governments, to force upon the Turk effective service of foreign loans. Various sources of revenue were assigned to the *Dette Publique*, which thereupon took over management of its assignments, and thereafter paid interest on loans from its own pocket. So effectively has the *Dette* administered its revenues that there is now an annual surplus of half a million sterling, after payment of interest on all of Turkey's original foreign indebtedness. To have a guarantee secured on the surplus revenues of the *Dette Publique*, of which one - quarter goes to the reduction of debt and three-quarters to the Government, is the golden dream of the investor of money in Turkey. For the present it is impossible for the Baghdad Company to touch the surplus of the ceded revenues, the half-million pounds mentioned, for it has already been mortgaged for several years ahead. In 1911, however, three-quarters of this sum again becomes available to the Sultan, and therefore available for the promotion of any preposterous enterprise supported by the Palace clique.[1]

According to Article 35, the Turkish Government is to hand over to the company the bonds of a State loan, representing the capitalisation of the guarantee, assigning for the service thereof various odds and ends of revenue. The guarantee consists of an annuity of 11,000 francs per kilometre, which capitalised represents a total of 54,000,000 francs, on the first section of 200 kilometres of the projected line. Besides this guarantee on account of capital

[1] The surplus has now been allocated to the Baghdad Railway—*vide* p. 325.

expenditure, however, there is a further provision against loss on the part of the railway company. To cover working expenses the Turkish Government agrees to provide an annuity of 4500 francs per kilometre, against which falls to be set off the kilometric earnings; which means that if the annual receipts per kilometre in a year amount to 2000 francs, the Turkish Government will only have to find 2500 francs per kilometre on account of the guarantee for working expenses. When the kilométric receipts exceed the figure of 4500 francs, the whole of the surplus goes to the Government, up to 10,000 francs, after which figure there are arrangements for division between the company and the Government in the proportion of two to three. As the prospect of an excess of earnings over expenses, however, belongs to the millennium, there would seem to be no advantage in dwelling upon this feature of the arrangements.

To proceed with examination of those terms of the Convention which excited distrust in England — the Statutes provided for the constitution of a company to exploit the railway. The company was to receive from the Turkish Government the state bonds for 54,000,000 francs, and to sell them in Europe. With the proceeds they were to build the first section of the railway, and subsequent sections were to be financed in similar fashion. Article 35 of the Convention provides that the bondholders are to exercise no control over the administration, which is entirely vested in the company. This is an interesting feature of the scheme, for the bondholders will have to subscribe some £20,000,000 sterling, whereas the capital of the company is no more than 15,000,000 francs, half paid up. So far as England was concerned, then, the crux of the whole question lay in the degree of control of the company allotted to British shareholders.

This was the rock on which the whole scheme struck, so far as concerned English capital. Article 12 of the Statutes provided for a Board of eleven members, three of whom were to be nominated by the Anatolian Railway Company, a German concern. Of the remaining eight, three were to be Ottoman subjects. Allowing for appointment of an equal number of directors from the countries concerned, say Germany, France, and ourselves two each, one to smaller countries, and one to Turkey, there remains the outstanding fact that Germany could command, out of the eleven directors, the votes of no fewer than six—the Anatolian three, her own two, and the Turkish one. The "absolute equality" which the German promoters prated of was in reality an impossibility under the terms of the Convention itself.

There were various other features of the scheme which did not commend themselves either to politicians or to financiers in England, and the country as a whole sighed with relief when it was announced that the Government had decided to take no part in the project. Germans, of course, were highly indignant at what they called our retraction, and many sarcastic things —many of which were true — were said about our Government's impotence against the ravings of the press. Germany declared herself perfectly able to proceed without our aid, and within a few months construction of the first section was actually commenced. Two hundred kilometres of the railway have been built, and the line has been open to traffic since October 1904. Since then nothing whatever has been done, and the cause of the delay resolves itself into an extremely curious story.

CHAPTER IV.

SECTIONS ONE AND TWO.

BETWEEN Konia and Eregli there exists the best
proof possible that the Baghdad Railway question
is a living issue. Two hundred kilometres of the
line have been already constructed, and are open to
traffic, showing that a substantial beginning has been
made. What the value of this beginning is, and what
are the obstacles that delay further construction, I
shall endeavour to show.

Certain points are important to realise in connection
with the scheme. The character of the country
between Konia and Eregli lent itself to easy inauguration of the line, for the route chosen passed over level
ground, upon which, with one small exception near
Eregli, there flow no rivers. Thus, embanking,
cutting, bridging, and all the forms of engineering
which render railway construction expensive, were unnecessary. Little more was needed than the placing of
ballast and the laying of rails. Under these circumstances it will be understood that construction of the
preliminary section of the Baghdad Railway was
extremely cheap,—as cheap probably as that of any
other railway ever built.

Let us now turn to the Convention again, and see
what were the arrangements made for provision of

capital. Under Article 35 the Turkish Government were to issue a State Loan for 54,000,000 francs, and to hand it over to the company which was to build the railway. The company was then to take the Loan to Europe and float the bonds. The proceeds of the sale of the bonds would give the company the required funds. It is necessary to remember that the capital of the company, 15,000,000 francs, of which only half is paid up, is quite apart from the Loan.

In due course the Loan was floated in Berlin at 86·40, and realised the sum of £1,868,000. The length of the section is fixed by the Convention at exactly 200 kilometres, so a simple sum in division shows that the amount available for construction was 233,500 francs per kilometre, or £14,944 per mile. Bearing in mind the nature of the country and the unique simplicity of construction, it is obvious that nothing like the sum provided was required. For permanent way, rolling-stock, stations, &c., it has been estimated by people who understand such matters that between £4000 and £5000 per mile is all that the section can have cost. Taking the higher figure, which is really an outside estimate of the expenditure, one finds that 200 kilometres = 125 miles × £5000 = £625,000, the total cost of the section. But the company had in hand the proceeds of the Loan floated in Berlin, £1,868,000. Clearly there must be one million and a quarter sterling pounds unspent. What has become of this money? Much of the politics of the whole question is involved in the answer, which is that the shareholders of the company, whose working capital is no more than £300,000, have pocketed a sum of, approximately, £1,243,000. A righteous denial of this soft impeachment is easily possible, for perhaps the shareholders have made no such profit at all. But the profit has been made sure enough, and if the books of the company do not show it, the accounts of the construction contractors, a subsidiary company formed to do the work, and composed principally of the interested parties, certainly must. With the exception of the backshish paid to palace officials, to whom even the blandishments of the German Emperor were as naught without a backing of solid recompense, this sum is sheer downright profit. Think of it—a return of capital *four times over* in one year! People make 400 per cent only in dreams—and in Turkey. Thus, in addition to the double annuity for construction and working expenses, there is enormous profit in the building of the line. If a similar profit could be extracted from the construction of subsequent sections, we might feel confident of there being very little delay in continuing work, if the matter depended solely upon the initiative of the company.

From Konia the railway proceeds over a dead level plain, unattractive in itself, but full of interest if considered economically. Here and there are tiny mud villages surrounded by odd patches of cultivation. What strikes one at once is the sparsity of population along the line ; also that the smallest fraction of the interminable stretches of country on either side is cultivated. From which arises the natural reflection that the neighbourhood is capable of supporting many times the number of people now settled in it. A hundred and one kilometres from Konia lies the town of Karaman, the ancient Laranda, dominated by the well-preserved ruins of a medieval fortress. Between Karaman and Eregli, the virtual terminus of the section, there is nothing to be seen but miles upon miles of bare plain, with here and there cowering villages, which merely emphasise the extreme desola-

D

tion. Everywhere the character of the soil is the same, and always one notes that cultivation is limited to areas ridiculously small in comparison with the surrounding wastes. Eregli would seem to be the point where the section should have terminated, but as the Convention stipulated for sections of 200 kilometres, the railway company, instead of arranging matters with the Turkish Government, continued to the bitter end so that not an ounce of their pound of flesh might be omitted. Eregli is an important little town, and marks the end of a comparatively populated stretch of country. Beyond it there is nothing but desert. Nevertheless the remaining ten kilometres of the stipulated 200 were duly constructed, and the terminal station built where it can profit nobody. The euphonious name of Boulgourlou was given to the station, for a village so called lay on a wide plain over four miles distant. Between Eregli and Boulgourlou there is not one single habitation. At Boulgourlou there is no house, nor any dwellings that I could see nearer than the village giving its name to the station. But even Boulgourlou station did not complete the stipulated distance, and for another kilometre the aspiring Baghdad Railway pursues its way into the lonely wilderness, to end with its pair of rails gauntly projecting from the permanent way, and pointing in dumb amazement where the Taurus shares the horizon with the very skies.

A mile or two beyond Eregli the great plain of which I have written ends, and there commences a gradual ascent into the foothills of the Taurus Mountains. The railway pushes just as far into the maze of low rolling hills as is compatible with cheap construction. It must have been rather a problem how to complete the 200 kilometres without actual

The last Station on the existing section of the Baghdad Railway.

*" . . . the aspiring Baghdad Railway pursues its way into the
lonely wilderness . . ."*

ascent, but it was managed by making a wide and unnecessary detour just before Boulgourlou, which added a kilometre to the length. A single hundred yards more and the route would have compelled cutting through rock, and that expense in construction of which the company has so natural a horror. This sort of meandering across country is a favourite device of concessionaires who are animated by the thought of kilometric guarantees, and is much in evidence on the Hirsch railways in Macedonia, and on the French railways in Syria. Poor Turkey seems to have learnt no wisdom from those modern examples of commercial morality, for in the clauses of the *Cahier des Charges* relating to the Convention of the Baghdad Railway the Government seems to have taken to itself insufficient power to prevent inferior work or undue extension of the line. Article 2 of the *Cahier des Charges* stipulates only for a longitudinal section, but not for the contour plans that would enable detection of unnecessary curves.

In October 1904 the first section of the Baghdad Railway was completed and opened to traffic. Every day a train runs from Konia to Boulgourlou and back —I had no opportunity of seeing whether it travels over the blank kilometre beyond the last station. The rolling-stock to support this daily effort need not be large, as can be imagined. My train consisted of an engine and four vehicles, in which were about twenty passengers, and a few empty sacks as freight. I have been told that in the wheat season goods trains have been known to run, but they must have been few and far between, for the total traffic, both ways, in the year 1906 only amounted to 25,000 tons. The kilometric receipts averaged only 1368 francs, giving a total for the year's working of a little over £10,000.

Owing to the scarcity of population and the impossibility of expanding cultivation, there seems no likelihood of improvement in the situation in the next few
years.   Perhaps in twenty years, if a new spirit is
infused into Turkish administration, there may be such
advance as will begin to justify the establishment of
so expensive a means of communication as a railway.

Meantime it costs Turkey 11,000 francs per kilometre
per annum to finance this concern, paid in the shape of
interest at 4 per cent on the State loan which provided
the capital for construction, together with 4500 francs
per kilometre per annum for working expenses, less the
trifle earned.   This means 2,200,000 francs, or £88,000
sterling, plus the allowance for working expenses,
which, in 1906, came to £25,000.   So that for the
whole concern Turkey is paying £113,000 per annum.
Of this amount £5650 represents the annual expense
of the utterly gratuitous extension from Eregli into
the desert beyond Boulgourlou.   One cannot contemplate the smug complacency of the backers of the
Baghdad Railway Company, with their million and a
quarter of loot and their handsome dividend besides,
without coming to the conclusion that whatever causes
Europe may have for holding up its hands at the
unspeakable Turk and his deeds, the Turk has just
as much reason to stand aghast at the treatment meted
out to him by Europe.   There is, of course, another
side to the picture which I have endeavoured to draw,
and it can be shown that the Turk himself is much
to blame for the impositions which have been inflicted
upon him.   But there is never much excuse for taking
advantage of ignorance, or wilfulness, or foolishness in a
child, for that is all that Turkey is in comparison with
the grown-up political organisations of Europe.

One more point is worth noting, for it throws light
on the question of working expenses in connection with

Eregli, typical of the Stations on the Baghdad Railway.

The Market-place of Eregli.

other railways to which I have made extended reference. In order to save the expense of setting up a full establishment, to operate so short a section of railway as the 200 kilometres built, the Baghdad Railway Company handed over the working of their line to the Anatolian Company, agreeing to pay for the service at the rate of £148 per kilometre. As the Baghdad Company is guaranteed by the Turkish Government for this purpose the sum of £180 (4500 francs), there remains for the shareholders the royalty of £32 per kilometre. £32 by 200 = £6400, or the nice little dividend of 2 per cent on their capital. This fact is interesting, as it shows what it costs to run a railway in Turkey, and because it suggests what a large margin remains for the shareholders of the Smyrna-Kassaba extension, discussed in the previous chapter, when their working expenses have been deducted from their guarantee.

The sketch on page 56 makes clear the difficulties that confront the engineers of the second section of the Baghdad Railway. We have seen how simple was construction of the first section, laid along the level wastes of the plateau of Asia Minor, and how delightful its completion, putting as it did so large a sum in the pockets of the promoters of the scheme. Section number two, however, falls to be constructed in that region where the great central plateau ends abruptly, and where there exists a sudden drop from 3600 feet to sea-level. The fringe of broken country bordering the plateau presents to the railway engineer no easy problem, for there are involved climbs and descents of no ordinary character. Nor is the financial problem more simple than the physical. I have already expressed the opinion that a great deal of the politics of the whole question is bound up in the difficulties of constructing the second section.

That is hardly an exaggeration, for while section one resulted in a profit of over £1,000,000, section two promises a loss of something like the same sum, owing to the expense of construction. The same financial arrangements hold good for both sections—that is, the Turkish Government issues a loan for 54,000,000 francs, which the railway company floats, taking the proceeds for construction expenses. The loan against section one fetched £1,868,000, and the state of the money market in Europe makes it probable that the flotation of the loan against section two would produce at the present time a smaller amount of cash. Yet section two will cost to build at least £3,000,000. In other words, the promoters of the Baghdad Railway Company, in order to proceed with the scheme, must disgorge the million and a quarter of profit already pocketed. This is more than human flesh and blood can be expected to do. Hence the halt at Boulgourlou for all these years.

From a mere company, especially one registered as Ottoman, no lofty standard of commercial morality can be expected, and one's sympathies go out to those wirepullers of the Baghdad Railway Company who would prefer to keep the fat profit in their pockets and to allow the grand, unselfish scheme for the regeneration of Mesopotamia to melt into thin air. But that is hardly possible. The German Government is behind the scheme, the Emperor William himself was personally concerned in obtaining the concession, and it is to the interest of the Fatherland that construction shall proceed. How then do the financiers manage to evade their responsibilities ? How is it that there has been so long a delay at Boulgourlou ? The answer is simple—the Turkish Government is always in financial straits, straits that only in the Orient are compatible with continued existence. Nevertheless the Turks

Scenes in the Gorge of the Taurus through which the Baghdad Railway will pass.

could manage to find the guarantee for section two, and if my information is correct, it has actually been intimated to the railway company that the necessary allocation of revenue can be made whenever the company is prepared to do its share. It is here the company takes up a strong and righteous position. No, says the company, we decline to construct section two by itself, for we should then be heavy losers. Provide your guarantees for three sections, however, and we will resume work at once.

Now the estimated cost of three sections is as follows :—

2nd Section (Taurus) . .	£3,000,000
3rd Section (Giaour Dagh)	1,600,000
4th Section (Mesopotamia) .	900,000
Total .	£5,500,000

against which the three State loans of 54,000,000 francs each are estimated to produce in the European money markets five and a half million pounds. In other words, the Baghdad Railway Company could construct the next three sections of their line without touching the profit already pocketed, provided the Turkish Government furnished the necessary security. But all the world knows very well that Turkey is better able to fly than to convince European financiers as to her ability to secure, satisfactorily, revenues for the service of loans aggregating 162,000,000 francs. Interest on the loans, and the guarantees for working expenses, would come to £360,000 annually, and it is a dead certainty that for some years to come Turkey cannot possibly find so large a sum.[1] The situation, therefore, plainly is that the railway company has brought

[1] In May 1908 the Turkish Government assigned revenues, which will be available in 1911, for the guarantees for four more sections—*vide* p. 325.

about a deadlock from which there is no apparent escape in the present condition of Turkish finances.

One thing may very well happen, and that is that the German Government may intervene and insist upon the company proceeding with construction of section two, loss or no loss. The disgorging of the million of loot, however, would be a bitter pill—the affinity between these two metaphors is so remarkable that the mixture may as well stand—and it is difficult to think that the German Government, which seems always to be borrowing, would venture to force it upon

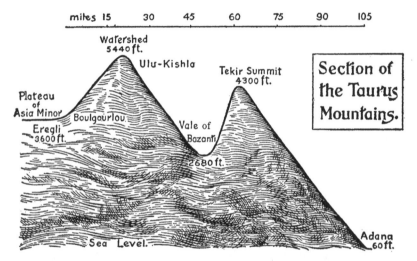

the financiers who are so useful in other directions. But rumour has recently been very persistent in connection with section two, and it is just possible that a move is about to be made.

Turning, now, to the actual country over which the Taurus section is designed to run, we find that it may be divided into four sub-sections, each of different character and each requiring different treatment. These are clearly shown in the accompanying sketch to be (a) the rise from the level plateau at Eregli to the watershed near Ulu-Kishla, (b) the drop to Bozanti Khan, (c) the transit of the mountain spur of which Tekir is the pass, (d) the descent to the sea-level.

Boulgourlou lies at about 3700 feet, and the ascent to the watershed involves a grade of about 1 in 50. The post road which runs from Eregli to Adana follows the proposed route of the railway, the grade at this portion of the line averaging about 1 in 63. The railway can choose its own grade as far as the watershed, for the country is open and rolling, allowing for wide sweeps and the avoidance of sharp rises. Underneath the coarse grass and gravelly soil there lies solid and very hard rock into which there will of necessity be much cutting. No engineering difficulties present themselves in the earlier portion of the section, the only bridges necessary being a few small ones over water-courses. The important feature is the open character of the country, which enables engineers to choose their own ground. Arrived at the watershed, the line will run along a level upland for two miles or so, and then drop down to Ulu-Kishla over country similar in character to that on the western slope of the watershed.

At Ulu-Kishla there occurs a remarkable change in the nature of the ground, and downward to Bozanti construction of the railway will be both difficult and troublesome, while expense will be on a very high scale. Near Ulu-Kishla there is the mouth of a long and narrow gorge extending for over twenty-five miles, and flanked by high and jagged hills which overhang the route. There is no choice but the gorge, for on either side of it lie impenetrable ranges of broken mountains. Throughout the whole distance there are practically no flats bordering the plunging stream that scours out the bottom of this remarkable gut in the mountains. The existing road, the result of thousands of years of tinker-

ing and building by the long list of conquerors mentioned hereafter, is to a great extent cut out of the
solid rock.   Considering that grades range from between 1 in 50 and 1 in 80, in a narrow ravine which
permits of no wide curves or sweeps, it will be understood that the railroad must go straight down, tacking
from side to side in the endeavour to reduce gradients
and to avoid broad spurs of rock.   Many bridges will
have to be built, nearly all of the track will have to be
cut out of the solid rock, galleries and small tunnels
will be numerous, while the amount of masonry embanking will be tremendous.   Work will have to be of
the most substantial character to avoid washouts.   The
post road, too, occupies at many points the ground that
would naturally have been taken by the railway, and
in view of its strategic value, in the event of a break-
down of the railway in time of war, it is certain that
the Turkish Government will not allow it to be inter-
fered with, or at any rate will insist on an expensive
alternative alignment.

The long ravine described above debouches into a
curious valley known in ancient times as the Vale of
Podandus, and in present days as Bozanti.   Completely
girt round by magnificent mountains, the Vale is one of
the most picturesque that the mind could well conceive.
About four miles long and one and a half broad, it
forms a deep pit in the Taurus system, from which
there is no exit to the south.   The sides of this strange
place are thickly covered with forest, from which project sharp spurs of weather-beaten rock thrown out by
the lofty peaks and ridges that surround it. ·- Broad
sandy flats are streaked by the silver of running water,
cattle feed in the bordering meadows, while the lower
slopes are green with growing corn.   Here camped
Cyrus with his Ten Thousand when the Vale was prob-

ably a busy and populous settlement. To-day, however, Bozanti is deserted but for a few lowly khans
and a hamlet or two in the neighbouring hills.

The grand problem of the railway scheme is, how to
get the line out of the Bozanti valley. The river
which flows down the long ravine from Ulu-Kishla is
here joined by another stream, and the two are henceforth known as the Chakut Su. South of the valley
there is a high ridge which blocks the natural outlet.
This ridge is nearly 2000 feet above the level of the
Bozanti valley, and over it the road is forced to ascend.
The Chakut Su, however, plunges into a deep and dark
canyon which winds into the heart of a mass of precipitous hills and ends in a blank wall of rock. Here the
river rushes into a great pool and disappears entirely,
to emerge, after an underground course some miles in
length, at the other side of the mighty barricade of
rock.

The German plan is to follow the course of the
Chakut Su until absolutely blocked by the main ridge,
after which it will be necessary to pierce the obstacle.
The railway will strike the ridge far above the level of
the river, and it is said that the main tunnel need not
measure more than a mile in length. At the same
time I have heard it estimated that the total amount
of tunnelling throughout the section will come to no
less than six miles, which means that construction will
work out on the most expensive scale.

The post road, meanwhile, leaves the banks of the
Chakut Su at Bozanti and climbs the opposing ridge.
In a distance of perhaps five miles as the crow flies
there is a rise of 1600 feet, which gives the severe
grade of 1 in 16. The road, however, winds in and out,
zigzags backwards and forwards, to such effect that
the distance is increased and the average gradient

reduced. Nevertheless there are some very severe ascents, and the road can only be compassed by the strongest of vehicles and the toughest of horses. It is the abrupt character of this ascent, entailing as it does gradients quite incompatible with railway traffic, that has forced the company's engineers to survey the difficult gorge of the Chakut Su. Personally I am inclined to think that the Chakut gorge may yet be deserted in favour of an alignment surmounting the ridge and crossing it *via* the Tekir summit, a small plateau on the top. This course would seem possible if the railway, instead of descending to the floor of the Bozanti Vale, struck up the side of the valley so as to encounter the ridge high above the point where the road meets it. Nothing but scientific surveying, however, can settle the feasibility of such a course, and the matter must rest entirely in the hands of the engineers. It is because German engineers are still wandering about these regions that I suggest the probability of their searching for a route alternative to the enormously expensive one of the river gorge.

Having negotiated the ridge south of Bozanti, the railway has to make the long and steep descent to Adana, which lies no more than sixty feet above sea-level. The actual distance is something like forty kilometres, but this length will have to be considerably exceeded by the railway if grading is to be kept within reason. On the whole the ground is open, and though the total drop is so great it can be obviated by curves and sweeps, such as would be practicable in the ascent from the Eregli plain. As I saw only a portion of this part of the route, that bordering the Adana plain, I cannot speak from observation, though I have been told that where the railway will emerge from the tunnel the ground is extremely difficult. Farther down, however, the foothills are low and rolling, presenting no obstacle of importance to the engineers. I should mention here, too, that I was unable to follow the gorge of the Chakut Su to the point where it disappears into the ground—no European has ever been able to do this, so far as I am aware, owing to the extraordinary nature of the ground and the fact that it is only possible when the water in the river is abnormally low. Natives, however, have often stated to reliable travellers the facts mentioned above, and there is no doubt whatever that the Chakut Su comes out at the other side of this ridge.

It remains to be remarked that there is practically no resident population throughout the whole length of section two, and that all the necessary labour will have to be imported, a course that adds materially to the cost of construction. As regards distance, from Boulgourlou to Adana is considerably less than the 200 kilometres prescribed in the Convention. The railway, however, will be forced to wander backwards and forwards at many points in the endeavour to attain a working gradient, with the result that its length may be spun out so as to achieve the required 200 kilometres between the terminus of section one and Adana.

The question of cost is one that can only be dealt with by experts, if any degree of exactitude is to be attained, and any remarks I can offer in that respect must, of course, be regarded as of merely general application. But it seems to me clear enough that if the first section of the Baghdad Railway cost to construct something like £5000 per mile, then section two must cost at least four times that amount. Judging from what I have seen of Himalayan and other mountain railways, I should say that parts of the Taurus route present engineering problems of the first magnitude, and that construction in these parts will parallel in cost that of any other mountain railway yet constructed. We know that where tunnels are concerned construction expenses frequently run up to untold figures, while many bridges and viaducts add infinitely to cost. How many of the latter will have to be built in section two is only for the engineers to say, but if what I saw in that portion of the Anatolian Railway which climbs from the plains to the plateau of Asia Minor is any criterion, then thirty to forty costly bridges and viaducts of varying sizes will be required at least. Without inflicting upon the reader further details, I will merely say that after calculations made according to my limited lights, I have come to the conclusion that every penny of £3,000,000 will be required for the building of this next section of the Baghdad Railway. In Constantinople I have seen other and lower estimates, made by people who had not seen the ground. What the official estimates are only those directly concerned know. If they were made public perhaps it would be more generally understood why there has been so long a delay in the advance towards Baghdad.

CHAPTER V.

EREGLI, I had hoped, would mark the end of civilised travel. Thereafter followed about a hundred miles of mountain, of so desolate a character that our Consul at Konia, in conjunction with the Turkish authorities, decided that it was necessary that I should be escorted by troops. I hoped to fit out a caravan, and to start in the good old fashion that makes travel so delightful and entertaining. But to my disappointment it turned out that pack-horses were not available, and that the only way to reach Adana, my next stage, was by means of a carriage which would occupy three or four days on the journey. Three golden sovereigns was the price demanded for this unpleasant variety of transport, and my mind went back to recent disagreeable experiences in Turkestan and Persia, when the absence of any other mode of conveyance compelled me to drive.

Arrangements were quickly concluded with an Armenian individual who possessed a specimen of the carriage of the country, and two creatures which he said were horses. My servant Socrate and the baggage were stowed in front, I reclined at length under a canopy in the rear, whilst my escort marshalled itself and its horse on the left rear. The Armenian then cracked his whip and we started. There had been rain in Eregli the day before, and no sooner were we clear of the roughly paved roads of the town than the carriage became bogged. The driver, Socrate, and self then descended, and after some pushing effected release. Thereafter we all walked. After some miles of laborious dragging through mud we left the plain and entered a region of low, rolling hills. Though out of the mud, we were now faced by an ascent, and the horses seemed so distressed by past efforts that I decided to continue walking. Thereupon the escort offered me his horse, which I accepted. As he tramped beside me I thought I could do no less than carry his rifle, and my proposal to this effect met with acceptance. It was a fearfully heavy old Martini, and though it gave me a thrill to find myself once more a mounted infantryman, I wished the weapon might have been the same light sporting piece with which I have shot so many Boers—shot at, I should say.

Except for my inspection of Boulgourlou Station and the lonely terminus of the Baghdad Railway, the day passed without interest. Just at nightfall we came to a village, and were informed that every house was full of people. The cold was very great by now, and we were all weary of walking, but were forced to proceed in search of shelter. To pass the time, the Armenian driver, the Turkish soldier, and my Greek servant all commenced singing the tunes of their respective countries. Each sang without any regard for the performance of his neighbour, and each seemed to find comfort in his own efforts to arouse the echoes of the surrounding hills. I bethought me how David had been wont to soothe the soul of Saul with sweet music, and regretted to realise that my own sense of harmony was much inferior to that of my namesake of long ago. It was weird work travelling in the midst of these old hills to such strange sounds. After a while, however, I began to find that the three voices chanting their quaint droning airs formed a curious symphony not unpleasing to the ear. It was Oriental to the backbone, and I remembered that the Greek boy had been brought up in Constantinople with Spanish Jews. He sang some old Hebrew air, with which the Turkish and Armenian tunes blended into something that carried the mind away from present surroundings and into the dim forgotten past. Xenophon had travelled this very ground with Cyrus, Alexander had passed it, St Paul had used it. The village that had been unable to take us in was the Faustinopolis built by Marcus Aurelius. Far back into the vast depths of ancient history this very road had been the grand route between the Orient and Europe. Hittites, Assyrians, and Greeks had used it; Romans, Byzantines, Persians, Mongols, Crusaders, Ertoogrul, the founder of the Turkish Empire, and a long train of conquerors, down to the Ebrahim Pasha of half a century ago, had passed and repassed with their armies, their captives, and their spoils. If only they might all move in panorama before one!

We travelled far into the night before obtaining accommodation. At last, however, an individual who sold chopped straw to passing camel-drivers said we could use his roof for the night. Stooping double, I entered a low mud hut which was piled roof-high with the commodity in which our host dealt. The only vacant spaces were a small platform on which lay the bedding of the owner, and about four feet square in front of a hole in the wall, supposed to be a fireplace. In we all crept, the Armenian, the Turk, the Greek, and the humble Scot who pens these lines. Our entertainer was a Kurd. I felt myself a veritable Daniel in a den of lions.

E

Socrate planned a pillav for the entertainment of my following. I had a cold chicken, which, when I had stripped it of limbs and every attainable scrap of flesh, Socrate said would impart a fine flavour to the pillav. So in went the skeleton into the boiling rice, together with pepper, salt, and a big lump of butter. I had made a frugal meal on the leg of the chicken and a hunk of bread, washed down with milkless tea. I was finished before the pillav was ready, but when once Socrate's party commenced work I realised that my appetite was far from appeased. I only needed an invitation to make a second supper. I chided Socrate for the manner in which he heaped up my plate. I lived to chide him a second time, and again a third time. I ask the polite reader if he has ever imagined himself eating three platefuls of plain boiled rice, flavoured with a pat of butter and a suspicion of fowl? Let him then travel for thirteen hours in winter air at 4000 feet above the ocean, and see what he can do. I had walked fully twenty miles uphill, and had suffered grievously from cold, so every mouthful of that pillav found room and to spare. When at last I could hold no more I lay down to rest in complete comfort. The smooth, easily-digested rice weighed no more heavily upon me than a down quilt. It aided sleep, quickened sweet dreams, and I awoke in the morning with a mouth like a new-born babe. What does the eater of the heavy dyspeptic dinner of Europe say to such an experience? Truly the East knows what is good just as well as the sophisticated West.

During the night, however, I was not altogether un-disturbed. Socrate found a corner amid the chopped straw, and I of course took the Kurdish proprietor's bed—trust the European for that. But the Turk, the Kurd, and the Armenian had nowhere to lay their heads, so they stopped up all night talking, Heaven knows what about. Perhaps they planned to rob and murder me. I had thought of it before I went to sleep, but cared not, for the pillav had brought me the peace that passeth understanding. Anyhow I was awakened during the night, and sat up to find the Turkish soldier and the Kurd struggling together. When I showed signs of consciousness they stopped, and sat down in apparent forgetfulness of the fierce contest of which I had been witness — another instance of the power of the intellectual Occidental eye over the untamed Oriental. It appeared that in the course of conversation the Kurd admitted possession of a revolver. The soldier then said that a damned son of a burnt father had no right to such a weapon, and demanded the revolver in the name of the Sultan. This characteristic attempt at robbery was defeated by no less than my humble self—who had apprehended violence to my own sacred person ! To what heights of egotism, to be sure, can one not attain.

Socrate woke me betimes, and we went forth to shake the chaff and dust from our clothes. We were promised fine weather for the transit of one of the most famous ranges of mountains in the world, a feature in history for the last 5000 years, and interesting in these days as the bugbear of those who would link Berlin with the Persian Gulf. As already mentioned, we were following the exact route described by Xenophon in the *Anabasis* that helped to make our youth burdensome. We began the day by waiting two hours for our escort. He had arranged the evening before for relief, but in view of the pillav had spent the night with us. In the morning he departed with his backshish and a full stomach, intimating that his substitute would arrive anon. Anon in Turkish we discovered to be the

equivalent of God knows when, and after long delay
we departed without a guard, hoping that he might
catch us on the road—a hope that was never realised.
Down the wild and narrow glen already described we
rattled at a great pace, for the road was good and
the horses fresh.   On either hand frowned high rocky
slopes, dotted with trees bearing the deep tints of late
autumn.   Great jagged peaks in every direction cut
fantastic figures out of the blue sky, while beside us
raced the foaming water of the Chakut Su.   Above
and beyond all there floated, serene and white, the
snow-covered ridge of the Taurus.   Contrast it is that
creates effect, not great bulk.   Placed beside the overwhelming masses of rock and glacier that look down
upon India, the Taurus would be lost to the eye.   But
in its own environment, supported by lesser purple-clad
hills, the Taurus has all the beauty and majesty of
greater mountain-ranges, and fills the heart with just
as much of still joy as comes from gazing upon Nature's
greatest symphonies in shape and colour.

We followed the road down the long ravine, passing
every now and then entrancing corners where houses
nestled close to the rocks, and where a few richly-
leaved trees grew peacefully by some little murmuring
canal.   Old-fashioned, high-peaked bridges took us
from side to side of the Chakut Su, deep rock cuttings through which the road proceeded opened out
new vistas of endless mountain scenery.   One of my
firm intentions was to visit the hot sulphur spring at
Chifte Khan, and to spend an afternoon and night in
the warm cave which covered its comfortable bubbling.
Friends had warned me to look out for this pleasant
interlude to the journey, and in the bitter cold of
late November I looked forward with anticipation to
a thorough boiling.   There also haunted my recollec-

tion an incident of the distant veldt of South Africa, when a much worn and dirty column arrived at Warmbad after a bootless chase of De Wet. There were warm sulphur baths there also, and we folks from India (Lumsden's Horse) rejoiced in the luxury of a real scraping and polishing. The baths were in much demand, and we had to arrange turn about. One man, who came from better-not-say-where, annoyed everybody greatly by occupying his bath for double the time allotted. We had the satisfaction, however, of knowing that he afterwards found himself so impregnated with the sulphur that he could not scratch himself without catching fire. But there was to be no sulphur bath for me this time, for the idiot of a driver took us miles past the place before we discovered the mistake.

An interesting feature of the ravine was the remains of the old Roman road which traverses it. At many places the modern road runs over the ancient bed, but every now and then there occurs a ledge at the side, showing where the floor of the old road had been blasted away to make the floor of the new one. Marks of blasting were numerous in the modern work, but all the ancient construction must have been sheer cutting of the solid rock. Like most Roman roads, this one used to go slap through everything, with the result that much cutting was necessary and also much embanking. At points where we saw the old road running at high levels, it was evident that there must have been much substructural work to support it. This latter feature of the road would have been responsible for its deterioration, for only constant repair would preserve such places from being washed out. The same feature lent itself to the defence of the Taurus, for when the defenders were defeated and were retiring

before an invader, they had only to destroy the sub-
structures to render the road useless.   In Byzantine
times one reads that the Arab armies were greatly
impeded by such tactics.

After a full day spent in negotiating this long
ravine, towards evening we suddenly emerged upon a
lonely hollow completely encircled by mountains, and
realised ourselves in the vale of Podandus, celebrated
in history as the Camp of Cyrus.   King Syeunesis
of Tarsus was waiting for Cyrus on the hills to
the south, and after a long delay at Podandus, the
latter appears to have eluded the Cilicians and reached
the plain beyond by means of the remarkable gut in
the mountains through which the Baghdad Railway
is designed to pass.   Alexander the Great, however,
adopted a different plan.   He occupied the Camp of
Cyrus, and from there reconnoitred the Cilician Gates
from the Tekir plateau.   Then during the night he
brought his troops up the hill by what is now the
post-road and rushed the Gates, thereafter marching
straight into Tarsus in a single day, a distance of
thirty-four Roman miles.   Overlooking the Vale is a
magnificent Byzantine castle, built of black marble, in
the neighbourhood of which are many relics of famous
crusaders.

We halted for the night at a lowly khan in the
Vale, and for the first time in Turkey I got thoroughly
warmed.   The reader knows the aromatic scent of the
fir, and how its sweetness curls round the cockles of
the heart.   How merrily the fir logs burned, and how
delightfully they smelled, are recollections more precious than fine gold.   Then early in the morning we
commenced the climb to the south.   The road was
truly abominable, and steep as any gradient dare be.
But on either hand were the firs, nestling among rocks

Where the Baghdad Railway will pass.

or thickly clothing an eminence, their rich scent hanging heavy in the morning air, their dark masses in warm contrast with the chill grey rocks that towered above them. There was no wind, and where there had been bitter cold the day before there was now the heat of a bright sun on a still morning. As we zigzagged up the declivity the voices of drivers and muleteers floated to us from above and from below, sometimes shrill and clear, again in deep reverberating shouts that rang from rock to rock in perfect harmony. Stately camels sailed noiselessly along in endless strings; bunches of tiny donkeys pattered by, care in their steps and deep wisdom upon their thoughtful brows; silly pack-horses neighed loudly as they recognised their own kind toiling up the hill-side. And everywhere beyond floated white peaks suspended in translucent air. How simple life would be if only the soul were content with sights for the eye and sounds for the ear.

On the Tekir plateau a modern conqueror has left his mark. The great Egyptian commander of seventy years ago, Ebrahim Pasha, halted here, and the boundary between the Ottoman and the Egyptain power was fixed in the neighbourhood. The plateau was selected for defence against the Turks, and eight forts, mounting a hundred guns, were built across in a line that measured two and a half miles. On the eastern side was erected a huge round watch-tower, which alone of so much work remains in a state of comparative preservation. The forts, however, have melted away before the ploughshare, and vindicated, here at least, the righteousness of peace as compared with war. Then not far below the plateau, down a ravine of the most exquisite beauty, we come to the Cilician Gates, the famous *Pylæ Ciliciæ* passed by Cyrus the younger, Alexander the Great, Cicero, Haroun-al-Rashid, and hosts of others classic in history. Truly, sacred ground. The gates are just a deep fissure in a mass of rock that blocks the ravine. The scouring of a small river, erosion, and the handiwork of man have widened the fissure sufficiently to hold a fine road. On one side there is the bed of the stream, and on the other, clinging to the perpendicular rock, and heavily buttressed from below, runs the road. On a rock in the middle of the stream is an inscription, clear as upon the day it was carved, cut by order of Marcus Aurelius. At every step in this wonderful land one encounters some remnant of the mighty past, some sign of great ones of other days.

The ravine of the Cilician Gates was soon passed, and we found ourselves on open ground overlooking in the distance the famous plain of Cilicia, where a dozen great cities once flourished, and were known to the whole world. Our horses made light of the descent, and we travelled at a great pace, greater indeed than seemed safe. But the springs of the Turkish carriage, or *yailieh*, are forged by supernatural hands, and they remain unbroken by a series of miracles that fill one with wonder. A place to lay our heads on the third night of the journey was difficult to find, for the road was alive with my old friends the hadjis, and every khan full to overflowing. But at one of the dirtiest places it has ever been my lot to rest at, the Greek proprietor gave me his own bed—a mattress stretched across a row of kerosene oil tins. I discarded the mattress and spread out my valise on the tins, praying the while that a cigarette end might not set the kerosene on fire. There was no window to this building, which was merely the back of a sort of shop and coffee-house. I shared it with Socrate, a pair of mules that were brought in through the shop with great difficulty, the owner being in desperate fear of their being stolen, and a few sheep. There was no ventilation, and the savour of the kerosene was almost welcome. If it had not been for the bitter cold I would have slept outside and escaped this dungeonlike corner. But one learns on the road to put up with minor difficulties, and one realises, too, that civilisation makes the senses somewhat dainty for practical purposes. I just cast my imagination back to the soul-satisfying odour of the previous night's fir logs, and slept a dreamless sleep by the side of the mules and the sheep in whose company I found myself. They, poor things, made no protest against my presence or my nasty tobacco smoke, or against the kerosene, but simply digested their food with a contentment and a placidity that mortals might well envy.

We started at three in the morning in bitter cold and almost utter darkness. I went without breakfast in my anxiety to get away and reach a particular point in the plain where there would be a train at a certain hour. It rained heavily all the morning, and we could see little or nothing of the surrounding country, besides which the wet entered the yailieh and caused much discomfort. I prayed for the train. After several hours' driving we came to the railway, to find only that we had been misinformed about the trains, and that there was none for several hours. There was nothing for it but to continue in the carriage, and an hour later we drove into Tarsus, the birthplace of St Paul, and no mean city even in these degenerate times.

CHAPTER VI.

ONE of the most remarkable corners of the Turkish Empire is that stretch of country known to both present and ancient times as the Plain of Cilicia. A glance at the map of Asia Minor shows Cilicia to lie upon the shores of the Gulf of Alexandretta, that wide indentation in the extreme north-east of the Mediterranean. Flanking the Gulf on either side are high mountain-ranges that run back from the water's edge straight into the heart of Asia Minor. In rear of the Gulf these ranges merge into one another, thus forming a great triangle, whereof part is sea and part dry land, the latter being the famous plain wherewith this chapter deals. Without further explanations the geographer will understand that the corner of land thus bounded by mountains on two sides, and by water on the third, has been redeemed from the sea by that everlasting and universal process of nature, the deposit of alluvium.

Three rivers that once bore the classic names of Sarus, Cydnus, and Pyramus, rise in the Taurus, Anti Taurus, and Amanus Mountains, and make short passages across the plain to the sea. The importance of these rivers is not to be measured by their length, but by their volume, which represents the winter's snow from three great ranges and the summer rain of a wide catchment area. Emperors and empresses used to voyage up the Cydnus in great sailing-vessels; on the Pyramus lay the port city of Cilicia, a centre of Greek trade and influence; the Sarus gave rise to a great scheme of land reclamation and harbour construction. But these glories belong to a period 2000 years old. To-day the three rivers whose banks were once lined with quays and wharfs flow unconstrainedly toward the sea, their waters roll over muddy flats or are lost in swampy wastes, their navigable channels have become impassable ditches.

Of the once famous Cilician cities, Mallus, Sis, Missis, Anazarba, Adana, and Tarsus, there remain only the two last, both greatly diminished in wealth and influence. The neglect of their waterways has brought them down from the position of cities in communication with the rest of the world to that of towns with only local influence. Cilicia was once of mighty strategic importance, for through it ran the only practicable road from Asia Minor into Syria, Mesopotamia, and the great old-time empires that lay therein and beyond. Every conqueror worth a mention in history relating to these regions crossed its rich and fertile plain. Ever a cockpit in which armies strove for its possession, Cilicia, nevertheless, was always prosperous, always wealthy. Its remarkable natural resources enabled it to survive all vicissitudes, to flourish where places less bountifully provided would have withered and died.

It has been estimated by a British engineer officer that there are in the lower plain of Cilicia 800 square miles of cultivable land, all stoneless alluvium. Between the lower plain and the mountains lies another tract of country, composed of shallow valleys and low

rolling hills, estimated by the same authority to contain 600 square miles of cultivable land. There is
no richer soil in all the world than that of the lower
plain; the quality of the upper plain is little inferior
to that of the lower. Besides these 1400 square
miles, there are great tracts of country in the foothills of the mountains at present neglected or covered
by forest. In both plains are many hundreds of
square miles of marsh and swamp, the consequence
of successive floods from rivers that have silted up
and are unable to deal with the water from the
hills.

Turning from the physical to the economic aspect
of this interesting region, we find a state of affairs
that is typically Turkish in one respect, and almost
typically American in another; for while there exist
in Cilicia all the drawbacks and anomalies of Turkish
administration, side by side with them there has arisen
an industry that has no parallel in Turkey, and that
has reached a stage of development amazing in such
an environment. Thirty years ago Cilicia had no
dealings with the outside world, nor with parts of
Turkey other than those immediately adjacent. To-
day there is a great production of cotton, a large
proportion of it ginned, spun, and woven on the spot.
Seventy thousand bales is the annual product, part
of which is exported to Europe raw, the remainder
in a manufactured condition being despatched inland,
wherever, and as far as, transport facilities offer.
Besides cotton, Cilicia produces sesame, wheat, and
barley in large quantity; oats, Indian corn, tobacco,
&c., in smaller degree. There is a small crop of
sugar-cane where there might be a huge production,
as soil and climate are especially favourable. Fruit

of infinite variety and fine quality is grown in great quantity.

It is to the cotton industry and to the commercial and agricultural potentialities of Cilicia that this chapter is intended to draw notice. In the year 1864 a Greek engineer named Trypani imported a small machine for cotton-ginning. This was the first effort of modern enterprise in Cilicia, and, incidentally, the beginning of the fortunes of the firm of Trypani Brothers, which now has established at Adana factories and machinery valued at £100,000. At the end of 1907 the machinery at work, and in course of erection, in Cilicia, comprised the following :—

Tarsus—
Ginning-machines	150
Spindles	6000
Spindles (being erected)	20,000
Weaving-looms (being erected)	400

Adana—
Ginning-machines	300
Spindles	12,000
Looms .	200
Flour-mills	10

District—
Threshing-machines	60
Steam-ploughs	4
Reaping-machines	1000
Pumps, large and small	200
Steam- and gas-engines	50

All of the above machinery is British, with the exception of the reaping-machines, which are American. But for one small German concern, which is only the beginning of a much larger project, the industrial machinery is owned and worked by Greeks, and the agricultural machines by Turks. One or two of the engines are German gas-engines, but the great bulk are old-fashioned steam-engines, built on the Clyde or in the Midlands. Most of this machinery has been imported by the Trypani firm for their own account, or for others, and the total import may be said to be due to their initiation. Thus, though there is not a born Briton at Adana or Tarsus, our reputation for the manufacture of machinery seems to have remained undiminished.

As in all countries deficient in communications, fuel has been one of the grand difficulties in Cilicia. There are several workable coal-mines in the district, but owing to the impossibility of obtaining concessions to exploit on reasonable terms, they remain untouched. For a long time wood from the foothills and mountain slopes was the only available fuel, its consumption, as it had to be sought for always farther and farther away, proving expensive and ineffective. Imported coal became available at the opening of the short Mersina-Adana Railway. Cardiff briquettes landed at Adana cost 44s. per ton,—a price that handicaps manufacture in no small measure. It is now found that gas-engines consuming anthracite are much more economical than steam-engines, with the result that all new engines are of this type, while it is probable that the other type will have to be discarded in order to reduce expenses.

A rough estimate of the total export and import trade of Mersina, the port for Cilicia, during the years 1904, 1905, and 1906, give an annual average of £1,500,000. This very considerable figure, and the remarkable development in the cotton industry, is attained, not, as might be imagined, owing to the fact that there is a large population engaged in ex-

Justinian's Bridge over the Sihun (ancient Sarus at Adana.

ploiting the total cultivable area, but from the cultivation of only some five - eighths of the land available. The upper plain of Cilicia lies almost fallow, not a third of it having been touched by the plough for many hundreds of years. There has been a steady increase of the area under cultivation in recent years, but the writer is assured by those who know the district well that production has not kept pace with cultivation : that, in fact, production has decreased, owing to inferior farming methods and the consequent exhaustion of the land. Shallow ploughing, ignorance in regard to the best rotation of crops, and so forth, have resulted in a deterioration of the soil that would be fatal in a region not so blessed by Nature. Cilicia has an average rainfall of some 25 inches per annum. The presence of three well-filled rivers, some lakes, and large expanses of marsh, produces, in the great heat of summer, a prodigious humidity that causes great discomfort to human beings, but which promotes fertility in the vegetable world. Cilicia is a veritable Garden of Eden in reality as well as in myth—it is one of the many spots in Western Asia assigned to our original parents —and no ill-usage can seriously diminish its powers of production.

But it suffers considerably, none the less, from the neglect of mankind. The deforestation on a grand scale, necessitated by the fuel requirements of the numerous factories established within the last twenty-five years, has seriously affected the rainfall. Where moderate and regular showers were formerly induced by a richly wooded hill environment, there occur now violent storms, due to the accumulation in the adjacent mountains of moisture - laden clouds. These storms burst suddenly, fill the rivers with rushing water that they cannot accommodate, and result in floods that destroy crops and property. In 1906 there occurred a flood that ruined £200,000 worth of grain. A succession of floods may end in the establishment of a permanent marsh. A curious feature of farming life in the neighbourhood of Adana is that people living within one or two hours of the town are frequently completely isolated from it for many months of the year. The soft stoneless soil does not lend itself to the construction of good roads, and upon such tracks as exist traffic is impossible in and immediately after the rainy season. One of the great anxieties of the farmer is whether the roads will be good enough at the critical moment for the transport from market of the seed for the ensuing crop. Deforestation is generally accepted as being responsible for much of the vagaries of the weather, and a recent governor made a laudable endeavour, following the Egyptian example, to correct the deficiency of trees. He ordered that every farmer should plant annually a certain number of saplings, and gendarmes were sent round in season to see that the order was carried out. The gendarmes reported the trees a'blowing and a'growing in every direction, but the fact was that the farmer was much too lazy and conservative to do a thing that produced no immediate or obvious result, and never planted trees at all. In the pleasant Oriental manner silence was secured on the part of the inspectors by the payment of a few shillings. So the efforts of the good pasha came to naught, and the plains around Adana remain treeless.

It will be observed that agricultural machinery figures largely in the list at page 77. In this connection there is room for exceedingly interesting comment. Twenty years ago it was customary for 60,000 labourers to visit Cilicia annually for the purpose of

Justinian's Bridge over the Jihān (Pyramus)
at Missis (Mopsouestia).

A bit of Adana.

assisting with the harvest. They came from all parts
of the northern mountains within a range of 200 miles
of Adana, and returned to their homes after three or
four months' work with sufficient money to keep them
in idleness for the rest of the year. This annual migra-
tion, for all practical purposes, has ceased within the
last few years, because the resident population, aided by
steam-ploughs, steam-threshers, and reaping-machines,
are now able to undertake the labour themselves,—a
magnificent object-lesson in the utility of agricultural
machinery, by which it would be well if other provinces
could profit. One reaping-machine, which can be purchased for £15, is said to do the work of forty men.
It is unfortunate that British reapers have not found
favour, the reason being that they are too expensive,
and too heavy for the light draught-animals available
in this country. British ploughs have been tried, and
have been found wanting for the same reason. Last
year American ploughs were tried with success, and it
is expected that hereafter they will have a great sale,
which hope, if realised, will effect much improvement
in the method of preparing the soil, and generally
cause reduction in the cost of agriculture.

In discussing the question of agriculture, it may be
mentioned that various endeavours have been made
to establish European enterprise, all failing, however,
owing to the difficulty of coming to terms with the
authorities. A German company proposed to start a
farm for the growing of beetroot and a factory for the
making of sugar. They wanted various privileges and
a monopoly, so perhaps the Turks were within reason
in refusing a concession. Several English syndicates
wished to start farming on a large scale and on scientific lines, but gave up their plans owing to the difficulties raised by greedy officials. A French company

F

wanted to drain the large lake near Tarsus, but could
not get a concession. The Sultan has estates aggregating some 150,000 acres in the upper plain, at present
practically untouched. An English syndicate offered
to rent this land and grow cotton upon it, but could
not arrange matters. For permission to mine coal,
iron, copper, lead, chrome, &c., there have been endless
applications, none of which has been successful.

The condition of the rivers watering the plain is of
extreme importance to the welfare of Cilicia. In the
entire absence of conservancy they are in a deplorable
state, and simply serve to flood the country at unseason-
able times, and to augment the already large marsh
land. The Sarus during certain months of the year
is navigable to lighters from the coast, and a few brave
the difficulties of the channel. Twenty years ago
steam-launches used to come up to Adana, but that
is said to be impossible now. The fact is that all three
rivers might be made navigable for shallow-draught
vessels, but, of course, at considerable expense. Much
expenditure is out of the question under present conditions, but comparatively little money would render the
Sarus navigable, and decrease the liability to disastrous
floods. There being a fair rainfall in Cilicia, the necessity for irrigation is not so great as in regions less
blessed. Still there are seasons of the year when water
would greatly add to the fertility of the land, and it
seems a pity that greater enterprise is not shown in
this respect. It is generally agreed that pumps,
of which numbers have recently come into use, are
more practical than canalisation, owing to the nearness
of the water to the surface of the ground. As the
utility of pumps becomes more generally recognised,
it is probable that there will be much increase in their

number, especially in the smaller kind that cost about a couple of pounds.

Enough has now been said of the plains of Cilicia to show that there exists a great field for the further development of the cotton industry, for agricultural enterprise, and for the importation of machinery that might as well be British as any other. It will be interesting, therefore, to see how British interests are represented in a region where there has been so much commercial activity in the past, and which promises so much for the future. During the last twenty-four years there have been vice-consuls stationed at either Mersina or Adana. Of these, three were unpaid, serving for an aggregate of thirteen years. The remaining two were military men, drawing pay on a special scale, who served altogether for nine years. For the last three years a Greek gentleman has acted as unpaid vice-consul, strangely enough during the period when enterprise has been most active, and when it might have been thought that a capable paid official would have been required to report on the progress being made. In the consular report of 1906-7 for Aleppo, under which is the vice-consulate for the Adana vilayet, there is no mention of Cilicia, or of Adana, or of the port of Mersina, through which passes £1,500,000 of trade. In the reports of the Constantinople Consulate-General, which usually gives a list of Turkish ports with their imports and exports, for the years 1902, 1903, 1904, 1906, the only ones in the possession of the writer, there is absolutely no mention of Mersina, though several other ports whose trade is not a quarter of that of Mersina are mentioned. In fact it may be said that, so far as British interests are concerned, Cilicia has hitherto been an entirely forgotten corner of Turkey. True, our cotton and machinery have enjoyed a fair share of the importations, but that share has been gained through the inherent merit of the goods, and the reputation for them which has been established in the past. But now other and cheaper goods are in the market, and we can hardly hope to maintain our position without energetic commercial action backed by official support.

It is satisfactory to note that the Foreign Office has recently begun to take an interest in Cilicia, and that in February it was decided to allocate to Mersina a paid vice-consul. The officer appointed to act has already shown aptitude in dealing with the commercial aspect of consular work, and there is every prospect that British interests will be satis- factorily represented. Much, however, depends upon the encouragement and support which the vice- consul will receive from headquarters. Nothing strikes the traveller in Turkey more forcibly than the immense influence wielded in the provinces by strong and tactful foreign consuls, amongst whom, without any arrogance, it is fair to say that British consuls are usually second to none. The presence of an efficient consul with a turn for diplomacy at the seats of local governments leads to marked improvement in social conditions, such as the administration of justice, the prosecution of public works, security, and so forth. When a consul is backed by his ambassador he is a great power for good in his district, he can do much to reduce abuses, and he can do something material to forward the interests of home commerce. Cilicia has had very little representation of this kind in the past, to the loss of all concerned except the officials, who profit by the absence of wholesome supervision. Some of the British efforts to obtain concessions in Cilicia for farming and cotton-growing might perhaps have been successful had we been represented by an influential consul.

Cilicia is in many respects behind the times. There is a short railway built mainly by British capital, which has now passed under the control of the Anatolian Railway Company, but there is an almost entire absence of roads and of many other things that make for advancement on modern lines. Administration is none of the best, nor of the cleanest. Broad questions, such as afforestation, navigation of rivers, public water and light, are all waiting discussion,—discussion which will be slow to take place where officials are ignorant, inefficient, and conservative. Let us be ably represented in Cilicia, and we will be doing something towards furthering the slow but sure progress of modern civilisation in Turkey, and something substantial, too, for British commerce. A consul cannot make a horse drink if he is not thirsty, but horses are sure to be thirsty sooner or later, and if the consul knows where the water is he may perchance lead the horse to the spot. If we are lackadaisical with regard to Cilicia, we shall find ourselves completely out of court when our great commercial rivals bring the Baghdad Railway to Adana, and find nobody to compete with them.

CHAPTER VII.

THE ROAD BY CARAVAN.

OUR arrival at Tarsus occurred in heavy rain, which had messed everything from top to bottom. I read in the guide-book that Alexander caught a dangerous fever in the local river; and the same authority informs me that Cleopatra, disguised as Aphrodite, sailed up the Cydnus in a magnificent vessel, and was received at Tarsus by Mark Antony. I read further that Tarsus was one of the three great universities of the pagan world, that the Emperor Julian lies buried here, that Justinian built a canal through it, that Haroun-al-Rashid of precious youthful memory fortified it; while we all know that the greatest of brands ever plucked from the burning, Saul to wit, came from Tarsus before he became a saint and an apostle. There are hosts of other great names connected with Tarsus, great memories and great events, that might well give pause to those who catalogue the attractions of this ancient and celebrated spot. But, alas! for the modern spirit, which respects neither persons nor places, but like a blue-behinded ape skips gleefully among the graves of Paradise—to misquote a recent writer in *Blackwood*. Nor is there much in the Tarsus of to-day to induce reverence. The old Tarsus lies deep down under the silt of her river, as if the majestic rampart of white mountain in the north had been ashamed of her fall, and were wishful to cover up her dust with dust from his own crumbling sides. Conspicuous chiefly in the Tarsus of to-day is an American college, half finished for lack of funds, a disgrace to America, even as another half-finished building that I wot of is a disgrace to the land of my own birth.

Instead of wandering around in this classic atmosphere, and braving the elements, I was content to wait in a dirty khan where I might be dry, for of such unromantic stuff is the journalist. Out of the window I noted a tattered beggar buying expensive hot-house grapes for a farthing a pound, saw the shopman cheat the beggar in the weight, and saw a small boy rob the shopman while he was busy with the cheating. When I discovered that the boy was the grandson of the beggar, I marvelled at the justice of Heaven. Two hours of the khan, and we load up the carriage again and proceed to the railway station; two hours in the station and the train comes in; three hours more in the train and we are at Adana, the modern capital of Cilicia. It still rains, and everything is wet and dirty. The tiny hotel where I am taken is squalid and uncomfortable. At this early stage I have nothing good to say of Adana.

But when next morning broke, and I saw stretching as far to the west as the eye could reach, and as far to the north-east, the white-capped ridge of the Taurus, one realised that to be at Adana was a blessed privilege. The town is encompassed in the far distance by the lovely vision of everlasting snow crowning purple mountain slopes. The season was almost mid-winter, so the distant whiteness was at its best, and would not fade away until the height of summer, perhaps not even then, for in the dark places of the climbed a hill and looked at the wall that had once surrounded Mopsuestia, a city founded by Mopsus after the Trojan war. The remains of the massive masonry of an acropolis and a stadium are clearly visible, as well as the defences which had looked down upon a battle between the two great crusaders, Tancred and Baldwin. These gleanings from the guide-book are not without interest when one can actually see the places discussed, and can find fault with the compiler. Besides, I have never before possessed a guide-book, and the novelty of using it is still upon me. This guide-book came into my possession by accident—never shall it be said of me that I deliberately bought such a thing. A friend in London referred to it in connection with my projected journey, and expressed surprise that I did not possess one. He said he would lend me his, but if I would excuse him he would first write his name on the title-page, as fellows were so infernally slack, you know, about returning borrowed books. He held the pen in his hand while I turned up the blank page at the beginning for him to write. And when I found it, lo ! there was already written the name of a mutual acquaintance. Fellows are slack sometimes, it would seem.

From Missis we proceeded due east until at nightfall we arrived at Hamidieh, a place not mentioned in the guide-book owing to the fact that it has only sprung into existence within the last few years. We were now in the upper plain of Cilicia, a region specially favourable to cotton cultivation. There had always been a small production of cotton in the neighbourhood, but owing to the great advance in the industry at Adana and Tarsus, dealt with in the previous chapter, there has been a strong impulse here in the same direction. A small ginning factory, established by a Frenchman, since deceased, is busily at work, and his widow is extending the concern by the importation of new machinery. A native has also begun a ginning factory, while on all sides cultivation is increasing. But the busy little town of Hamidieh, the consequence of this activity, is still in its infancy, and if the resources of the upper plain in which it is situated are to be developed it will certainly blossom out into a city. If the Baghdad Railway comes this way, as it is planned to come, the future of Hamidieh is assured. I wonder if any British business people have ever heard of Hamidieh, and if they realise that the values there of to-day will be increased fifty-fold within ten years ! Hamidieh is further notable on account of the failure of a scheme for the immigration of Circassians. After the Crimean War the Turkish Government brought about seventy families from the Caucasus and settled them here. To-day there is hardly a Circassian alive in the town, though the burying-ground is full of them. The change of climate kills them off like flies. A similar experiment at Ras el-Ain, also on the line of the Baghdad Railway, has met with still more disastrous failure. Forty years ago no fewer than 12,000 families of Circassians were imported, with the result that to-day there are only about 100 families left. Such is the consequence of the change of environment upon people who earn their living by the sweat of the brow. Sedentary work may be carried out under all sorts of conditions, but the moment hard physical labour is involved the human constitution declines to adapt itself to radical changes of climate. The fate of these Circassians is interesting, for it bears upon the frequently discussed proposition of the possibility of settling German farmers along the line of the Baghdad Railway. Anybody who

knows this country will at once agree that north
European labour could never flourish under the conditions that prevail in summer in southern Asia Minor
and in Mesopotamia.

En route for Osmanieh, a place about fifty miles
distant from Adana by the road, we pass several wonderful old medieval fortresses perched upon tall rocks
in a marvellous manner, that would seem as if it must
have made them utterly impregnable in days prior to
the invention of artillery. The existence of these old
defences, in such magnitude and frequency, proves how
valuable in ancient times were these regions that to-day
are almost neglected by mankind. Osmanieh itself is
a beautifully situated little town resting beside the
foothills of the great Amanus range of mountains,
known locally as the Giaour Dagh, and constituting
the second great obstacle to the construction of the
Baghdad Railway. This last fifty miles of the route
we travelled was of marvellous richness, hardly a mile
of it that might not grow the richest of crops, though
much of it at present lies fallow, used only as pasture
land for cattle. Here we observed several little hold-
ings marked by huts of the dirtiest and most primi-
tive description. These were occupied by Roumelian
peasants recently imported by the Turkish Government from European Turkey. They had been able to
improve their condition considerably, and doubtless
they have a future before them. But curiously enough
these little settlements were not placed where the
ground was best, but where it was stony, and decidedly
inferior to soil in the immediate neighbourhood. As
already remarked, the Turkish Government often
makes most laudable endeavours at improvement, but
generally damns its own efforts by hopeless methods.
Immigrants who cost the Government a good deal of

money are left to the tender mercies of local officials, who hate to spend a penny on them, and who do not care a fig for the fulfilment of promises.

To live under Mussulman government, strange as it may seem to those who have heard something of it, is the ambition of many good Mussulmans, especially those in the Balkans who have sampled Christian government, and if the Turks would only carry out their immigration schemes in a proper manner, they could obtain from the Peninsula, and from Russian territory, an endless stream of immigrants of a desirable kind. But the treatment meted out to those who have trusted the Turk has become known, and immigration has grown difficult in consequence. At Konia are colonists that would give their ears to return to the country they have left, but who are powerless because they have spent their all in getting to the land of promise. At the same time, it should be admitted that some immigrants have fallen on their feet and are really doing well. But the whole business seems to be an utter lottery, wherein are far more blanks than prizes.

At Osmanieh, the most easterly town on the Cilician plains, the question of the Baghdad Railway obtrudes itself once more. Right in the track of the projected line lies the great wall-like obstruction of the Giaour Dagh, whose steep scarped sides solemnly overlook the great and wealthy country stretching westward to the foot of the shining Taurus. To penetrate the mighty cliff-like ridge that bars advance to the east is out of the question for a railway planned on economical lines, so search must be made for a break in the obstruction. Two are to be found in the immediate neighbourhood,—one the Aslanli Bel, the other a pass of which I have been unable to obtain the name or height, but across which I believe the railway is designed to proceed. The Aslanli Bel lies 3140 feet above the sea, and the other pass must be approximately of the same height, and is probably higher, as it is a little frequented route across the Giaour Dagh. Thus the problem involved in the transit of the Giaour Dagh is an ascent from Osmanieh, 470 feet, to a pass, say 3100 feet, and a descent on the other side to 1700 feet. No very great feat for engineers, one would suppose, but the fact is that, owing to the restricted nature of the ground, construction will be both difficult and expensive.

Osmanieh has been touched with the modern spirit that pushes Adana ahead of the times and its environment. Cotton buyers and others come up from the lower plain at seasonable moments to purchase what they can, and perhaps to trade for the payment involved. So a khan has arisen where polite food and lodging can be obtained. My room contained two very decent beds guarded by mosquito-nets, a small table, and several windows. Washing arrangements, of course, and other conveniences, were absent, and it would be folly to expect them in Turkey. Nor was there a dining-room on the premises, a deficiency supplied by a restaurant and coffee-house that did a roaring trade next door.

While I sat in my room and bit my pen in the interests of unborn literature, a knock came to my door, followed by the apparition of a Turkish officer, with satellites. Needless to say that here, as elsewhere in the Orient, no person of dignity ever moves without attendance. My visitor's friends brought chairs for their superior and for themselves, and Socrate proceeded to collect his wits for the purpose of interpretation. Coffee opened the conversation, and the inevitable cigarettes. My whence-come and my where-go having been discussed, we tackled broader subjects, and gradually fixed upon military matters. Socrate, off his own bat, told the Turk of my remarkable experience of war and battles, and I heard in return of my guest's service in the Russo-Turkish War, in which he had fought thirty years ago. In the east the Turks had been victorious all along the line—according to him—and would have won the war entirely but for the muddle that had been made of matters in European Turkey. At this stage I discovered that my guest was drunk, and so the value of his declaration that Turkey could whip a dozen Bulgarias was discounted. I advanced the opinion that all Europe thought the Bulgarian soldier extremely efficient, without eliciting any acquiescence. The Turk said that the Bulgarian was a dog, and I was afraid he was going to say that all Christians were ditto, when he slipped from his chair, fell across the charcoal brazier around which we were all seated, and began blazing. When the fire on his fur coat was extinguished his friends carried the Turk away, and Socrate was free to remark that all Turks were dogs,—a sentiment which he would never have ventured upon in any language within earshot of an Ottoman. Brave lad!

Next morning we sallied forth to climb the Giaour Dagh, Yusuf the muleteer displaying a large sackful of magnificent oranges which he had purchased for tenpence. Socrate had also bought some for me at twopence each, a discrepancy which I remarked upon, and with regard to which he could only reply that an Arab would rob his own mother. For a few miles our road lay across the plain in a north-easterly direction, until we struck the Bagche Su, a tributary of the Pyramus. We followed this stream up a valley that gradually closed in and finally became a narrow gorge through which the river roared and tumbled. Ten miles from Osmanieh the track divided, one half proceeding along the gorge to Bagche and thence over the Aslanli Bel, the other following the more easterly line leading to the southern of the two passes. The latter road ran through magnificent scenery, climbing an abrupt spur at the severest possible gradient, and twisting and turning in a bewildering fashion. After steadily ascending for about two hours we suddenly found ourselves on a wide plateau or shelf thrown out by the main range. Beyond was a low gut in the great ridge that barred the way, and I was astonished to find that we had practically attained the height of the pass we intended to cross. There can be no doubt that the Giaour Dagh will prove to be an expensive obstacle to the Baghdad Railway. I calculated that from the point where we left the plain to the point where we reached the plateau could be little more than five miles. In that distance we ascended nigh on 2000 feet, which gives an average ascent of 1 in 13, a gradient quite out of the question for anything but a purely mountain railway. Moreover, the track we followed ran along the edge of a sharp spur, on either side of which lay deep gorges, and which offered no alternative ground whatever to a railroad. So far as I can make out from inquiries made, the other route *via* Bagche is much of the same character. The problem confronting the engineers is therefore a difficult one, and there will be nothing for it but a plunge into one of the two gorges, much bridging of torrents, much embanking, blasting, and building of galleries, and doubtless one long and terribly expensive tunnel. Hitherto I had been under the impression that the transit of the Giaour Dagh would be comparatively simple, but it would seem as if the difficulties are almost as great as those presented by the worst part of the Taurus. The chief difference is that the transit of the Taurus involves a distance of nearly a hundred miles, whereas that of the Giaour Dagh will require little more than twenty miles from the western to the eastern side. But I shall be surprised to hear that this distance can be compassed at an expense less than thirty or forty thousand pounds per mile. In this calculation, of course, I include the descent on the eastern side of the Giaour Dagh, which I shall mention hereafter.

Having attained the plateau we were rather puzzled to see in front of us a long line of arabas, or native carts. The track we had ascended had once been a road of sorts, but it seemed quite inconceivable that any vehicle could have passed along it in its present condition. Nevertheless, when we overtook the arabas, we found that they actually had climbed as we had done, with disastrous results, for two bullocks had succumbed from the exertion. Anything more pathetic than the story of the people with the arabas can hardly be conceived. According to their own story they were Roumeliotes, who three years before had been happy dwellers in a Macedonian village. A murderous night attack by one of the notorious bands left them homeless and ruined, and so placed politically that the future had no hope for them. Accordingly they had accepted the Turkish offer to emigrate to Asia Minor, where they were promised land, homes, and allowances for starting life afresh.

Travelling to Rodosto on the Sea of Marmora, crossing to a port near Broussa, and awaiting the decision of the Turks in regard to their future, had taken up no less than eighteen months. Most of the poorer of them had a little money and property in the

G

shape of bedding and cooking things, while the richer appeared to be well off, as they had been able to sell their land. These richer people had been consulted as to the journey to the ground selected for settlement, a valley on the eastern side of the Giaour Dagh. For some utterly inexplicable reason they appear to have chosen to proceed overland, a distance by road of nearly a thousand miles, rather than by sea to an adjacent port. After eighteen months' travelling over mountains, in the deadly cold of winter and in the burning heat of summer, they had reached Cilicia to find compatriots, who had chosen the sea route, already settled in comparative comfort. They themselves were in a deplorable plight. Something like a third of their total number had died from the privations of the journey, many of the bullocks they had bought on the Marmora coast to drag their carts and property were dead, and the remainder of the party was utterly exhausted in body and spirit. I camped the night at a village called Hassan Beyli, and there heard their woes from a deputation that waited upon me. They were then within one or two days' journey of their destination, and I was able to assure them that the valley they were bound for was a veritable Garden of Eden, which raised their hopes somewhat. But the trouble was that they had absolutely exhausted their own money, and that the subsistence allowance promised by the Turks had not been paid, which made them doubt that other promises would be kept when they reached the land reserved for them. . Without some capital to build huts, to provide animals for ploughing, and to purchase seed, the finest ground in the world would avail them nothing, and they were greatly dispirited. I did my best to buck them

up, but it was a difficult task to infuse hope into
such worn-out, hollow-eyed creatures, surrounded by
tired women and starving children. Heaven knows
what has since happened to these poor folk, but their
unhappy experiences at once illustrate the immense
capacity of the Oriental to endure suffering — I am
assuming that Mussulman Roumeliotes are Oriental
—and the ruthless disregard for the welfare of its
people frequently exhibited by the Turkish Government. One must make allowance, of course, for the
very fact that what seems unendurable hardship to us
is almost a matter of course to those accustomed to
Eastern rule. Nevertheless this picture of long-drawn-
out human distress is a haunting one. What had
these simple people done that their God should have
forgotten them, that God whose name was ever on
their lips, and in whom their faith was absolutely
unabated? Perhaps life holds something for them
yet. *In sh'Allah* they chorused when I bade them
hope.

Hassan Beyli is an Armenian village, and here for
the first time I encountered a community of another
people who would seem to have been deserted by
their God, and who remain faithful. But of Armenians in general more anon. For the present I am
concerned with the Armenian woman who was our
hostess for the night we spent at Hassan Beyli. She
began by very busily sweeping out a most uninviting
room, and afterwards did service in the matter of procuring water and eggs. When I had finished my
evening meal and had dismissed the Roumeliotes she
and her family descended upon me. The mother herself was middle-aged and had dyed her hair a deep
carroty colour to conceal its greyness—she was quite

frank on the subject when I asked her how her daughter's hair was black while her own was red. The daughter was aged fifteen, dark, plump, and subdued in manner, and sought in marriage by a young man without money or prospects—ye Gods! that it should be ever thus. Mention of the suitor made the girl hide consciously behind the mother, and never a word could I get out of her thereafter. Next was a tall and good-looking boy of twelve, the only one of the family who could read and write. For him the mother was anxious, as he had outrun the village schoolmaster and she wanted him sent to college. It was after the relation of a long family history that I got to the root of the matter, which was that my benign influence would serve to obtain for the boy a place in one of the missionary schools. The father had been killed in the massacres of '95, before the boy was born, husband number two had lost his leg in an accident, and all the family—there were two little ones besides—were kept alive by the exertions of the mother. But there was no possibility of finding money for college fees, and so the promising boy must go without education unless something were done. And so I wrote a touching account of the position to some kind American missionaries I had encountered in Cilicia, and expressed the hope that they would inquire into the case. What has been the result of my letter I cannot tell, for I carefully omitted to put an address in it for fear the good missionaries should mistake my meaning and write to me for the dollars to make the lad a doctor, or a lawyer, or a clergyman. In justice to my unborn children, and in view of the parsimony of publishers, I am compelled to practise an inglorious economy. Perhaps the poor mother thought she had found a rich but pudding-hearted Englishman, who would do the needful with a flick of his money belt—two five-pound notes will make an M.A. in Turkey. But she found the canny Scot, who would do no more than write the letter, and give a trifle extra for the eggs.

CHAPTER VIII.

AMONG THE KURDS.

MORNING at Hassan Beyli was bitterly cold, and as we marched out of the village the watercourses were frozen and the local mill-race a mass of ice. In the ravine leading to the pass, however, there was no wind, and a bright sun soon made travelling mighty pleasant. What in the world is there to equal the lights and shadows of early morning in a mountainous land, the wafted scent of firs, and the song and laughter of newly-waked birds? In an hour we reached the summit of the ridge and looked across the beyond that ever awakes the curiosity and stimulates the imagination of those whose route is confronted by a mountain-range. Here, indeed, was a satisfying view.

An immense valley lay stretched out athwart our line of vision. A projecting spur of the Giaour Dagh blocked the prospect to the north, but to the south the eye roamed unchecked down this mountain-girt plain to where ancient Antioch and its swamps lay wrapped in haze. A full hundred miles we could see from north to south of a valley that seemed no less than ten miles in width throughout. Here and there tiny villages could be seen, but they were mere spots on a limitless expanse. Across the valley lay the long line of the

Kurd Dagh, a limestone range that in the north towers up to 5000 and 6000 feet, and which dwindles away in height until in the extreme south near Antioch it disappears altogether. The Kurd Dagh is the last mountain difficulty lying in the path of the Baghdad Railway, for beyond it lie the plains of Mesopotamia, a region flat almost as the palm of one's hand, and with only a few river-beds to give pause to the rail-road engineers.

Severe as had been the ascent of the Giaour Dagh, the descent on the eastern side seemed equally if not more severe. The plains below looked little more than a stone's-throw from where we stood, and it seemed as if a line drawn to the village at the foot of the ravine by which we were to descend would involve a gradient of 1 in 3. Climbing down was a hard business that occupied us about two hours, for we followed a goat-track that puzzled our horses with their heavy packs. There is an old road across this pass, but we left it to follow a short cut, which like many short cuts took longer in the end. Arrived in the valley below, we looked up to realise that railway-making up this steep wall will be no child's play. A long ramp giving a suitable gradient will perhaps be the plan adopted for reaching the top; but the rounding of spurs, the cutting into rock, the galleries, viaducts, tunnels, and all the other expedients of rail-way construction, will cost a pretty penny.

Travelling south we crossed the bed of a dried-up lake, and in two hours reached Islahieh, the seat of a Kaimakam, and the little town where my friends the Roumeliotes were to find rest after their three years of weary journeying. May Allah be with them and their carts during the descent to the plain, was my inward wish, as I contemplated the land where they were to settle, and realised that it was indeed the best of soil, well watered, and surrounded by good pasture for such animals as the bounty of the Turkish Government might provide. But, curiously enough, this pleasant region is almost devoid of inhabitants, while cultivation is almost nil in comparison with the immense stretch of country awaiting the plough. We struck across the plain diagonally, and in ten miles did not encounter a single soul. Then we came to a low line of hills in the middle, the which having crossed, we found ourselves confronting the western slopes of the Kurd Dagh.

Here we met with a new phase of existence under the Turkish Government. The range is inhabited by Kurds who are entirely jealous of their own happy hunting-grounds, and have no liking for other people, whether they be fellow-subjects of the Sultan or not. Their predatory instincts have made cultivation of this valley almost impossible, and it is only in quite recent times that the village of Islahieh has come to be regarded as a point around which agriculture may be developed. The instruments of the development are not to be the needy Armenians of these regions, who would immediately be eaten up by their neighbours the Kurds, or by Turks who, away from Anatolia, seldom demean themselves by manual labour, but by the poor Roumeliotes, who may or may not be vouchsafed protection by their careless patrons. Anyhow, whatever cultivation is done in this great valley is confined to the western side, the eastern being entirely reserved by the Kurds for themselves and their herds.

From the top of the low hills mentioned I saw a great tract of pasture-land literally covered with cattle. How many were actually in sight it would be hard to tell, but I do not think it is exaggeration to say

A Mesopotamian Well.

that they might have been counted by thousands.
Having reached my point of observation considerably
in advance of my caravan, I proceeded alone into the
valley below to ask some of the shepherds which of
two or three villages in sight was the one where we
meant to spend the night. The presence of a stranger
was soon noticed, and several of the shepherds gathered
around me. A more villainous-looking lot it has seldom
been my fortune to meet, and every one carried a gun
of sorts, in addition to knives, swords, and revolvers
stuck in their belts. There was a hard calculating
look in the face of one man, which, subsequent experiences under the Turkish flag assures me beyond
doubt, meant that he was wondering to himself
whether this was a suitable opportunity for murder
and robbery. But my being utterly alone, and
obviously unarmed, barring camera and glasses, which
might have been newfangled kinds of weapons, made
him suspicious of powerful protection handy, and he
just gazed doubtingly at me. Soon afterwards Socrate
turned the corner, and came up with the idiotic confidence of utter innocence. The potential robber at
once · asked him what was the thing fixed to the
pommel of his saddle—my camera-stand—and Master
Innocence replied that it was a small English cannon.
Thereafter we were directed to our village and allowed
to depart without molestation, my understanding of
the feelings of the ravening wolf when the woolly lamb
is snatched from his jaws being greatly enhanced by
the expression on the faces left behind. This experience, instead of acting as a warning, merely assured
me of what I had always comfortably imagined—that
the European traveller in Turkey was safe by the mere
light of his presence ! !

Our destination was a Kurdish village said to con-

tain a guest-house. In the midst of a half-nomadic
and half-settled collection of tents and huts we came
to a long low building, one end of which formed a
tolerable room, and the other end a stable, the usual
accommodation provided for travellers where there are
no khans to take them in. While my kit and the
horses were being bestowed, the Agha invited me into
his own quarters, where blazed a roaring wood-fire.
Cushions and rugs were spread out, and I was invited
to make myself comfortable and to drink coffee.
These attentions satisfied me that the rather cold
reception of the Agha had not been intentional. In
fact it turned out that the poor man was ill in bed
with fever when I arrived, and that he had dragged
himself up to show me politeness. I judged his
temperature to be somewhere in the neighbourhood
of 103° F., and his appearance and weakness proved
him to be very ill. Of course he expected me to
doctor him, and though my diagnosis of his case
was kidney disease, I gave him a dose of the only
medicine I could rake up — phenacetin. A handful
of five-grain tabloids delighted him, particularly when
given with exact instructions when to take and with
what food. I warned him that the medicine was not
a cure but merely something to ease his headaches,
and that for proper treatment he must go to a town
and consult a doctor. But he was quite satisfied to
give the phenacetin a fair trial, and when in the
morning he said that my prediction as regards violent
sweating had been fulfilled, it was evident that he
regarded me as an accomplished hakeem. I wonder
what the precise effect of the phenacetin could have
been under the circumstances. I guarded myself
against a subsequent charge of murder by warning

him on no account to take more than one tabloid per day.

The tabloids came in very useful later in the evening. The great drawback to the guest-house as an institution is that it makes every villager your host, each one a host who considers it his duty to inflict his company upon the traveller from the moment of his arrival until far, far into the night. To the poor wayfarer who has toiled over hill and dale from early morning these limpet-like visitors are the very devil, for there is no getting rid of them. They ask one question every quarter of an hour, and sit like graven images in between. Their slow minds all the time are taking in one's clothes and appearance, and particularly the food one eats. No European had ever visited their village before, and so I and my equipment were a greater wonder than usual. Having eaten and smoked I was ready as a man could be for sleep, but politeness enjoined that I, and everybody else present, should wait until the Agha retired. But the blockhead, though in high fever, meandered on and on about nothing until I felt fit to murder him. It was then that I played up the phenacetin, and swore that a man who took that medicine and did not go straight to bed and cover himself with blankets, might easily die for it. But his Aghaship was ready to die if God so willed it, so long as he could take his cursed pleasure by conversation with me through the yawning Socrate. Fortunately his friends dragged him away before anything happened, and we were left in peace.

In the morning I did a little washing at a bucket in the open air, my usual apparatus having been packed in a hurry. This action procured for me rather an embarrassing amount of public attention, not on the part of the men, who do not stimulate one's sense of delicacy, but on the part of the ladies of the village. A large bevy of them, mostly quite young, had been away somewhere to draw water, and on their return journey they halted close to where I was busy at my ablutions. The ordinary Mohammedan woman would have veiled at once, and died rather than pass the place where a Giaour was so engaged. Not so these Kurdish girls. They expressed a frank curiosity in what I was doing, freely admired my white skin, and made abundant jokes, at the full tenor of which God forbid that I should ever guess. My inclination, of course, was to retaliate by catching hold of the prettiest and forcing upon her an acquaintance with soap. I am sure all concerned would have been delighted with such a *dénoûment*. But the male Kurd is a bloodthirsty ruffian, and my heart failed me. I afterwards had occasion to know that the Kurd women are most enthusiastic about cleanliness, and that my devotion to their creed earned me much favour in the village. The Kurd gentleman is much too much of a swell to bother about such a minor matter.

The grateful Agha, cured for the moment of his fever, bade me farewell, and accepted a medjidieh (3s. 4d.) with formal protestations against the shame of taking. I told him that it was the will of God that he should prosper, and that it would be a sin to interfere with the workings of Providence. *In sh'Allah*, said he, and took the money. The folks in Turkey are as great upon appearances as anybody in our own country with a long pedigree and a short purse. It is always a shame to take money in exchange for hospitality, but most take it directly or

A Kurd Woman.

indirectly. Sometimes you have to give to the servants, but one always does so with the knowledge that the master will grab what you give as soon as you are clear of his door. Big men of course do not trouble about such trifles, and it would be unjust to tar everybody with the same brush. But there is considerably more prating than practice of the duty and virtue of hospitality, and much cant in regard to the shame of doing this and that. I know an individual in this country who some day may well occupy an exceedingly important post, and who has private fortune, birth, and position at the present moment. This gentleman is a regular taker of backshish, and has, to my certain knowledge, requested certain subordinates never to mention the matter, as it would be a shame for him if certain other people knew what he did. The shame lies in the thing being known, not in the doing of it—and having said so, one is fain to admit that all countries are very much alike in this respect; the major crime is always that which is found out.

The Kurd girls laughed and waved when we marched out of the village, and for the moment I almost thought that there were better things than the study of the Baghdad Railway question. But we made straight for the Kurd Dagh, and soon found ourselves involved in a maze of low foothills that skirted the main range. This we found in the course of a day's journey to consist of a central ridge flanked by lower ridges on either side, with two flat depressions between. We crossed at a point where the Kurd Dagh has almost melted away into the plain, and the total climb involved could have been little more than 800 feet. Both ascent and descent are easy as regards grade, while there is a wide choice of ground owing to the character of the country. Along the route we followed—the one to be taken by the railway, I believe—there are no difficulties worth speaking of, and beyond the fact that there will be a good deal of minor rock-cutting, it would seem as if the Kurd Dagh possesses no terror for the engineers.

To cut this terribly long story short, we reached Killis, on the eastern side of the Kurd Dagh, on the second day, and then left the route of the railway, the second section of which ends a few miles farther east, to visit Aleppo, one of the most interesting cities in Turkey, and one which deserves a chapter to itself. But before leaving the Kurd Dagh, I must mention a very pleasant custom of the inhabitants which I had several opportunities of observing.

In crossing the first of the three ridges constituting the range we went through a picturesque little pass, on the eastern side of which was a delightful grassy glade surrounded by trees, and cut in two by a purling mountain burn that in one corner spread out into a miniature lake. I was in front of the caravan and came upon the spot quite suddenly, and so quietly that my horse had carried me right into the middle of it before either I or they realised the situation. In the glade was the total female population of an adjacent village, every one of them as naked as the day they were born. Of the squeals and laughing that greeted me there was no end, and I saw some scampering towards cover that was worthy of the chamois in his native haunts. Evidently I had hit on the local washing and bathing place. Huge pots were simmering over fires, and before each squatted an old woman busily washing the contents. The younger women were mostly standing up and tramping the wash-tubs with their feet, while

all the young girls and children were splashing in the
water or running about like the nymphs of mythology.
A prettier scene, I am sure, has seldom gladdened the
eye of man, for here was the female form divine, at all
ages from two upwards, in a state of pure nature.

The spot was made for the fairies, and who were
these creamy brown-skinned creatures but the very
fairies themselves, at play in the sunlight and among
the shadows of the trees, flashing their full round
limbs as they raced across the grass or glistened wet
after a dip in the limpid pool! *Ma sh'Allah*, 'twere
a sight for the gods. But the charm disappeared like
magic, for the ancient crones screamed admonition, and
the smooth brown figures laughingly hid themselves
behind festoons of wet garments. Some of the half-
grown girls remained unabashed, and stood up to
take full stock of the stranger, forgetful of their own
budding attractions. It is bad manners to look in
Turkey, and I passed on as slowly as seemed decent,
casting my eye hither and thither, as upon a dream
that must fade, never again to appear. One more
glimpse I had, for no sooner was I fifty yards away
than the young ones were at their play again, and
oblivious of the mere male who cast looks at them
over his shoulder. But it was a scene that was to
recur again and again, for every day, and all day,
the Kurdish women are at their washing and their
bathing, almost indifferent to the eyes of the passer-
by, and as unconscious of their nakedness as a marble
Venus of her undraped limbs.

CHAPTER IX.

ALEPPO.

THE ride into Aleppo would deserve no mention but for the headman of the first Arab village I had ever encountered. This sportsman received me with great *empressement*, and I gathered that I was sampling the real Arab hospitality—and so I was. I was given a clean place for my kit, and carpets and pillows for my comfort. I sorely needed my tea, but Socrate was too busy interpreting to make the necessary preparations—the young dog loves the flowers of speech much better than the vegetables of duty. My host was so infernally polite that my own convenience had to be postponed entirely, and where I would have loved to lay me down I had to sit upright and swap ornate compliments. In a strange land one must go slow, for the double reason that one feels it a duty to humour the inhabitants, while upholding the British reputation for *savoir-faire*. Nor dared I suggest the preparation of a meal from my own resources. A fatted turkey had been slain on my arrival, and in an hour it would be ready. To cook my own goose would be a mortal insult to my host—and a beastly nuisance to Socrate, who sat contentedly smoking cigarettes and drinking coffee, the while he substituted his own impressions of travel for the pearls of wisdom that I laboriously concocted for transmission to an ever-widening circle of listeners.

The turkey appeared in pieces that had to be fished for in an immense pyramid of pillav, made of tough wheat instead of toothsome rice. I hated it from the beginning, and hated still more the turkey, into whose thighs or breast my teeth vainly endeavoured to penetrate. My host ate with me, and after we had begun Socrate readily responded tŏ an invitation to join us. He found the pillav to his stomach's taste, and his teeth knew what to do with the turkey. He ate just like a dog, shovelling the food into his mouth and past his palate with no consciousness of flavour or texture; he got the taste only when it was safely settled in his belly. Then he leaned back and gave vent to the internal trumpet that all over Asia signifies repletion. While the servant fed, the master starved and cursed, and finally decided upon the broaching of a tin of tongue.

That put me in a better humour, and gave my host an opportunity to unfold his mind of a long-cherished design which he proposed that I, his distinguished guest, should forward on his behalf. And then came the old, old story, the wanting of something for nothing. He desired to have his son made a dragoman to the British Consulate at Aleppo, half a day's journey away. I countered him there, because the son could speak neither English, French, nor Turkish, but only his native Arabic—a dragoman being an interpreter, used as a linguistic go-between by foreigners resident in Turkey. The old man, however, had never meant to fly so high. The request for more than he really wanted was merely an opening move; his real object was to have his son made a kavass at our Consulate. A kavass being a mere messenger sort of person, it

puzzled me mightily to understand why such an inglorious billet should be the object of so much diplomacy
on the part of a man who was a notable in his way.
Moreover, the son was willing to be kavass for pure
love, without a piastre of pay. The mystery deepened,
and I wished then that the innocence of my youth
might have descended upon me again, and that I might
once more be able to accept statements at their face
value. Then this fine young fellow, tall, slender, with
long drooping moustache, with the face of a Greek,
and with the manners of a prince, would surely have
my support. I did not then know enough of Turkey
to understand the significance of what was wanted;
but much contact with the Aryan brother has sophisticated a mind naturally simple. I temporised. To be
kavass to a foreign consulate in Turkey, I discovered
later on, is to be a perpetual joy to one's self and to
one's relatives, to be a rich man among poor, to be a
power over the weak, to be the anointed of Allah beside the sufferers from His wrath. A man of substance
in Turkey gives one son to the Church, one to the
Government, one to Business, and the fourth, if there
be such, to the Devil. But if it be possible to import
a kavass-ship into the family, the Church, the Government, and the Devil are all forgotten, and only the
mantle of the kavass is remembered. The kavass
henceforth takes all his connections under its ample
folds, and all prosper in goods and influence, all can
laugh freely in a country where there is much gnashing of teeth and rending of garments. Meanwhile I
promised to bring the young man to the notice of
the consul, a promise that evoked many thanks and
much appreciation of my high qualities. When I
left that house I presented the servants with a
mejidieh, wondering whether my host himself would

Aleppo Castle.

collar the coin within the hour—Yusuf, the muleteer, said he would, with a laugh that I should have thought any other course possible. Trust an Arab to know an Arab.

Six hours' riding brought us within view of Aleppo, a city redeemed from plainness of appearance by its citadel, than which Europe and Asia can surely show nothing more graceful. Miles away it may be seen projecting over the rolling down-like hills, a red sandstone castle sitting on a perfectly symmetrical base of green hill. The town is approached through country that is yellow and uninteresting beyond words, for in winter there is no vegetation to cover up the nakedness of the land. But when close at hand the traveller's eyes are gladdened by a long strip of green that comes from somewhere in the north-east and runs right up to the foot of the castle hill, only to leave it again to melt away in a dark line to the far south. It needs no practised observer to say that running water is the father of this refreshing band of verdure. Hidden behind the foliage of trees and between high tortuous banks flows the Kowaik, at present a lazy brook, but at other times a rampagious river—witness its treatment of the Crusaders' camp, when, many hundreds of years ago, it arose in a single night and forced the Unbelievers to raise the siege. The standard of Islam floated from the walls of the citadel, and well might the Faithful cry praise unto Allah for timely aid. Saladin himself lies buried at the very gate, the champion of a cause that has spread, until to-day it looms large among the influences that shape the world's destiny, looms larger and larger as we realise that its power is based on its fitness to the needs and necessities of its followers. There is a stratum of the human species, product of hard natural conditions, in which

spirituality and sympathy have little place, where the
demands of the body restrict the flights of the soul,
where grim justice overshadows kindly mercy.   And
here it is that the creed of Mahomet flourishes, relent-
less to its enemies, Spartan in its practices, frankly
sensual in its rewards.   It is a creed born of the desert,
where life is severe, often brutal, where passions over-
ride emotions, where stern conditions harden the heart.
The core of the stratum is the people of the desert, the
outer edges those races in whom environment has
generated low nervous organisation.   For such none
but the alternative terrors and pleasures of Islam have
any attraction ; for them the humanity of Christ holds
no appeal.

Aleppo is not in my guide-book, and I cannot palm
upon the reader the reflections and observations of
better men than myself ; so follow the coruscations of
an open mind, undefiled by the simple wisdom of actual
knowledge.   But the citadel of Aleppo is a living fact,
and the entrance thereto is surely the finest thing of
its kind that ever grew under the eye of mortal archi-
tect.   The slopes of the hill, a natural mound perfected
in shape by human hands, are covered with rich green
grass except where the masonry facing has been de-
nuded of soil.   The light terra-cotta walls and redoubts
against the green of the foundations form a colour-feast
for the eye, the massive approaches, whose ornamentation conceals orifices for boiling oil and red-hot lead, fill
one's geometrical soul with joy, and the deep dark
cavern of the actual gateway makes a mystery of the
wonders inside.   It is a stiff climb up the flagged floor
of the long tunnel inside the gate, and one easily
imagines the march of mailed riders echoing among
the vaulted arches overhead.   A flickering match
makes visible in the darkness above the heads of two

Gate of the Castle at Aleppo.

Hittite lions projecting from the sides of an inner gateway, relics 3000 years old. Kufic inscriptions of 1000 years ago fix the date of the construction of the existing edifice, probably itself only the great grandchild of a fortress that defied its besiegers when the planks of Noah's Ark were yet but saplings. From the top of the tower Mehmed Ali Bey showed me the minarets and roofs of the city, the suburbs of white stone, the great barrack built by the Egyptian conqueror Ebrahim Pasha, the terminus of the railway that will soon be linked with Europe, and whose other end even now is close upon the sacred cities of Islam. We descended the tower to visit the water-supply of the fortress, a well over 200 feet deep whence comes water clear as crystal and cold as if drawn from the heart of a glacier. Then to a little courtyard sunk deep in the ground, built of stones old and worn. Here dwelt in the days of long ago the aged patriarch Abraham, his daily task the milking of a white cow at the gateway for the benefit of the poor children of the town. Hence the Arab name for the city, Haleb-es-Shahiba (White Cow), in these days shortened to simple Haleb. Then to a huge ruined chamber where lies a wrecked gun-carriage, and where are strewn the great iron balls for the cannon of sixty years ago. Thousands of small round bullets litter the ground, escaped from the canisters that once filled the ammunition boxes piled against the wall. Curious that these boxes are an almost exact replica of the ammunition boxes of the British army of to-day, and that they should have painted upon them in English characters the artillery calibres of the contents. There was no maker's name to show their origin, but it was clear enough that the Egyptian forces were content to use English ammunition. Aleppo citadel has no more need of ammunition, or of artillery, or of soldiers. It stands empty, a monument to the chivalric days of Saracen and Crusader, a ruin of former greatness. The Turk treats it kindly, for infantry guard the gate and protect from the ravages of man what the will of God has made obsolete.

Mehmed Ali Bey belongs to a class of which the Turkish Empire holds many. Once a personage of the palace in Constantinople, and filling a post which brought him into contact with his sovereign, he is now an exile in a far city, condemned to dwell in the cold atmosphere of royal disfavour. His offence cannot have been great, else he would hardly be allowed to hold an appointment under the local administration. But his friends and his heart are elsewhere, and he lives in hope of the Sultan's gracious pardon. All Englishmen who have met him will join in this hope, for he has a soft place in his heart for our country, and has done kindly service to many of us who pass. And no wonder, for the keeper of his hearth is an Englishwoman who remembers well her ain countree, and brings her children up to speak her own language, good little Mohammedans though I suppose they are. Hospitality is a Turkish as well as an English virtue, and Mehmed Ali Bey and his wife practise it faithfully towards the ubiquitous traveller. May they be rewarded, as the Arabs have it.

So far I had had but small dealings with the Turkish official, but at Aleppo it was to be my fortune to encounter my first pasha. The pasha of one's imagination is surely a being set upon a divan, sucking at a hookah, turbaned, bearded, cross-legged, and red-eyed with the lust of slaughter. But His Excellency Nazim Pasha, Governor-General of the province of Aleppo,

was no such being, nor is it possible to imagine that
either he or his forebears, or his descendants, could
ever fill the popular bill. Mehmed Ali Bey accompanied me when I went to call, and my first shock
occurred when our carriage pulled up before a large
white villa that savoured much more of Park Lane
than of the Arabian Nights. The Pasha's reception-
room destroyed more of my illusions, for it was
furnished like an ordinary drawing-room, with numerous sofas, chairs, and little tables. There was neither
sign nor smell of hookah. The Pasha himself sat in
a comfortable arm-chair at the top of the room, and
rose to receive me with the same degree of kindness
and courtesy that one would expect from an elderly
gentleman elsewhere. A greeting exhausted his
French, and I was relieved to know that our conversation was to be carried on in Turkish and English,
Mehmed Ali Bey acting as interpreter. The only
things Turkish about the Pasha were his language
and his fez, the latter an adornment that no loyal
Turk dare omit from his toilet. Otherwise the Vali,
the Turkish equivalent of Governor-General, wore
frock-coat, trousers, and fittings according to Piccadilly.
If His Excellency's mind matched his appearance,
then indeed was another of my preconceptions fallen
from me.

And so it happened. Our conversation ran upon the
construction of roads, upon the introduction of a motor-
car service, upon the development of the country, upon
education, trade, female suffrage, and other curses of
civilisation. I had thought to find myself in full
agreement with His Excellency upon these matters,
and had hoped in a humble sort of way to harden
his heart against the encroachment of the modern
spirit. But I was the reactionary, he the progressive ;

it was I who deprecated European interference in Turkish domesticity, he who lauded the blessings bestowed upon his country by foreign powers. Aided by cigarettes and coffee we roamed over the fields of politics and philosophy, theology and science, the Pasha always the optimist, I always the pessimist. I marvelled greatly that my host should show so much partiality for the European and his ideas. An acquaintance explained the reason a few days later. Nazim Pasha many years before had been Governor of a port city, wherein a European had misbehaved himself. The European having been jailed, his country sent a battleship with orders to obtain release of the prisoner, or to bombard the town. The Pasha's advisers suggested a gridiron with the European on top and a bonfire underneath, the latter to be lit when the man-o'-war commenced to fire. But the Pasha had so much respect for the guns that he delivered up the captive, since when, quoth my informant, His Excellency has been a fond lover of, and a firm believer in, the European. I wonder! Is a pasha not as other men are?

Bekir Pasha, on the other hand, is the real old fire-eating Turk, who wishes all innovations to the devil. He is commander of the division stationed at Aleppo, a soldier whose recollections go back to the Crimea, and whose wounds and honours rival the sands in number. He also received me most kindly, and whatever disapproval he may feel for European people and things in general, he showed none of it for the wandering Scot in particular. Mehmed Ali Bey having informed him that I had done a bit of soldiering in my time, we had no difficulty in making friends and finding subject for conversation. The yarns of an old soldier are always worth listening to—provided he is not an egotist—and I heard some things about the Turkish army that I did not know before.

Few places can compare with Aleppo in length of history, for it is probably one of the oldest cities in existence. It has never been known to fame as Babylon was, or Athens, or Rome, for its function in the world has always been commercial rather than military, though it has suffered often enough from the vicissitudes of war. We know that it existed in Hittite times, for the proofs are to be seen, while there is reason to think, apart from the fact that Abraham once lived in the citadel, that it must be much older still, for it lies on what has always been the grand trade-route between the Indian Ocean and the Mediterranean. Tadmor was once the most important depot in the Middle East for goods brought from the Indies, long before the route round the Cape of Good Hope was thought of. Tadmor declined, its successor, Palmyra, fell, and the mantle of their greatness fell upon Aleppo. In comparatively modern times the Levant Company had an important agency at Aleppo, and it would seem probable that the agent for the company was among the very first English consuls ever appointed. There are numerous archives at the consulate, among them volumes dated 1580, recording the courts that were held, the dispatches sent to London containing lamentations over bad trade, prayers for deliverance from plague and pestilence, dissertations on local politics. There is a little Protestant cemetery, too, where old stones record the burial of English and Dutch worthies three hundred years ago. Within the city there are bits of ancient walls still to be found, of masonry grandly massive, and yellow with age. Aleppo has its own unique style of architecture. The houses are built

of glaring white stone, with never a window on
the ground floor, but only an iron-studded door, for
when, not so long ago, the Arabs of the desert roamed
close to the very gates of the city, they sometimes
entered and plundered the bazaars. So private houses
were built with a view to such contingencies. Instead of windows as we know them, the houses have
great latticed oriels let into the upper walls; here and
there are little balconies of delicately twisted iron, all
of them painted a rich green or a dull blue, that in
contrast with the cream of the masonry gives one's
æsthetic soul a pleasure that money cannot buy. And
the streets are so old, so narrow, and so tortuous.
They wind in and out between tall blank walls, unbroken save by the low forbidding doorways that look
as if they could never be opened, pass under broad
arches supporting curious old buildings, and dive
into long tunnels that are pitch dark, moist with
dripping water, and foul with the accumulated dirt
of ages. For there is no conservancy here but the
dogs, which swarm in their thousands, mangy, sore-
eyed, and unclean. And for the people, they also
swarm, degenerate town Arabs for the most, many
Syrians, some Armenians, a few Turkish officials, and
perhaps 15,000 Jews, of the old original stock that
crucified our Saviour.

Aleppo has a cross to bear, a toll which all who
dwell within its gates must pay. You may find yourself afflicted after a single week of residence, or you
may live here for twenty years and escape all the
while, only to return to your native country and find
yourself at long last the possessor of the Aleppo
Button. The button is a pimple, not unlike a wild
strawberry, that appears on the face, or arms, or
ankles, and stays there for six months, impervious to

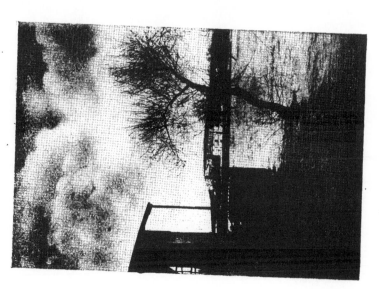

A corner of the old British Consulate, and a house built in the Aleppo style of architecture, both flooded by the Koweik.

treatment or coaxing with unguents. Then for another six months it gently suppurates, and no power
can stay the issue. Then, as suddenly as it came, it
goes, and its place knows it no more, but for the mark
that will endure to the grave. If you are careful you
may confine the number of buttons to one, but if you
are careless of the matter you may find yourself the
possessor of six or even more. It is a painless visitation, but a troublesome one, and leads at times to
undesirable consequences. One unfortunate British
consul reared a button on the end of his nose, with
the result that when the button had run its course
there was no nose left. For which, ever since, the
Foreign Office, for consular pensions, counts every
year of service at Aleppo as eighteen months. Nobody knows what causes the button, whether it be
the water, or the food, or the climate, or an insect.
But most people at Aleppo regard it as a sign of
heavenly displeasure at an evil deed. From time
to time sufferers confess their wickedness, and occasionally their buttons have fallen from them. Of
late not many people have been so lucky, and confession as a cure is going out of fashion.

CHAPTER X.

IN London an individual thoroughly acquainted with
the resources of Aleppo had told me that there
might be obtained tents, camp equipment, servants,
and all the essentials of travel in a foreign land.
When I got to Aleppo I found that nothing of the
sort was procurable for love or money. So I had to
make up my mind to retain Socrate, to forego a camp-
bed and sleep on the ground, to put up with horrid
little Arab tents, and generally to be content with
the absence of all the conveniences one is accustomed
to on the road. I worked off some of my feelings
in silent anathema upon the well‑informed friend,
and the remainder I kept for gradual infliction upon
Socrate. With Yusuf, who had brought me from
Adana, I arranged for the hire of six horses, himself,
and an assistant called Ebrahim, all to accompany me
whither I listed into the deserts of Mesopotamia. Yusuf
was full of doubts as to the practicability of the route
I proposed, and tried hard to divert me, failing completely to realise that a Briton who meant to follow
the line of the Baghdad Railway would surely follow
it while he had strength to be pig-headed. This same
pig-headedness seemed to have a hypnotic influence on

Yusuf, for he consented to proceedings that no sensible Arab would have shared or countenanced. At the time I complacently supposed that I was exerting force of character; it was afterwards that I came to know that it was pig-headedness.

On the 19th of December I planned to march. On the morning of that day Socrate overslept himself, and then came to announce that it rained heavily. If I myself had observed the rain first I would have deferred departure until a more auspicious moment, but being enraged with my domestic for being late I insisted upon his packing up immediately and setting forth in the wet. The endurance of physical discomfort is a small matter to the mind inflamed with wrath, and I wanted my creature to realise the discomfort of soaked garments on an empty belly. I had breakfast while Socrate and Yusuf loaded up. Yusuf also had come late, and, moreover, had brought with him an extra horse, dead lame, which he proposed should undergo a cure by marching until it got better. So I was cross with all my follow ing, and took my revenge by making them taste the disagreeable.

Getting into a wet saddle is certainly nasty, and so is rain down one's neck, and a horrid wind that makes a cigar burn on one side only. Nevertheless, a string of loaded horses, a lonely route, and an unknown destination are powerful aids to happiness, and a mile or two out of Aleppo found me as contented a man as ever bestrode a horse. We marched for eight long hours in the wet, over utterly uninteresting country, and in a driving mist that would have graced a Highland moor. Curious that the projection of the mind into the future should make the body so com-

pletely indifferent to the present. There lay before
me the Euphrates and her sister Tigris, Nineveh and
Babylon, Kerbela and Baghdad, Arab tribes and
Kurdish rovers, all the fascination of the free life of
the desert. *Ma sh'Allah!* it was surely good to be
alive, despite the raindrops.

Arrived at the village of Achterin I funked the
tents, and agreed to seek the dry comfort of a khan.
But Achterin being off the main road offered but poor
accommodation, and once more we found ourselves
lodged where the host kept chaff for camels. We
shared quarters with the chaff, which lay piled from
floor to ceiling, and dribbled down when one so much
as sneezed. The chaff got into our food, our mouths,
noses, ears, and lungs, and, worst of all, into my bed,
where it scratched me like live pins all the night
long. And still it rained in the morning, and still
we proceeded, only to arrive after nine hours marching
in the wet at another poverty-stricken village, where
there was no khan at all, and where we had to make
the best of the hospitality offered to us by a poor
Kurd farmer. His home consisted of one low thatched
building, the roof of which was supported by posts.
Our seven horses marched in and joined company with
a few donkeys, two or three calves, a handful of sheep,
many fowls, and one tall camel for whose head and
neck there was insufficient room. The floor was about
twelve inches deep in dry dung. In one corner of this
dark windowless apartment was a low mud platform,
railed off as kitchen, dining - room, and bedroom for
the farmer and his family. One side of this oasis in
a desert of uncleanliness was handed over to our party,
and Socrate at once sat himself down to rest instead
of preparing my tea. But I threatened to tie him up

between the hind legs of the camel if he did not immediately commence work, and soon I quaffed the cup that dries wet clothes, that soothes chafed limbs, and mends broken hearts. While Socrate peeled the potatoes, the camel, a tame and privileged animal, doubtless attracted by the unwonted waste, protruded its long nose over his shoulder and tried to lip up the peelings. Socrate cursed the brute in Greek. A dog took the chicken that Socrate had left unguarded, and Socrate chased him amid the horses' and the donkeys' legs in the vain hope of recovery. While he was so engaged a kitten fell into the pan of milk that had been procured after much trouble from a neighbour, and was designed for a rice pudding. Only the fact that I had a bottle of Horlick's Malted Milk to accompany the high tea that took the place of the lost dinner saved Socrate's life. A Greek is of little account in Mesopotamia, and nobody would have bothered if I had righteously done him to death for his sins.

Day number three broke threateningly, and once more we proceeded with the disapproval of the elements. But our pertinacity perhaps wearied the powers above, for towards afternoon the skies cleared and the sun broke forth. By that time we were involved in the low ridge of broken hills that fringes the bed of the Euphrates, and expecting every moment to obtain a glimpse of one of the world's greatest rivers. We were long denied the hoped-for view, and it was only when the sun had begun to fall low upon the horizon that I climbed a high knoll and from the top saw the sheen of water. Scarce a mile away lay the mighty Euphrates, steely bright in the evening rays that shone behind us. North and south

it stretched into the far distance, in broad expanses
that lay upon the darkening land in shimmering lakes.
Straight ahead only a ribbon of water was visible, for
the high banks concealed all but the farther shores.
Immediately beyond the river frowned a rampart of
drab-coloured hills, deeply scored with ravines, and
completely devoid of vegetation. From my feet to the
river there extended a flat brown plain unrelieved by
a single note of colour. Not a tree, or a bush, or a
blade of grass was in sight; only desolation the most
dreary, sadness the more sad because of the living
water that gleamed brighter and brighter in the
slanting light of a sinking sun. I sat watching this
panorama of present loneliness and ancient memories
until dusk fell upon the land and blotted out the
changing colours and soft outlines of distant mountains. Scrambling down to the plain at my feet
I passed close to a great mound, the earthly remains, as yet untouched, of the capital city of the
ancient Hittites, Carchemish of the Scriptures. The
mound conceals the relics of an old-time civilisation
that once covered these regions, that has left endless
signs of might, but of whose history, recorded in
countless rock cuttings, not one word can be read by
savants. All the greatness of Carchemish and its
people has vanished. The rolling river that nourished
its inhabitants flows quietly past the site of the ancient
capital, wondering perhaps why humankind one day
work busily on its banks, fight fiercely another day,
and are gone the next. The power of Carchemish,
in a desperate battle between Nebuchadnezzar and
Pharaoh Necho, was broken on this little plain nearly
three thousand years ago, and hardly fifty years ago
the Turkish army, with von Moltke in command of

the artillery, was beaten by the Egyptian forces on the selfsame spot.

Now sordid commercial enterprise is about to invade the solemn silence that hangs over this ancient battle-field, and soon passing Philistines of every nation may stop a day on the road to Nineveh and Baghdad, that they may wander among the pillars of Carchemish and wet their feet in the waters that flow down to Babylon.

We spent the night at a small village of mud-huts in the neighbourhood of the great mound of Car-chemish. Jerabulus sits fairly on the western bank of the Euphrates, and here the Baghdad Railway will essay the first crossing of the great river. The surveyors of the railway were considerably puzzled where to place the bridge owing to the divergent conditions of the bed of the river at different times of the year. Sweeping southward in a succession of wide curves, the Euphrates flows in a shallow valley about two miles broad, which the water crosses from side to side with almost mathematical regularity. When the river is low the stream is comparatively narrow, and flows between well-defined banks. When the spring rains commence, and the hot sun begins to beat upon the snow - covered mountains of Asia Minor, there is a tremendous increase of water, and the river rapidly rises, till at the end of May it races southward in turgid fury, thick with suspended mud, overwhelming islands and bordering flats to a breadth very often of nearly two miles. Birejik, the principal ferry on the northern Euphrates, did not commend itself to the engineers, as the eastern bank is high and precipitous, and would require a severe climb in the first mile after the crossing. At Jerabulus, how-

ever, the high western flat is above flood level, while
the lower hills beyond the eastern bank are scored
with deep ravines, along one of which it will be simple
to attain the general level of the surrounding country,
which is perhaps 200 feet higher. The bed of the
river at Jerabulus is thus contracted by the high flat
on the western side and the low hills on the eastern
bank to about 1500 yards. The stream is here cut
into three by two islands which are said to be flush
with the water in flood-time. These islands, however,
will greatly simplify the construction of the bridge,
for they offer firm ground for the erection of piers.
The main stream is about 200 yards wide, the other
two about 150 and 100 yards respectively. Unfortunately the middle channel is very deep, ranging from
30 feet at low water to 60 at high water. The current
varies between three and six miles per hour, according to the season. The greater part of the bed of the
river, including the islands and the two narrower
channels, should give little trouble to the engineers,
but I imagine that the spanning of the central current
of 200 yards presents rather a difficulty. The whole
problem, however, is not to be compared with any of
those involved in the bridging of the big Indian
rivers, with their great breadth and ever changing
beds. At Jerabulus the course of the Euphrates is
fixed, the bottom is firm gravel, and the possible
variations of rise are easily calculated.

At Jerabulus I suffered great annoyance, for it turned
out that there was no ferry, and no possibility of crossing the river but by travelling twenty miles north to
Birejik, or twelve miles south to a smaller ferry. We
chose the latter, and proceeded to march down the right
bank of the river. On the way we passed several of the

Old Crusading Castle at Birejik.

A Turkish Yailieh.

mounds which mark the sites of ancient buildings, and also for the first time encountered the cave-dwellings which are a feature of existence in this part of the world. The soft chalky rock is easily cut, and the straight precipices which continually present themselves to the river invite excavation. When we came to one hole in a wall overlooking the river I climbed up into what looked like a tomb, a vaulted chamber about ten feet square, with three shelves that could serve no purpose that I could imagine but to rest the dead. There was nothing to show whether this place was ten years old or ten thousand, for the creamy whiteness of the hewn walls was just the same colour as the rock itself when chipped by a knife. Most curious was the echo. Even a whisper was rustled about from wall to wall and ceiling to floor, until it died away in distant sibilance. A loud shout shook the rock to its very depths, reverberated in one's ears like stage thunder, and died hard, with a sound like that of far-away lowing cattle. The crack of a whip gave a result like the rattle of a Maxim. Every noise in this curious little chamber set the air quivering, and seemed, literally, to make the whole hill shake as if an earthquake had stirred its foundations. An eerie place to live in with a quarrelsome wife. A mile farther on we came upon a whole village cut out of the rock, and heard something of what the shrill voices of women and children could do. They were an evil-looking lot, and screamed to us loudly and rudely to ask why we went with our ears uncovered. It is a curious custom among Arabs of every age, degree, sex, and country to envelop the head and neck in a cloth that completely covers up the ears. For these appendages to appear in public struck these half savage, wholly

villainous rock-dwelling Arabs·as positive indecency,
not to say absurdity, and they expressed their opinion
of us with an impudence I have never seen surpassed.
If their men-folk had been of equal temper I expect we
should have fared badly, but they were evidently from
home, and we saw but one scowling brute armed with
a long flint-lock, and a pair of eyes that completely
withered Socrate. He, Socrate, bitterly protested when
I stopped to take photographs, and even Yusuf advised
immediate departure. In front of this village were
several heaps of stuff that looked like broken-up
bushes, black in colour, dry and dirty in appearance.
The stuff was *sus*, and its collection in season was the
only source of livelihood, besides robbery, which these
degenerates possessed. *Sus* is liquorice, and the founda-
tion of the delectable sweet that in days long past
turned one's teeth black and one's inside out.

In due time we came to the ferry and endured the
agony of impatience that all must suffer who would
cross a river. Here the Euphrates runs in one narrow
stream, scarce 200 yards broad, at the rate of an express train. The boats were plain deal boxes rather
longer than broad, and with one end cut away in a
lip that protruded over the river-bank. After endless
belabouration and objurgation we got three horses into
one of the boats, and then pushed off by the aid of long
poles. We reached the other side nearly a mile down-
stream. Meanwhile the other boat, no sooner than I had
left, took on a load of sheep, leaving the remainder of
my caravan to be dealt with by the first boat. This,
having vomited out self, Socrate, and the three horses,
proceeded to tow up-stream for a mile, then cross, then
tow up again—anyhow it meant a whole day wasted,
and another blackened page in my book of life,

Ferry-boat on the Euphrates.

Embarking a Yailieh at Birejik.

for I cannot rule my tongue when my spirit is vexed.

We were now in Mesopotamia in reality, and we signalised the event by putting up the tents. This performance interested Socrate tremendously, especially the hammering in of tent-pegs, of which he mushroomed the tops of half a dozen in complete happiness. Any tomfoolery pleases him, but .the boiling of water for tea is more difficult to him than work to a British navvy. My experience of him in the matter of charcoal fires, in the cooking of the simplest of food, in getting up in the morning early, are all too agonising for reproduction in print. Yusuf and Ebrahim I found had their work cut out, dividing the night into watches, and I realised why they preferred a khan to the pitching of tents. We were near a village with a very bad reputation, and it was never safe to leave the horses unguarded for a moment.

Mesopotamia is an expression that requires some definition. It refers particularly to that portion of the plains lying between the Tigris and Euphrates rivers, south of the mountains of Asia Minor and north of the ancient coast-line running between the two rivers not far north of Baghdad. Mesopotamia, however, is generally used to include all the above country, together with the immense alluvial flats lying between the old coast-line and the junction of the two rivers near Bussorah. This latter is the region that constituted the great wealth of ancient Babylonia, and which prophets foretell will one day recover its former richness under a modern system of irrigation. Mesopotamia proper, however, is outside all these schemes of the future, for though a flat plain generally speaking, it is irregular in surface and con-

siderably above the level of the great rivers which
enrich it. In contrast to the absolutely and mathemat-
ically level flats of Babylonia, which lend themselves
to irrigation, Mesopotamia is not suitable for canalisation, and indeed has never been irrigated in this
manner except to a small extent at isolated points.
The great value of Mesopotamia proper, a value very
little understood by the world in general, lies in the
fact that the greater part of it is blessed by a rainfall
that alone is sufficient to nourish a rich harvest. It
is not irrigation that Mesopotamia lacks, but security
and population.

After crossing the Euphrates our objective became
Haran, a district three days' journey to the east,
and lying in the same latitude as Jerabulus. By
striking north-east from the ferry we soon regained
the exact route of the Baghdad Railway, and thereafter had but to steer by the compass in order to
follow it step by step. The country offers no obstruction to engineering, and the exact track must be
that practically in a straight line between Jerabulus
and Haran. From the level of the Euphrates, about
1100 feet, there is an easy rise to 1700, whereafter the
height does not vary by 200 feet throughout the next
200 miles. On entering the basin of the Tigris, however, the level falls away by degrees until at Mosul the
altitude registered is only 800 feet, though Mosul is
nearly 600 miles from the Persian Gulf in a direct line.

Picking up a guide here and there we proceeded
across a country of low, rolling hills, alternating with
plains of high agricultural value. The most important
of these is known as Serouj, a great flat expanse dotted
by 360 villages said to contain 45,000 people, practically all Kurds. Next in value to Serouj comes the
plain of Haran, with 15,000 Arab inhabitants. Note

that these two rich and populous regions, as well as minor plains of similar character, lie within the first seventy miles of the railway's route in Mesopotamia, a region popularly believed to be a desert and of no present economic account. Our last camp in these parts was pitched in a curious oasis known as Ain el-Arus, an hour's march west of the Haran district.

Here are two features of interest to people brought up as Presbyterians, for few others of the Christian faith have any real knowledge of their Bibles. One small roof covers at once the burying-place of Abraham and the spot where bubbles up the water of the Well of Rebecca. Not many miles away is the city of Nahor to which Abraham migrated from Ur of the Chaldees. Serouj was originally settled by a patriarch of that name seventh in descent from Shem. Nahor was a son of Serouj; Haran, who founded Haran, was a grandson of Nahor; and Haran begat Lot—facts recorded in the eleventh chapter of Genesis. The Bible says that Abraham was buried in the cave of Machpelah in the field of a Hittite named Ephron. There is nothing to connect Ain el-Arus with the cave in question except the fact that Hittite remains are to be found in the neighbourhood. At Ain el-Arus, however, there is the unmistakable tomb, but no cave. Which is the more reliable, Holy Script or Arab tradition, is not for me to say; enough that the tomb is there, sacred in the eyes of all Mesopotamia, and the object of many a weary pilgrimage.

At one end of a low building is a dark chamber, whereof the greater part is railed off to enclose the actual tomb, a massive slab of stone with upright stones at head and foot. The stones are covered by a green cloth, there is a little Arabic writing on the wall, and no ornamentation of any kind. The walls and low dome were once whitewashed, but now are covered with dust and cobwebs, the stone-flagged floor is littered with straw and sheep droppings, the only light comes through a door so small that one must stoop to enter. In such humble quarters rests the father of Israel. The other end of the building consists of a much larger chamber, perhaps twenty-five feet square, a replica of the other but for the railing and the tomb. In the centre of the floor is a tank four feet square and about as many deep, full to the brim of the clearest water, wherein hang suspended with waving tails and fins about two score small fishes. From the tank runs a little stone canal through which the constantly rising water is allowed to escape into the open. Outside, the well-water runs down a short slope into a small pond, beyond which there is a much bigger pond, and beyond that again a lake nearly two miles long and about one hundred yards in width. The ponds are fed by numerous underground springs that rise hot from the ground. In the warm water are millions of tame fish ranging in size from an inch to four feet. The lake is covered with water-lilies that gleam snow-white amid patches of floating leaves, broad and velvet green. Between the tomb and the lake is an open space surrounded by mulberry trees. Hanging over the water and sweeping its surface with their drooping branches is a line of willows, now bare of foliage, but exquisitely graceful as they sway in the wind. In the little open glade we pitched the tents, and tethered the horses in a long row. A few poor Arab huts were near, and the people came and sat overlooking our arrangements. They spoke but little. There was a peaceful subdued air about the spot that enforced respect from all. At evening the sun sank out of sight in a splendour of red and gold light, and no sooner was he gone than a crescent of gleaming moon transformed the scene into a marvel of silver whiteness and black shadow. A simple and lovely corner of the desert is Ain el-Arus, and here Abraham sleeps the long sleep undisturbed by the noise of the world.

CHAPTER XI.

AN ADVENTURE.

AT Ain el-Arus we asked about guides to escort us across the desert to Ras el-Ain, on the road to which there was no habitation. Nobody cared, however, to accompany us into the country of the famous Kurd chieftain, Ebrahim Pasha, who has at his beck and call no fewer than 20,000 lances. Owing to the ravages of his men, part of Haran, once thickly populated, is now desolate, and unsafe to the persons and property of those who dwell to the westward of his haunts. In the night, however, two men came to say that for five pounds they would go with us for three days' march. This offer I declined, as we were not yet on the border of Ebrahim's territory. In the morning—it was Christmas Day—we marched for an hour, and then came to Aktchi-Kalaah, an Arab village in Haran, and the last populated place on the eastern route. Near by flowed a small river running north and south, a dividing line between the populated part of Haran and the region where ranged the lawless followers of Ebrahim Pasha. Here I hoped·to get soldiers from the Turkish official who, according to my information, was stationed at Aktchi-Kalaah with a guard of 100 men. The first thing we discovered, however, was that the Kaimakam and his guard had left five months before, and that there were now no officials at Aktchi-Kalaah, but only two soldiers in charge of the tumble-down barracks.

The soldiers declined to go with us, for they had no horses, besides which they could not leave their post without permission. They took us into the village, however, and did their best to persuade some of the people to accompany us as guides. The Arabs for reply pointed across the plain to several clusters of houses which they said were the ruins of villages recently ravaged by Ebrahim Pasha; the Pasha was a very bad man, and his people killed everybody who entered his country. Nobody would venture. After a long delay, however, one man, under pressure from the soldiers, agreed to come, and went off to saddle his horse. Meantime Yusuf laid in three days' corn for his animals.

After a long delay our prospective guide came back horseless and confessed himself afraid. He would not go. There was now nothing to be done but to wait several days until a military escort could be obtained from the town of Urfa, nearly forty miles away, or to proceed without. Needless to say which course we adopted. The talk about Ebrahim Pasha was true enough in regard to the ravaging of villages and the killing of people from Haran. But I knew that the cause of it was the existence of a desperate feud between the local tribes and those adhering to Ebrahim. Ebrahim himself had shown the greatest courtesy to European travellers, and whatever dangers his enemies ran in his country, foreigners had always been safe. There seemed to me no good reason for not proceeding alone. It was a simple matter to march straight east by the compass until in three days we struck the stream on whose banks stood Ras el-Ain. Water on the way was rather a difficulty, but my two Arab muleteers would surely be able to locate the holes that I knew to be comparatively frequent. Unfortunately we had no firearms. Hitherto I had always travelled with rifle and gun for sporting purposes, but during the present journey I had been told that I should see no game, and that carrying weapons and ammunition about would be useless. Hence our unarmed condition. I calculated, if indeed I thought about the matter at all, that Socrate's cannon, the camera stand, would be quite sufficient for any potential robbers whom we might encounter by the way. Alas! I calculated without full knowledge of the conditions, and without a sufficient understanding of the bold and ruthless character of the Arab of the desert.

An Armenian lad accompanied us for a mile or so, to show us the way to the ford across the river. That passed we were fairly launched into the wilderness, and with every prospect before us of not seeing a soul for three days. A wandering shepherd and his flock we might meet by chance, and always, of course, a band of freebooters. But these last I had no faith in, and no fear of if we chanced to encounter them. Clothed in ignorance and innocence we marched eastward, Socrate whistling indifferently, Ebrahim singing lustily, Yusuf, the owner of the horses, sullenly silent, feeling that he was doing wrong, but unable to combat the force of character, hereinafter recognised as pig-headedness, which made my will prevail against his. So we marched for two hours, until we were far out of sight of Aktchi-Kalaah and deep in a desolate region of low hills.

Then Socrate came up to me with an uneasy manner and drew my attention to a horseman cantering in rear. I said at once it was the guide who had turned

The Man who caught him, Bimbashi Muslim Bey, A.D.C. to H.M. the Sultan.

and

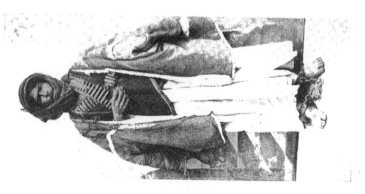

The Man who did he Deed,

AMBROSIA.

afraid, but who had now repented and was coming after us to earn the promised douceur. That satisfied Socrate, but not Yusuf, who pointed to another figure converging upon us from the far right. Socrate glanced fearfully around and said it would be much better if we had been escorted by soldiers. I said in reply that I would escort his back with my whip if he didn't keep his mouth shut. Yusuf made the horses close up until he had them all in a heap, a precaution that annoyed me, for so much apprehension on the part of my followers somewhat shook my own confidence.

Then the horseman from behind came up and from the offing began shouting questions. He was not the man I had supposed, but a very wild-looking Arab armed with a Martini carbine, which he carried across his saddle instead of slung on his back. He professed himself afraid to come near as we had the appearance of soldiers, and he did not want to be caught. As he shouted this information he took a cartridge from his belt and deliberately loaded his rifle. When Yusuf asked why he did this near inoffensive travellers he said it was merely a precautionary measure in view of the Effendi's military appearance—not an unreasonable statement, I thought, if he was as timid as he professed to be. Then it was our turn to ask questions : who was our friend, and where was he going ? Oh, he was the servant of Ebrahim Pasha, and he was bound for his master's camp at somewhere towards the south, nine hours distant.

Now to visit the famous Ebrahim had long been my desire, and I had hoped to hear at Ras el-Ain how and where to find him in the desert. If he was camped only nine hours away it was best to take him on the way to Ras el-Ain, for by so doing I should save two

or three days' journey.   Here then was the means
of obtaining my desire.   I told Socrate to tell Yusuf
to ask the Arab if he would guide us to his master's
camp, for which service we would pay him well.   The
gentleman graciously assented, and between him and
Yusuf there then ensued a long conversation, the gist
of which Socrate translated to me as soon as Yusuf had
told him in Turkish what it was all about.   Yusuf
was full of suspicions, and cross-examined the man as
to his connection with Ebrahim Pasha, finally getting
him to swear by the eyebrows of Mahomet, a sacred
oath, that he spoke the truth and cherished no evil
designs.   Even then Yusuf was not satisfied, and
Socrate was decidedly tremulous as he explained
the situation in English.   All of my following were
extremely averse to accompanying the fellow, and
strongly advised me to have nothing to do with
him.

Easier said than done, however, for we were unarmed while our friend had a loaded rifle in his hand.
Throughout these negotiations he had maintained a
position of tactical advantage, riding along on our
right rear at a distance of about 60 yards.   The rifle
carried across his saddle was thus always pointing
towards us, and ready for action at a moment's notice.
It is the traveller's business to observe these little
matters, and I realised that we were dealing with a
tough customer, whether his actions were prompted
by timidity or by aggressive intentions.   I was inclined to believe what he said, for his Martini carbine
was a weapon which I knew was carried by many of
Ebrahim Pasha's men, having been supplied to them
by the Turkish Government.   I had never seen it
carried by any of the numerous armed Arabs we had
passed here and there, and I supposed it could not be

obtained otherwise than through the Government. If the man meant robbery he could accomplish his object at any moment without any humbug about guiding us to Ebrahim Pasha. The mere fact that he refrained argued honesty. By diverging from our course a few points to the south, and travelling in company with him, we 'put ourselves in no worse position than we were already in, for he could pick us all off one by one whenever he fancied. • Subsequent consideration of the circumstances has led me to think that the presence of another man, mentioned earlier as having been seen on the far right, delayed action on the part of our timorous guide. The distant figure appeared to be a shepherd accompanied by a dog, probably in search of a lost animal, and as we marched along they crossed our line in rear and disappeared to the left. Our man probably caught sight of the shepherd about the time he loaded his rifle, and thought it better to wait developments before showing his hand. Hence the guide story, and the quaint experiences of the next half-hour.

Having decided to accept our friend's services, we now, according to his directions, swung off a trifle to the south and continued our march, he still maintaining his advantageous position on our right rear. After a little time, however, he gained confidence and came nearer, so that I was able to talk to him through my pair of interpreters. It was rather a slow business, as Socrate and Yusuf were behind, and both decidedly sulky. Finally I offered the man a cigarette, and he came up and took it from my hand. He then rode beside me for some distance, the muzzle of his rifle, however, always within a few feet of me and pointing straight towards my body. He wore two bandoliers full of cartridges, an equipment which further suggested the probability of his belonging to Ebrahim Pasha's organised body of desert horse. While decidedly amused at his precautions against surprise, I was none the less conscious of the formidable character of those rows of big bullets. Perhaps the reader, accustomed to small-bore rifles, does not realise what a huge lump of ugly lead goes to the Martini cartridge.

Conversation soon languished, and I then took from my pocket a volume of Chaldean history and began reading. The Arab's horse walked faster than mine, and in a few minutes he had forged ahead and fallen into line. My horse had his head to the leader's tail, and confidence seemed completely established. Our guide seemed content that we should all be behind him, out of his line of sight. Occasionally he looked round to see how we were getting on, and then I would look up from my book and exchange grins with him. My suspicions were now almost lulled. The others trailed on behind, and I did not bother about what they thought. A little later our guide slackened his horse and waited till I drew level, noticeably on my left side, so that the rifle no longer commanded my defence-less body. He asked for a cigarette and I passed one to him, and lit one for myself. He then requested matches, but failed to get a light as a breeze defeated his endeavours. So then he wanted my cigarette at which to light his own. Having succeeded, he held out my cigarette, now reduced to half its original size. He was a trifle in front and had to extend his right arm rather backwards towards me. To avoid burning myself I had to grasp the cigarette between thumb and forefinger, the rest of my hand thus spreading over his for a few seconds as the movement of the horses made it difficult to catch hold at once. As I took the cigarette from him I noticed that in his hand there was a spare cartridge, presumably ready for reloading in case he had to fire. But this business of the cigarette seemed to suggest that he had full confidence, for his left hand held rifle and reins while the other was completely at my mercy as he held it out with the cigarette. At that moment I could have gripped his wrist, whipped my other hand over it and pulled him out of the saddle without difficulty. By falling on top of him on to the ground he would have lost his rifle, and then we would have been equal in a struggle until my three men behind should have come up and secured him. It was a perfect opportunity, and I suppose I shall regret all my life that I did not take advantage of it. But all things considered I don't think I then had justification for taking him to be a robber. As it was I did nothing. He then drew ahead again into his former position, slung the rifle over his shoulder, and proceeded peacefully, my doubts thereafter being completely allayed.

For three-quarters of an hour we followed our guide, under the impression that we were being led to the camp of the Kurdish chief. I smoked and read Chaldean history, and generally felt that the world was going well. The day was clear, the sun bright, and the air pleasant, for it blew fresh and cool from the snows in the north. The man in front sat his horse well, carried his rifle and bandoliers with perfect ease, and gave the impression of a man who was thoroughly at home in the saddle. He was of the small and wiry kind, very dark in colour, and with a hawk-like brown eye that showed a great deal of white. His feet were bare, and played in and out of the stirrups at random. He was for ever looking round, as if existence consisted in observation rather than in contemplation. I took him to be a bit of a devil who would not care much

K

what he did. His high staccato voice suggested independence and action. His attitude towards me was
one of perfect equality, with perhaps a dash of con-
tempt, natural enough no doubt towards one he meant
to rob and murder. He soon tired of holding us all in
the hollow of his hand.

We were approaching a sky-line which looked as if it
would afford a wide view to the south-east. In every
other direction we could see for miles. Not a man,
nor a beast, nor a habitation was in sight. Putting
his feet into the stirrups and kicking up his horse, our
guide cantered slowly forward to the sky-line, where he
stood silhouetted against the horizon for some minutes.
He then turned back and walked his horse to meet
us, but at an angle that took him to our right flank.
At eighty yards' distance he halted and shouted
something in a loud voice. No interpretation was
needed; I knew at once it was a case of your money
or your life. His demand was for forty pounds for
his master, Ebrahim Pasha.

I shouted to my followers to reply that we would
settle with his master when we got to him, not before.
There then ensued a lot of bawling between the robber
and my Arabs, and all I could make of it from Socrate's
agonised translation was that I must pay or be killed.
The rascal now began shouting at me direct in a
blustering manner, and I threatened him with my
whip, and started kicking at my horse's ribs. If only
I could get the brute going I would be safe enough,
and could probably run the fellow down between his
first and second shots, for I had now no doubt whatever that he was prepared to shoot. Unfortunately
my nag was young, foolish, and pig-headed, and instead of answering sharply to whip and heel it swerved
violently sideways towards the caravan horses, who

were now bunched together about twenty yards away from me. Despite everything I could do he halted near the other horses for a second, the while I brought up both hands to the reins to slew him round. At that moment I looked up, saw the rifle pointed, and a tiny puff of smoke issue from the muzzle. A dark grey line seemed to hover for an instant between the rifle and myself, I felt a thud somewhere below, and then I had got my horse moving again, and given him a couple of sharp whacks with the whip. But the brute would not go straight, but kept swerving sideways, and I was still thirty yards from the robber when he fired again, almost straight in my face. I saw his eyes glaring diabolically along the sights, but was too keen to get at him to bother much about consequences. Shot number two, however, completely scared my animal, and he whipped round and bolted back. I was surprised to find how little control I had, and now for the first time discovered that both hands were deluged with blood, and that one finger was hanging by the skin. When I tried to pull up, the reins slipped through my fingers, and I noted an unusual lack of strength in the right arm. While I was realising the damage the robber fired again, and I heard the bullet whistle past me towards the caravan, one of the horses of which immediately began to plunge violently. When I came up with a rush the whole lot stampeded. I cannot now remember whether a fourth shot was fired or not, but I saw the robber follow at a canter, and when the horses were stopped he was still about eighty yards away, shouting, and threatening with the rifle. By now my saddle and clothes were drenched in blood, and I realised that I was helpless. I slipped to the ground and told Socrate, who was desperately excited, to pass the word that I would pay all the money I had. Ebrahim then came to me, and I told him to fish a little bag out of my breeches-pocket and give it to the robber. Feeling suddenly faint I then lay down with my head on a stone. Out of the corner of my eye I saw Ebrahim run forward and put the money-bag on a tiny mound fifty yards away. The robber then shouted him off and came up with great caution, leading his horse.

My faintness had passed away the moment I lay down, and I was glad to realise that whilst I was bleeding profusely there was none of the spouting of blood which indicates the breakage of an important artery. Yusuf got out a large handful of cut tobacco and wrapped it round my left hand. By this time the robber had discovered that the bag contained less than half the money he had demanded. He threatened to kill us all if the full sum was not produced. I cunningly prompted my men to reply that their master was already dying, and that he was welcome to all their lives and all their property. At the moment Socrate, Yusuf, and Ebrahim were all kneeling down around me in the most touching manner, and their solicitation, and the fact that the horses had been left to wander at will, bore out their statement that I was *in extremis*. Nevertheless Yusuf pressed me to give the fellow something more—say the yellow leather bag wherein I kept my papers. But I wasn't for that at all, and made a counter-proposal to give up the tiffin-basket. Yusuf got quite cross with me, and said that all our lives would be sacrificed if something was not done. Then I decided to give way, and was ordering the extraction of the papers from the yellow ·leather bag when the robber moved off a couple of hundred yards and occupied himself with a pair of saddle-bags that had fallen to the ground. The horse that had been wounded by the third shot had bucked them off.

Having examined the contents of the saddle-bags—potatoes, rice, charcoal, and tent-pegs—the robber slung them over his horse, cast many doubting looks towards us, and then rode slowly off, much to my astonishment, for I hardly expected that such a tough customer would have let us down so lightly. But he seemed really off, and soon he disappeared over the sky-line half a mile away. We were all intensely relieved, myself probably more than the others, for I felt extremely disgusted with myself for having brought these three ignorant fellows into such a predicament by my wilfulness. I had hitherto been in much anxiety lest our robber friend should see fit to polish them off altogether so as to be rid of witnesses. It is a rule in the desert to leave no traces of deeds of violence, and it has been a matter of amazement to all who know the story and the customs of the Arabs that a single one of our party was allowed to escape. But my three followers showed no fear on their own account, but the greatest sympathy for me. One and all declared that they would willingly have given their lives to save me my wounds, and I verily believe they meant it at the moment. Kinder, anyhow, they could not have been. Much blood made my damages appear more serious than they were. One corner of the palm of the left hand was pretty well smashed, and the forefinger severed. There was a big bullet - hole in the right forearm, and an exit hole in the wrist just below the pulse, evidently a near shave of the main artery. For a long time afterwards I had the idea that the first bullet did all the damage, but latterly I have come to think that it is possible the second bullet was responsible for one of the wounds.

One curious thing is that I felt no pain whatever when I was wounded, and thought indeed that only the flap of my thick shooting jacket had been struck. I was able to hold the reins with the damaged left hand, and to whack my horse soundly with the whip in my right hand, although the radius was literally pulverised. It was because the reins became slippery with blood that I could do so little to control my horse. It has to be remembered too that the hand is one mass of nerves, and is probably the most sensitive part of the whole body. Yet this great lump of a Martini bullet, so different from the little pencil of nickel from a small-bore rifle, had ploughed its way right through one hand, and in a lateral direction for some six inches through an arm. Writers of stories should note these facts, for they are at considerable variance with the assertions commonly made in books that wounded men groan and faint and do other untoward things. It is only when inflammation sets in that pain is experienced, and then it is seldom so severe that it cannot be borne, unless in one of the vital organs, when nature gives relief by unconsciousness.

With the departure of the robber we all became quite chirpy, and I stood up to see how I felt. A cummerband was twisted round my body with both arms inside, and I found I could walk easily enough, though my head was a trifle dizzy. The horses were then collected, and with a man holding each of my arms we commenced the return journey, our seven horses following obediently in rear. There was no doubt about what to do, for Urfa, where was a German Mission hospital, was only thirty-six miles distant from the village of Aktchi-Kaalah, which we had left behind only three hours before. After ten minutes' slow walking I concluded that there was no longer any likelihood of a fainting fit, which I had feared owing to loss of blood, and with some trouble I was hoisted into the saddle, where I found myself quite comfortable. But very soon afterwards I began to be disagreeably conscious of my wounds, and of the shaking of the horse, but as there was absolutely no other method of proceeding I had to put up with it, little relish though I had for ten miles of riding in such circumstances. Story - tellers should here again note that I never felt the slightest inclination for water either down my throat or upon my heated brows. Nor would I have looked at a brandy flask if anybody had offered me one. Nothing particular happened on the way back, except when recrossing the ford in the river. The bed of the stream is a deep trench little more than thirty feet wide, with perhaps three feet of water running at the bottom. Getting up and down was very awkward, and Socrate fell off his horse and into the water. By a merciful coincidence my camera, which he was carrying, fell on the soft mud, and was picked up undamaged. I got across without falling, but I would much rather have had my hands and arms loose. During our march we observed far to the south a horseman riding parallel with us, and we had no doubt that this was the culprit watching to see what we were about. I was afraid when he saw that I was alive and kicking that he would come back and have another go at us. But he did not, and doubtless to - day he is bitterly regretting that he did not cut us all off utterly.

I was mighty thankful to arrive at Aktchi-Kaalah. The whole village soon surrounded us, and bitter were the curses rained down upon the head of Ebrahim

Pasha and his infernal brood. There seemed no doubt in anybody's mind that one of his men had done the deed, and by this time I had come to believe that the Kurdish chief was all these people painted him. The unblushing hypocrites. I discovered afterwards that every man in Aktchi-Kaalah knew who my assailant was, why he had attacked me, and that he no more belonged to Ebrahim Pasha than to the man in the moon. But that is another and rather interesting story.

Meanwhile I was taken to the hut of the headman, tenderly lifted from my horse, and bestowed on rugs and pillows in the darkest and dirtiest of chambers, whence fowls, sheep, and goats had to be turned out to make room for me. All the male population came in to sympathise and to hear the tale of woe related by Yusuf. The first thing to be done was to send word to Urfa. Socrate wrote a letter in Greek on the pages of his note-book, with my name printed in Roman characters, and a messenger was engaged to take it. The Armenian boy said there were several people at Urfa who could read Greek, and the letter, together with the explanation of the messenger, we supposed, would be quite sufficient to bring the doctor to me without delay. On promise of payment of a sovereign the messenger agreed to cover the thirty-six miles to Urfa in six hours, which would land him between nine and ten at night. There being a bright moon, the doctor would probably agree to travel all night, and so reach me in the early morning. I was now beginning to suffer considerably, but a brew of tea and something to eat bucked me up, and I was quite able to join in the conversation conducted by about fifty Arabs squatting around. The burden of it all was what a scoundrel Ebrahim Pasha must be.

Then the Arab hakeems came to me and proposed to dress my wounds. As it must be a long time before the doctor could arrive I consented, thinking it would be better to have them washed and bandaged rather than remain open to the air in such a foul and dirty place. They hurt me considerably and I yelled with much vigour. They bound pieces of hairy goatskin over the wounds and then bandaged them up with dirty rags. I suffered too much to protest, and indeed did not care what they did so long as they quickly made an end of the business.

Here I cannot but think it appropriate to interpolate a little advice to readers, in case they may ever find themselves in a like predicament. It was a fatal error allowing these Arabs to touch me, and I endured long months of suffering in consequence, not to speak of great danger to my life. The first thing to do to a wound is to shut it up from contact with dirt or foul air. If no antiseptic bandages are available, a clean white handkerchief, or any other linen or cotton, in the folded condition in which it has come back from the wash, is the safest. Unless water is known to be absolutely pure, it should not be used. If there is no antiseptic liquid available for dressing and washing, it is imperative to use boiled water that has been carefully protected whilst cooling. Boiling will render any bandages antiseptic. If poison can be kept away from a wound until a doctor arrives little harm can ensue. But poison is everywhere, and infection can be avoided only if everybody's hands are carefully washed and perfectly clean water and bandages are used. The hands of these Arabs were filthy, and their bandages traps for every kind of microbe under the sun. In consequence of their handling my wounds were furiously poisoned, and I am lucky to be alive to tell the tale to-day. Most people know these things, but there may be some who are as lamentably ignorant on the point as I was until bitter experience brought me knowledge.

My first night at Aktchi-Kaalah was no pleasant vigil, apart from the fact that I was missing my Christmas dinner. Inflammation rapidly increased and with it came fever and much pain. There was never a wink of sleep to be got, nor any relief by change of position. Both hands were propped up with pillows, and I could not move off my back without an explosion of language that shocked the grave people who sat by me smoking, and cursing Ebrahim Pasha. Then, too, there was always coming the memory of those diabolical eyes and their ruthless owner who shot at me as callously as if I had been a wounded bird. As my visitors dropped off in the middle of the night, and my own weary fellows slept, I could think of little else than the occurrences of the day, and there came to me plenty of the fearfulness that bothered me but little when the bullets were flying. How brave we could all be if we were not afflicted with consciousness.

CHAPTER XII.

A CITY OF TERROR.

MORNING duly arrived at Aktchi-Kaalah, but no doctor with it. I calculated that the messenger's horse had failed him and that he did not reach Urfa in the time expected. But at peep of day he must have been there, as the doctor was even now hurrying towards me, more alive even than myself to the danger I ran from lack of attendance. By midday he would arrive. I endeavoured to practise patience, although I was bored and tired beyond words of the pain and discomfort. In the morning came the Arab hakeems for another dressing, but I said I would wait for the European doctor. At midday there came no doctor, nor at two o'clock, nor at four, nor at six. Then the Arabs pressed again to be allowed to dress me, as they said there was danger in keeping the wounds tied up. So I let them. They could not cause me much more pain than I was already enduring—so I thought in my ignorance.

They had prepared some thick sticky stuff that looked like treacle. One man took a lump of this concoction and rolled it between his palms until it lengthened into a pencil—this to be thrust into the wound in my arm to make it better. Taking off the bandages was an experience in itself, and the whole village collected to know what the noise was about. Then they commenced operations with the pencil. To make it slippery they borrowed some of my salt butter from Socrate. Yusuf, with much rough tenderness, held my head and shoulders during these proceedings, and Socrate stood near to help. When I cursed, Socrate changed my English into Turkish and Yusuf transformed it into Arabic. By degrees the hakeems got to know what I thought of them. The first half-inch of the pencil revealed to me potentialities of pain far beyond the most morbid of dreams. I roared like Job when, covered with boils, he sat down in the ashes. The bloody bandages, my furies, and the sight of the pencil being pushed home, was too much for Socrate. He staggered to the door, and there fell down in a dead faint. Not a single Arab saw the humour of it, and I was the only one able to raise a laugh. I didn't laugh long, however, for the pencil business went on while I yelled and called upon all the powers of darkness to consume the terrible men who tortured me. With Socrate stretched lifeless in the doorway there was nobody to translate my sentiments, and the pencil was duly thrust home. That quite satisfied me of hakeems, and when Socrate recovered I explained to them that they could dress my wounds again when I was dead, but not before. I was so upset in mind that I insisted on getting up and going outside, where I walked up and down for ten minutes in the cold. I looked a good deal in the direction of Urfa, but there was no encouragement coming from there.

All the evening I expected the doctor, and even up to twelve o'clock I had hopes of him, but he never appeared. My left hand was now swollen up like a cocoa-nut and the arm was treble its usual size, conditions that were productive of quite enough pain to put sleep hopelessly out of the question. My fever increased, but even yet, O story writer, I never once called for water, or to have my brow laved. Certain touches to my pillow, I will confess, were welcome, even when administered by the rough hands of Yusuf. Several times during the day I had drunk a cup of tea, and eaten flaps of Arab bread anointed with my own tasty salt butter—that nipped so when introduced into my arm. That night was very weary, and again in the silent hours I had horrid visions of smoking rifles, glaring eyeballs, and threatening Arab figures. I buoyed myself up with the certainty of the doctor arriving in the morning.

But the third day brought no doctor. It was time for action on my part now, for long-neglected wounds have a way of turning on their owner. I wasn't very fit for travelling thirty-six miles on horseback, but if Urfa would not come to me it was clear that I must go to Urfa. Yusuf packed up quick enough, and at seven o'clock I was hoisted on my horse with a liberal amount of swearing on my part, and much consolatory groaning from all the females of the village, gathered to see me depart. We now had a sergeant and two soldiers as escort. They had been out in the district to keep a tax-gatherer company, and came quickly to my rescue when I needed them little. They added to the volume of curses against Ebrahim Pasha, and offered to lend me money to tip all the people in Aktchi-Kaalah who had sympathised with me. The first ten minutes' marching made me think how little the average human being knows when he is well off. Thereafter, however, I felt a trifle easier, and was able to take a dim sort of pleasure in the keen morning air. After an hour's riding a man came cantering towards us and said a carriage was following him with doctors and lawyers and bimbashis. A few minutes later came the carriage, and I realised that henceforth my troubles were removed to another plane.

I was greatly disappointed to find that the carriage contained none but Turkish officials, one the municipal doctor of Urfa. The German doctor had not come, and these people knew nothing about him except that I was to be taken to the German hospital on arrival. We were eight hours getting to Urfa—over country roads and in a country carriage! Towards the end of the journey I was so beat that I actually slept for an hour. Then in the darkness we drove up a steep hill and halted outside a gateway. Almost immediately I heard " Poor man " from female lips, and thereafter I knew I was all right.

They helped me inside the while I explained how long I had been without attention. Immediate dressing was of course the verdict. I wanted a cup of tea very badly, and that was being prepared. Then I said I wanted chloroform, as I was tired of hearing myself roar when I was hurt. Doctors and nurses looked at each other when I said that, but they agreed to it, stipulating that I should go without the tea. Then I was laid flat and had my clothes cut off with scissors. Next they put a mask over my face and commenced dropping the chloroform on it. I was very cheery by now, anticipating the pleasure of complete unconsciousness after much weary experience of the other thing. The chloroform seemed slow to work, and in the course of conversation I said it must be of German manufacture. This cheap joke I thought I made before I went off, but afterwards they told me I had waked up in the middle of the examination to make it, to the entertainment of all concerned. My next remembrance was waking up and asking for my tea. Somebody

Ancient Viaduct at Urfa (Edessa).

Armenian Nurses.

sleeping in a bed beside me looked at a watch and said it was nine hours since the chloroform, and that I should have the tea in five minutes. Nine solid hours of forgetfulness! The tea was made over a spirit-lamp, and had no milk in it, and all they gave me to eat was sweet biscuits. What bitter disappointment. I could have eaten three large meals at once. But kindness prompted these measures, chloroform having strange effects on ordinary stomachs.

Then I was comparatively easy until the afternoon, and was able to tell them all about it, learning too where I was and in whose hands. Two Swiss doctors were in charge of this German Mission hospital. There was also a Swiss house-father, Jacob Kunzler, who was a trained hospital assistant, and his German wife, who had done her three years in a hospital at Perth, and spoke English as well as I did myself. Besides these there were an Armenian apothecary, Abraham Effendi, and three pretty Armenian nurses. The head German doctor had gone off to meet me, but had taken the wrong road. He was now back, and all concerned were to dress my wounds in the afternoon. Then Gracey came in, a wild young Irishman belonging to the American Mission, and he fell on my neck and wept over me.

They said I would not need chloroform this time, and I let them lay me flat in the operating-room and take the bandages off. Gracey held one arm up while the rest played with the other. This hurt considerably until I found Gracey's one paining too. I looked at Gracey in indignation, for instead of supporting the broken arm he was leaning on it, and gazing in a fascinated manner at the other hand, exposed to view in all its bloody ugliness. Then a nurse darted round, pushed Gracey away, whereupon he fell flat on the floor

in a faint. That was my second scalp, and I felt quite
pleased over it. When it was all over they said my
injuries were not serious. The hanging finger was
done for, but everything else would mend in a few
weeks, including the smashed radius of the right arm.

Next day all the people of Urfa of any consequence
came to see me. The most friendly was an Effendi,
whom I afterwards came to know was the owner of the
village of Aktchi-Kaalah, a thoroughly accursed place,
as I shall demonstrate later on. I had a good deal of
fever at the time, but felt quite cheerful in the warmth
of so much sympathy. My hands were of course
absolutely useless, and I lay in bed with them propped
up, so that I could not move from my back. I had to
be fed like a small child, and when I smoked the cigar
had to be lit for me and taken from my mouth when
the ash got too long. Other people seemed to have a
much worse idea of my condition than I had myself.
Miss Shattuck, the kind American lady whose mission
work is famous throughout Asia Minor, came to see
me. Like all Americans in Turkey, she thinks smoking one of the most serious vices, and when she walked
into the room and found the poor maimed and fevered
Britisher smoking a long cigar she was sadly taken
aback. I couldn't even take the cigar out of my
mouth, and the others present were so tickled at the
situation that they forgot to come to my rescue. But
Miss Shattuck was not the woman to deny her sympathy for so small a reason, and to her thoughtfulness
and kindness while I was in Urfa I owed the allevia-
tion of many a long-drawn-out hour. Another visitor
of mine that day was Padre Josef, the pastor of the
Syrian Protestant Church. He hung on for a long
time, while others came and went, waiting for an
opportunity. It came when three solemn old Turks

sat in the room with nobody to interpret. Down on his knees dropped Josef, with a most unctuous *Let us pray*. And he prayed for a full quarter of an hour in his best Turkish, for his English wasn't good enough to lay before the Throne, he afterwards explained. The Turks took this infliction very well, and at every hope for the recovery of the sufferer they interjected a pious *In sh'Allah*, spoken in the deep reverent voice that makes one think the Moslem the most sanctimonious humbug in the world.

These were early days, before my troubles descended upon me, and I had time and spirit to hear about things local. Urfa was a city of terror, for here in the days of the Armenian massacres terrible deeds had been done. Early in the autumn of 1895 there had been a small massacre, when several hundreds had been murdered. The town was full of ruthless Kurds and Arabs who thirsted for the blood of Unbelievers. Then came some months of outward peace but much inward tremor. Half the population of the city was Armenian, nearly all of whom were poor folk who earned their living in menial occupations. Hardly one was rich enough to leave the place, and those who had the money could not get official permission to go where they might find safety. Men went to their shops or their work in the morning, having said good-bye to a family whom they might never see again in this world. Staying at home meant starvation, perhaps precipitation of the massacre of which they went in daily fear. At the end of December the bolt fell.

One morning a gun was fired at sunrise, whereupon killing began. Every Armenian man in the streets was ruthlessly shot down or hacked to pieces. At sunset a gun was fired and the massacre ceased. Next morning the gun was fired again and the massacre was resumed.

During the night three thousand women and children took refuge in the Armenian cathedral, which was filled to overflowing. They had been assured of safety there by the Turkish authorities. But in the morning the rioters surrounded the church, placed tins of kerosine and heaps of firewood against the doors and set the building alight. Every one who came out was cut to pieces with knives, the cathedral burnt with ghastly fury, demented fanatics ranged around it pouring volleys in at doors and windows, and in a few hours the building was a heap of smoking ruins, covering the ashes of the three thousand innocents. Altogether between 6000 and 10,000 lives were taken in Urfa. There were several hundred orphan children left, hence the American and German orphanages, which have fathered and mothered them since those terrible days.

That long period of waiting between the first and second massacres was almost worse than the massacres themselves, so said the few I met who had been through it. I said that those days were over, that there would be no more massacres. But they shook their heads and said recent events made them go in daily fear. Signs and portents were ominous. , Urfa was one of the most lawless places in all Turkey, where the people were most fanatical and most independent of the central Government. The local Governor was a bad man, and he was quite capable of projecting a massacre without instructions from headquarters.

Meanwhile I had other things to think of, for abscesses had developed in my wounds, and caused me great pain. Three geese outside my window troubled me much by their noise. They had voices that curdled my blood, and caused the rafters of my room to vibrate. A cat bereft of her young moaned continu-

The Pool of Abraham at Urfa.

A Swimming-pond at Urfa.

ously for a week. Every hour of the day and night two bugles in the Turkish barracks close by rang out a discordant call. And a certain dog in the compound, when chained, never ceased to lament his fate by howls, miserable as those of a lost soul. The dog was hard at it one day when the Doctors and the Nurses and the Knives and the Iodoform and the Bandages came in to pay me their daily visit. Programme for the morning was the cutting of abscesses in right arm and left hand, and the amputation of the finger that had been left hanging. Right O, said I to the doctor, for they might have cut my throat for all I cared, so long as I floated in the sheltered deeps of Chloroform Bay. When I woke up the doctor said he'd cut off the finger, and at that moment I noticed that the dog was now silent. I addressed myself to Jacob in tones of deep reproach.

"Jacob, you have given my finger to the dog."

Quoth Jacob, equally reproachful — "Oh, Herr Fraser, neffer would I gif the meat of an Englishman to a dok." Whereat I was satisfied.

Dr Fischer, the kindest and best of men, now developed enteric. So ill did he become that the others despaired of his life. The Armenians, too, were in great anxiety at this time, for the Governor of the city had been overheard to remark that the Armenians were raising their heads too high and that they must be taught another lesson. A dead Armenian had been found in an adjacent village, and not even an inquiry was held. Crowds of patients were coming to the hospital, some of whom cried and moaned in bitter agony. After a fortnight my fever had left me, though the pain of dressing still necessitated chloroform—after much pleading on my part, for they were very reluctant to give it to me—and opiates were still the only road to rest. They let me go out for a drive one day, with Mrs Kunzler, and the baby. Three times stones were thrown at us in the course of the drive. I began to conceive a horror of Urfa, and longed to get away. After much discussion I was deemed fit to travel to Aleppo, four days distant by carriage. The faithful Gracey agreed to accompany me, and having had five long weeks of Urfa I left it and my kind hosts with much gladness. I fancied my troubles were nearly over, and that in the house of some hospitable friends of my own nationality at Aleppo I should soon be convalescent, and able once more to take the road.

If the yailieh were not the most wondrous carriage in the world it would surely be in a chronic condition of smash and upset. But although at the present moment of writing I have travelled in it no less than 500 miles I have never yet suffered accident, nor have I ever seen one in trouble in the course of my wanderings. Being something like a shallow boat hung upon springs, there are no seats, and the traveller must recline on the floor. Seated thus, with pillows behind and a good mattress underneath, considerable comfort may be attained. Above the body of the carriage are stiff ribs that curl right round the top. These are covered with a hood of thin wood or waterproof canvas, which effectually keeps out sun and rain. Flaps all round may be drawn up or secured down, according to desire. When the carriage upsets in a rut it rolls on its ribs and suffers little damage. People inside escape hurt according to the age of their bones and the number of iron-cornered boxes they may have beside them. This was the carriage which was to take me to Aleppo in four days. It was driven by one of the fattest men I have ever encountered, an

Armenian called Moxes, or Moses, who had the reputation of being the finest whip in Asia Minor.

But the finest of whipping cannot dodge the inequalities of the Turkish road, and we did some rolling and lurching that caused me much agony. The broken arm was fixed in a starched bandage that had stiffened into boards, else it would have suffered further breakage many times over. The other poor cocoa-nut I held suspended in the air when we came to bad places, and prayed that we might not go beyond 45 degrees. And we never did, whether owing to the driving or my prayers I cannot say. Gracey kept me alive by his conversation on theology, anthropology, and politics, subjects he discussed with the force and originality given by Heaven to the Irishman to make up for general cussedness. Priestcraft summed up Gracey's ideas of the root of all Irish trouble. If ye don't do what the priest tells ye, yer sins won't be forgiven. And for an Irishman, ye know, the worst thing that can happen to him is not to have his sins forgiven. Yes, I acquiesced, in a tone that made Gracey look at me and ask what made Scotsmen so damnably dry. Being a missionary, of course he used another word having the same meaning. Then Gracey fed me with a spoon three times a day, lit my cigars though he disapproves of tobacco, procured me Turkish whisky though he is a teetotaller, and never once remonstrated when I used language appropriate to the road. He joked out of the window with our escort of mounted police, and beat one with his stick when the man made a difficulty, for which they all loved him the more. They took half the usual backshish from Gracey, and evinced twice the usual gratitude. Gracey once made a carriage journey with three solemn Moslems. When Sunday came round Gracey called a

halt, for he wasn't going to break the holy Sabbath
day. The Moslems remonstrated, and said they hadn't
required the carriage to stop on Friday, *their* Sunday.
Gracey was obdurate, and the others gave in! Gracey
always gets what he wants, and I never heard anybody
deny that he deserves it.

At Aleppo I was still alive, and very satisfied to find
myself in the hands of a motherly countrywoman and
four charming daughters distributed over a total period
of seventeen years. There was much competition for
the feeding of me, and if I could have absorbed all
that offered I should soon have been worth killing for
foie gras. The first thing to happen to me was an
operation that entailed two and a half hours under
chloroform. When I woke up I ate a large meal and
felt quite happy. Then the band began to play. At
night the doctor came again, and I delivered an ulti-
matum—morphia, or hari-kari. He mixed a full dose,
and the prick of the needle was the sweetest feeling I
have ever known. In ten minutes the murderous agony
in my left hand was stilled, and life was once more
worth living. Blessed sleep ensued, and in the morning I was only troubled by the nausea that succeeds
heavy saturation of the system with chloroform. In
this matter of chloroform I became a marvel to the
whole faculty in Aleppo. The first operation was
succeeded by several others, to all of which I walked
a mile to the doctor's dispensary. There I would be
subjected to twenty-five minutes' carving, with forty
minutes under the chloroform. On waking up I used
to eat an orange, watch other operations taking-.place
beside me, then ten minutes later rise up and walk
home alone through the crowded streets of Aleppo.
Then a large tea, followed by a long and strong cigar.
That's what early porridge does for one.

Herewith endeth my tale of woe, for in the middle of May I was ready for the road once more. Of my intention to proceed to Baghdad after all, much disapproval was expressed in Aleppo. Yusuf held his hands up and begged me to take note of the warning of Allah. Nevertheless he was prepared to go with me again, if I would ride and wanted his pack-horses. I was generally supposed to be mad, with *toujours Baghdad* for my *idée fixe*. And so it was, for it was the getting to Baghdad that was to make up for all these long months of weary idleness.

CHAPTER XIII.

LOCAL POLITICS.

Now for the Mesopotamian politics with which I so unfortunately got myself mixed. The adventure which I have described has much more to it than simple robbery.

The common understanding of the word desert is a place where nothing profitable grows, and where nothing profitable would grow if encouraged. In this sense Mesopotamia is no desert at all; it is desert only in the sense that it contains no settled inhabitants, except at a few points on the outer fringe. In the interior there are no towns and hardly any villages worth mentioning. Nevertheless, a considerable population roams over the immense plains that lie between the Tigris and the Euphrates, and it is the enmities and friendships, the feuds and alliances between the different divisions of these nomads, that constitute the politics of Mesopotamia. Of one of these feuds it appears that I was the unfortunate victim.

Not to delve too deeply into ancient history, let it suffice to relate that a certain Kurdish chieftain, about a generation ago, was summoned by the Turkish Government to the city of Aleppo to answer for his misdeeds. Doubtful as to the date of his return, the chief took the precaution of depositing his valuables with a wealthy friend who lived at Urfa. When the Kurd got to Aleppo he was given coffee and died, and his son was exiled to Egypt. In the course of time the son, the now celebrated Ebrahim Pasha, was allowed to return to his own country, and to inherit the leadership of his tribe, vacant since the assassination of his father. On his return to the tents of his ancestors he asked for delivery of the valuables deposited for safe custody. The original friend was dead, and his son, who reigned in his stead, denied all knowledge of the valuables. And that was the beginning of a great and desperate enmity.

The offender possessed much landed property in the plain of Haran, adjoining Ebrahim's country. A long series of differences culminated in a raid by Ebrahim's people into the country of his enemy. Fifteen villages were burned, many men were killed, and all the cattle were taken. Ebrahim was chief of a tribal confederation that could put 20,000 men in the field; his enemy was merely a town notable, owning country villages boasting no tribal organisation. So military retaliation was out of the question. Circumstances, however, were such that reprisals of another kind were possible.

Ebrahim Pasha's large following was composed to a considerable extent of truants from justice, cattle-lifters, ravishers, murderers, deserters from the army, and individuals who were wanted for the satisfaction of blood feuds. Indeed a goodly fraction of the scum of Mesopotamia had collected under the banner of Ebrahim, and each one of such had people looking for him. Everybody who injured one of Ebrahim's enemies ran to Ebrahim for protection, and got it, together with a rifle, a horse, and a place in the continually moving camp. The tribes settled in and

around Urfa and Diarbekir had particular cause to hate
Ebrahim and his following, for all their delinquents
took refuge with the Kurdish chief. The notables of
those two towns were also hurt both in pride and
pocket by the exactions upon their flocks. Caravans
passing between the towns were forced to pay blackmail, and occasionally a village would be burnt. In
addition to the private individuals who had grievances
against Ebrahim and his men, the local officials had
bitter complaint to make because of flouted authority,
and the impossibility of making money for themselves
wherever the hand of Ebrahim reached. He took all
and left nothing for them.

Now Ebrahim Pasha was a great favourite with the
Sultan, and annually sent to Constantinople presents
said to be worth £10,000. So it had always been
very difficult to get Constantinople to take any notice
of accusations made against him. The burning of the
fifteen villages aforesaid, however, brought matters to
a climax, and it was no more possible for the Porte
to ignore the behaviour of the Kurdish chief. The
notables of Diarbekir at the psychological moment
took possession of the telegraph office and wired to
Constantinople to inquire who was the ruler of the
country, and were they to pay taxes to the Sultan
or to Ebrahim Pasha. In consequence Ebrahim was
ordered to Aleppo to confront his accusers. A commission was sent from Constantinople to investigate
the truth of the charges. But Ebrahim's father had
gone to Aleppo under similar circumstances, and had
never returned. Ebrahim wrote to the Governor-
General at Aleppo to say that he was sick and could
not appear before the commission. A man with 20,000
horsemen at his back can afford to be sick when it
suits him. Ebrahim's enemies were enraged beyond

words, and all the local authorities foamed at the mouth. The true inwardness of it all was that, although Ebrahim was hopelessly involved with the Turkish Government, he remained friends with the Sultan. He actually possessed a cipher code by means of which he could hold secret communication with the Sultan, to the utter confusion of all local officials, who could make nothing of the telegrams. There was only one way of obtaining revenge, and that was by discrediting Ebrahim Pasha with the Sultan. Every endeavour had been made to effect this, but Ebrahim still remained sick, and all Mesopotamia was laughing at the discomfiture of his enemies.

At this moment, unfortunately for me, I set foot in Mesopotamia. Whether the events which followed were part of a deep-laid scheme, or whether minor parties merely snatched at an opportunity to further what they knew to be the designs of their principals, cannot be said for certain. Several circumstances and local gossip point to the former conclusion, while Ebrahim Pasha openly states that the whole business was planned from start to finish. What actually happened was this. Half an hour after I left the village of Aktchi-Kaalah, a Shammar Arab, notorious as robber and cattle-lifter, saddled his horse and followed me, to the knowledge of all the village. This man was subsequently captured, and when brought to Aleppo I identified him as my assailant. After some persuasion he confessed his guilt, and said that he had spent the night in Aktchi-Kaalah and in the morning had gone after me at the instigation of the villagers. They had told him that I was a Russian, that I had killed many Turkish soldiers, and that it would be merit to kill and rob me. The blame could be put upon Ebrahim Pasha.

This village of Aktchi - Kaalah is the property of Nedeem Effendi, the man who is said wrongfully to hold Ebrahim Pasha's valuables, and Ebrahim's greatest enemy in the world. No sooner had news of my misfortune reached Urfa than word was sent to Constantinople that Ebrahim Pasha's people were the culprits. Nothing more annoys the Sultan than to have foreigners maltreated in his territories. The injured nation usually makes a terrible fuss, particularly those with effective fleets. There could be no better way of getting Ebrahim Pasha into trouble than by showing that he was the cause of an ambassadorial demand for explanation of a dastardly attack on the sacred body of a British subject. Ebrahim, however, countered this move on the part of his enemies by declaring that he had nothing to do with the matter, but that he knew for a fact that Nedeem Effendi had deliberately planned the attack, and that a particular Arab, resident near Aktchi-Kaalah, was the man who had carried it out.

It is instructive of Turkish methods to examine what happened immediately after my accident. My messenger, instead of going straight to the German hospital at Urfa with my letter, went to the house of Nedeem Effendi and gave him the letter. In the course of the following morning the letter was sent to the Turkish Governor, who spent the whole day procuring a translation and making up his mind what to do. Meanwhile the messenger had spread the story in the bazaar, and the details were known to the whole town, including the fact that the messenger had been promised a pound for his services. Miss Shattuck of the American Mission heard that a wounded Englishman lay at Haran, and she sent her clerk to the Governor to ask if the story were true. The Governor denied all knowledge of the matter, though at the moment he had already given orders for a carriage and a doctor to be sent to meet me. He knew perfectly well who I was, for some days previously he had received telegraphic instructions from Aleppo to see that when I passed through Haran I should be looked after and given an escort. Curious that Nedeem's villagers should have a professional robber ready on the spot to go after me, and that no official measures had been taken to provide me with escort when I got to Haran. Nedeem was hand in glove with the Government at Urfa, and he may or may not have made the plan. Subsequent events made the affair look even more suspicious.

No sooner had I arrived in Urfa than, according to the Governor, a hundred soldiers were sent to Aktchi-Kaalah to catch the robber. They were accompanied by a magistrate to investigate. Yet the magistrate and the soldiers returned and said that there could be no doubt that the culprit was one of Ebrahim's men. They were able to find out nothing at Aktchi-Kaalah. Yet all Aktchi-Kaalah had seen the robber go after me, knew what his purpose was, and knew he had accomplished it.

The fact is that the Turks never made any real effort to find the guilty man, but confined themselves to accusations against different men of Ebrahim's. One particular man they demanded that Ebrahim should send for trial. Ebrahim agreed to send him to the British Consul at Aleppo, on condition his return was guaranteed by the Consul if I could not identify him. Meanwhile our Consul had written to Ebrahim Pasha asking him to search for the culprit. Ebrahim replied that he would search for this man if requested to do so by the Turks. This was the last thing the Turks wanted to do, for the production of the real assailant would

knock the bottom out of their case against Ebrahim.
But the Consul pressed the matter, and finally the
Turks were compelled to invoke Ebrahim's aid. Doubt-
less Ebrahim had had his eye on the man all along, for
in a very short time he was captured and brought to
Urfa under the care of Ebrahim's Bimbashi.

There now ensued a tussle for possession of the
prisoner. The man had made desperate efforts to
escape. Once, at a big camp where 300 people were
seated in the principal tent, he had strolled outside
for a certain purpose, and had suddenly leaped on a
horse and bolted. But the long ropes that support
the tents of an Arab encampment had hindered him,
and the people caught him by the robe and pulled him
off the horse. At Urfa, when sitting in the Bimbashi's
house, he had slipped out of his clothes, and when a
favourable moment offered darted away naked. Again
they caught him, however, and this time his feet were
shackled. When brought to Urfa the Turks blandly
asked the Bimbashi for delivery. No fear, said the
Bimbashi, for he wasn't going to have the man die by
misadventure in the hands of the civil authorities.
After much telegraphing between Urfa, Aleppo, and
Constantinople, it was agreed that the prisoner should
be handed over to the military authorities, an important
officer giving his personal guarantee to our Consul that
the man should be brought safely to Aleppo.

The preliminary trial was an imposing affair. All
the Pashas of Aleppo were seated in state, with myself
in a big arm-chair suitable for an invalid. In came a
wild-eyed, bare-footed figure, strangely disreputable
amid so many brilliant uniforms. I knew him at once.
He was told that I was the injured man, when he
immediately ran towards me and began kissing my
boots. I thrust him away with a good deal of vigour.

I took this to be a sort of admission of guilt, but not so, for the rascal declared he had never seen me before, that he was a man of Ebrahim Pasha, and that he knew nothing of this business. After a great deal of talk, however, he broke down utterly and confessed that he had done the deed. Then we got the story as already related. My man was now a very different being from the truculent ruffian who had demanded my money or my life. He grovelled on the floor, embraced everybody's knees and wept bitterly. A month's confinement in towns and under the guard of soldiers had taken all the spirit out of him. "Let me go, let me go," he wailed. "I want to see the world, I want to see the world." A limb for a limb, and a life for a life, is the base of all desert law. He begged that they would take his hand and let him go. Then he held up his wrist and made a cutting motion, did the same to a foot, and declared himself willing to sacrifice both for freedom. Then with his head on the magistrate's feet he begged that his life might be taken quickly, for he was afraid of living in a house, and of being surrounded by so many great people. Hysterical, frightened, and haggard, the poor devil was indeed a pitiable object, and most of my animosity against him evaporated, for, after all, he had never been anything but a wild wanderer in the desert, getting a living as best he might according to the usage of his fathers, and no more responsible for his misdeeds than any beast of prey. A few days later he cut his throat in prison, in an unsuccessful endeavour to escape the fifteen years' imprisonment that will be his fate when justice takes its course.[1]

[1] *The Times* of Christmas Day 1908 states that the Arab who wounded Mr Fraser has died of typhoid fever in the Aleppo prison hospital.

CHAPTER XIV

DIARBEKIR.

INSTEAD of three or four weeks of convalescence at
Aleppo, I dwelt there seventeen weeks, all of them
devoted to a daily struggle with various ills consequent on experiences related. Having lost nearly
six months of precious time, I had nothing to spare
for convalescence, and the moment daily attention
ceased to be a necessity I became a starter. Socrate's
successor, an Armenian lad, could henceforth do all
the dressing required under my own experienced eye,
and if complications arose, were there not doctors on
the road at intervals of four and five days? Alas, for
the manner of my going! Riding was out of the
question, for I could not hold the reins; sitting in a
saddle was torture, owing to a chronic lumbago that
had seized upon me; while mounting and dismounting
were athletic feats beyond my power. My old enemy
the yailieh was my only possible friend in the circumstances, for in and out of it I could crawl with assistance. Nor was my old route across the desert from
Haran any longer possible. For carriages there was no
road, and if I made an effort to ride I must surely die
in the terrible heat. Baghdad and the Persian Gulf in
the height of summer were no fair prospect, and if ever

The Good Samaritan who took me in—the
Rev. W. M. Christie of Aleppo.

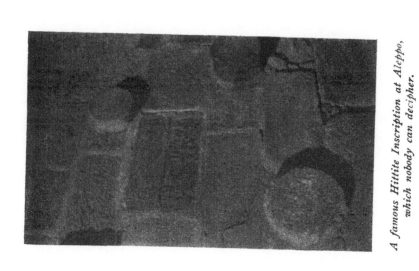

A famous Hittite Inscription at Aleppo,
which nobody can decipher.

AMARILLA 3

I was to see my native land again I must take the least trying road.

And so it was that one morning late in May there awaited me a three-horsed vehicle, instead of a caravan of pack-horses. Parting from the kind friends who had taken me in, and who had unexpectedly been called upon to keep me for so many long weeks, was a sad business. My host had dressed and undressed me morning and night for months on end; my hostess had washed my face and brushed my hair every morning with as much solicitude as if I had been her own youngest born; four sweet little maids between them had given me more food in spoons than I had ever dreamt it possible one man could contain; and there was George, aged five, and more Scotch than Robbie Burns, who took me for unnumbered walks, who spilt gallons of coffee on my chin, who lit hecatombs of cigarettes for me, who opened thousands of doors to let me through, and who dreamt o' nights of shooting with a gun the man who tried to kill me, and of cutting his head off with a sword. Of all these faithful friends and loving comforters I took a melancholy farewell, and once more faced the wilderness.

On the fourth day we reached Urfa, and now I was well enough to look upon the town with other eyes. It was a mighty pleasure to go into the room where they said the echo of my groanings might still be heard, and laugh until the roof rang. They killed one of the geese that used to make my head vibrate, and I ate my share of the brute with apple sauce. The cat had forgotten its stolen babies, and the dog fawned upon me that would have eaten my finger. The finger itself, in medicated salt, awaited me. The good Swiss doctor was better of his enteric and had gone hence to his own white mountain land. Brother Jacob and his

M

kind wife received me gladly, and told me things that
formerly they had withheld. How they feared I would
become a morphinist, and how they sometimes injected
water instead of the real thing—which explained how
the poor man often found his opiate ineffective. Gracey
nearly tore my arm out by the root when we met, and
when we talked of the painful journey I had made
under his care, he said that now I was well he would
stand no more cursing and swearing.

At Urfa there was a parting of the ways. Either
I must here take horse and re-enter the desert, picking
up the trail where my blood stained the ground, or I
must continue in the carriage. On horseback we could
follow the exact route of the Baghdad Railway, could
visit my friend Ebrahim Pasha and his twenty thousand freebooters, could pass the place where Tiglath-
Pileser had hunted tigers from elephant-back, besides
touching places where half the prophets and worthies
of the Scriptures had lived or died. The carriage
route offered no attractions, and was indeed both
desolate and disagreeable. Yet I chose the carriage
route, not because the spirit prompted, but because
the flesh was weak and trembling. Truly humility
followeth a fall.

From Urfa we passed through the village of Julmen
to Suverek, where stand the ruins of a crusading castle,
and thence along the northern slopes of the Karaja
Dagh, a great mountain mass that overlooks the plains of
Mesopotamia. In the north stretched the great snow
wall of the Taurus, pierced hereabouts by the tumultuous waters of the mighty Euphrates. The road we
traversed was one of the most uncomfortable I have
ever known. Its surface consisted of stones so set
that the carriage wheels were for ever springing and
plunging over them with a noise worthy of the *pavé*

that makes the street of a French town a place of martyrdom. Our progress had the effect of a series of shocks from a galvanic battery, and when I began to see things out of the window I wondered if it was possible for an overdose of electricity to do for one what a long course of whisky does. The first thing I saw, that made me wonder for my mental balance, was a tortoise walking across the road. I observed it a long way ahead, but neither Shuckri, nor the driver, nor any of the horses appeared to see it, and the carriage passed over it with a crunch. But when I looked behind there was the creature toiling along as if nothing had happened. While I was pondering the matter we whisked past something else that wriggled along the road—a horrid grey snake with a white belly. At once I shouted to the driver to stop, thinking that a little walk would do me good. Out I got, without looking backward, and commenced stepping gingerly along the side of the road. I hadn't gone fifty yards when I saw an enormous beetle crawling across my path. He was fully two inches long, of a most brilliant yellow colour, with shiny black enamelled points. I rolled him over with my stick, and so much hated to see the way he clawed the air with his legs that I left the spot in a hurry. A moment later I almost trod on a large lizard with pink eyes. That decided me to get into the carriage again. But I had hardly settled myself among the pillows when the carriage stopped, and I found the sterns of three or four camels pressed up against the windows on one side, while a row of necks of the same beast barred the view on the other. I shut my eyes for a few minutes while we scraped through a caravan of several hundreds of these brutes, and then opened them to see a sorcerer hanging on to three captive monkeys who were skipping violently about the road, immediately under my nose. Ugh ! they were playing with a large black scorpion. The last thing I saw was the most terrible. A man was herding a donkey from whose back and sides protruded about twelve long, thin, red necks that swayed and curved and reared and waggled like serpents. They were only turkeys being carried to market, but I thought that if any more signs of the zodiac presented themselves, I must surely take refuge in a lunatic asylum.

On the fourth day out from Urfa we reached Diarbekir, one of the most ancient and famous of the cities of Asia Minor. The great dark walls are built of black basalt, with square and round flanking towers of the same forbidding stone. The city is placed on the edge of a plateau overlooking a broad valley wherein flows the silver Tigris on a wide band of dazzling sand. Immediately below the eastern walls there is a sheer drop of several hundred feet. From the river the town looks unspeakably majestic, set square and dauntless on the bluff above. From the city walls the scene is no less impressive, for the broad flat below, held within a curve of the sparkling river, is a mass of every shade of green conceivable by the human retina. Pale patches of budding vegetation are surrounded by rows of tall and dark poplars ; fields of brightest emerald corn are flanked by thickets of rich-hued mulberry bushes ; walnut trees, peach trees, apple trees, border beds of lowlier fruits of the earth ; all the strength and youth and brightness of spring seem here combined to sing in the one joyful key. These well-ordered gardens speak of peace and prosperity, the mighty walls above of well-guarded security. But the gold is false, despite the glitter. Nature's colouring may be perfect, and man's handi-

" Bringing home the sheaves "—of mulberry leaves.

Old Carvings and Inscriptions on the Wall of Diarbekir.

CALIFORNIA

work satisfying to the eye, where all the while lurks a ghastly skeleton. Seeming and reality are here wide apart as the poles, for in Diarbekir Oriental misgovernment is at its height, and within its walls there is neither justice for the righteous nor protection for the weak.

Few of the places of the earth chosen by mankind to inhabit have seen greater vicissitudes than Diarbekir, Amida of the ancients. Tossed about between Romans and Persians, Armenians and Parthians, Arabs and Turks, it has ever been a city of martyrdom, once no fewer than 80,000 of its inhabitants being put to the sword. In 1750 its population was said to have numbered 400,000, where to-day dwell no more than a tenth of that number. Thirteen years ago a thousand Armenians were murdered, where many thousands more would have died but for spirited defence by the persecuted and timely action by a stiff-backed British Consul. Diarbekir is rich in remnants of its former greatness. The walls have been built and rebuilt, each period showing clearly in the massive masonry. Stones let into the walls bear inscriptions that show them to have been carved and used originally by long-forgotten architects. There are the remains of an ancient palace, where the richly carved pillars and capitals and friezes of marble and porphyry indicate forgotten art and civilisation. Old Jacobite, Greek, and Armenian churches are intermingled with a host of Mahomedan mosques. The streets are so narrow that no vehicle can pass through them. Overhead, projecting windows of latticed woodwork almost shut out the light of day.

Diarbekir is full of character. Its position overlooking the bed of the Tigris gives it an appearance of command, and the old well-preserved walls look forth severely upon the surrounding country. The gardens below the eastern wall smile up at the town, and send continuous streams of porters with peace-offerings in the shape of great bundles of mulberry branches, to feed the greedy silk-worms within. All Turkey at this time of the year eats lettuce day and night, to fill up the void that aches with longing for the abundant fruits of summer, now fast ripening. Little donkeys labour underneath huge loads of the fat green bundles that are ready for human teeth. The smallest imaginable copper coin buys half a dozen heads, and no urchin in the street is half a man unless he carries a lettuce in his hand and another under his arm, casting aside the outer leaves with lordly in-difference, devouring the sweet crackling inside with animal voracity. Then you have to go cannily in Diarbekir, for the city is full of scorpions of three different colours and virulent stings. An Armenian doctor told me the cure—just score the part with a razor or a sharp knife until the flesh all around the sting bleeds freely. If permanganate of potash is handy rub it in. If not it does not matter much, for the poison of a scorpion, quite different in its action from that of a snake, is slow to penetrate the blood, and profuse bleeding, if quickly procured, will surely result in its ejection from the wound.

Half the population is Christian, the other half Moslem, with Kurds in the majority. The Christians are of Armenian and Syrian races, and their religious subdivisions are without end. People in Turkey are classified not according to blood, but according to religious persuasion. All Moslems are liable to con-scription for the army, and those chosen cannot escape except by payment of a large sum of money. But the Christian is entirely exempt, paying in lieu a tax of no more than five shillings per head per annum. Payment of the *askarieh*, or army tax, is made through

A Street in Diarbekir.

. . richly carved pillars and capitals and
friezes of marble and porphyry . . . "

the local church organisations, which declare to the
Government so many souls on their books, for which
they pay a total sum. The poorer Christians frequently are quite unable to pay any ready money at
all, and then the better off ones of the community
are supposed to make up the amount. The Turk, however, is very lenient, and most churches are largely in
arrear, besides which quite a third of the Christian
population is never registered at all. Immediately
after the massacres of 1895 Europe was astonished to
see that the Christian population, as evidenced by the
askarieh collections, had actually increased in some
places where thousands of Armenians were known to
have perished. The reason of the increase is not
uninstructive. When European charity came forward
with large sums of money to succour the distressed,
all and sundry put their names down for assistance.
When the assistance was paid out the Turkish tax-
collector was there, and noted the unregistered.
One of the obstacles to emigration from Turkey by
Christians is the difficulty of obtaining permission,
owing to unpaid taxes. One individual may have
paid his own and his family's taxes regularly to his
church, which as a whole may be in arrear. Perhaps
the money has been sufficient all along, but corrupt
elders may have put the payments down to friends
of their own, or stolen it outright, as has often happened. In any case, the individual has no redress
against the Turk, for it is his own people who have
put him in the cart.

The various Christian churches are one of the puzzles
of Turkey to the newcomer. I had no opportunity of
going into the subject as regards the whole of the
country, but while at Aleppo, Urfa, and Diarbekir I
took the trouble to find out something of the subdivisions of which there are representatives in those

three towns. Christians belong almost exclusively to
Greek, Armenian, and Syrian races, though it is hard
to tell exactly what a Syrian is, beyond the common
understanding, which is that he is an individual belonging to Syria who is neither Moslem nor Jew. The
Greeks are remnants of the Byzantine Empire, and
are presumably in greater part of Hellenic origin. In
some parts of Turkey they are extremely illiterate and
debased, eating with their fingers, treating their women
with Mahomedan despotism, dirty, and superstitious.
In the west, on the contrary, they are extremely well
educated, intelligent, and active, with all the originality and independence of western character. A Greek
in Turkey is always a Turkish subject, Grecian subjects
proper being known as Hellenes. In religion they are
divided into three—Orthodox Church, Roman Catholic,
and Melchites or United Greeks. These latter recognise the Pope as head of the Church, but they say
mass in Arabic, allow their clergy to marry, and in
many other respects differ from Roman Catholics.

Armenians are of three different kinds—Gregorian,
Roman Catholic, and Protestant. The Gregorian
Church is practically the old and original Armenian
institution, the Roman Catholics are a separate community having their Patriarch at Constantinople, with
priests educated at Venice, and the Protestants are
Armenians who have come under the influence of
American missionaries and set up churches of their
own under American control. There remain churches
belonging to people of so - called Syrian extraction.
Principal among them are the Nestorians, followers of
Nestorius who was Patriarch of Constantinople 1500
years ago, and who broke away from orthodoxy for a
variety of reasons. The Nestorians have no confession,
disbelieve in purgatory, and allow their priests to marry.

The Kharput Gate.

Diarbekir—the Mardin Gate.

They are remarkable for their wonderful missionary propaganda, which penetrated in pre-Mahomedan times as far as India, Central Asia, and China. An offshoot of the Nestorians are the Chaldæans, who in the seventeenth century forsook their old Church and joined that of Rome. From them again spring the New Chaldæans, who deserted Rome and formed a sect of their own, with their own Patriarch. Another offshoot of the Nestorians are the Jacobites, who in the sixth century, under a bishop called Jacobus, broke away from their parent Church. Their Patriarch now lives at Diarbekir, and their distinctive doctrinal principle is belief in the monophysite nature of Christ—whatever that may mean. Then from the Jacobites there have seceded to Rome a community calling themselves Syriani, with a Patriarch at Aleppo. This by no means exhausts the religious divisions of so-called Christians in the Turkish Empire, for in European Turkey, Palestine, and other parts are other varieties which I forbear to mention.

Common to all, however, is that non-Christian spirit which is characteristic of Christian countries where there is more than a single Church. Among the dozen divisions enumerated above there is only one that seems to have a reasonable hope of salvation, and that is the Protestant Church, the members of which have been rescued from an idolatrous prostitution of true Christianity, and refined upon the best American Congregational lines. Unfortunately for peace, hope, and charity, each of the remaining eleven divisions firmly believes that it itself is the chosen one, and no more thinks it possible for a member of a rival Church to enter the kingdom of heaven than for a camel to pass through the eye of a needle.

CHAPTER XV.

AFLOAT ON A RAFT.

IN my time I have sampled most kinds of transport, including torpedo destroyers, Atlantic greyhounds, ocean tramps, yachts, house-boats, motor bicycles, yaks, camels, Cape carts, buck-waggons, and the God of Communications knows what else. But never before had I tried the kelek, a contrivance sacred to the river Tigris since the days of Adam and Eve. From Diarbekir to Baghdad as a crow might do it the distance is somewhere over 400 miles. As the kelek does it the distance is nigh upon 1000 miles, and the time occupied anywhere between eight and twenty days. It was a long journey to make, and a novel one. I made my preparations with all the excitement and anticipation, all the heart-sinkings and soul-risings, all the fears and tremblings and spasms with which a coming bride collects her trousseau. A new road, a new country, a new steed!—these are the joys that quicken the blood.

The kelek is easily constructed. Take any number of inflated goatskins from 100 up to 800, and tie them in rows underneath a framework of light poplar poles. One or two pairs of great oars complete the ship, and she is ready for crew, cargo, and passengers. If

Ready for sea.

A fleet of Keleks on the Tigris.

the materials are ready, a kelek can be prepared for sea in a couple of hours. Cargo usually consists of bales of merchandise or sacks of corn, which are easily laid across the wooden framework, and which form a comfortable deck for the passengers. When a globe-trotter ships aboard a kelek some of the cargo is left behind, and upon the space thus left vacant a hut is erected. A light wooden framework is hung round with cotton walls that roll up or let down according to the desire of the occupant. In addition, the roof has a thick grass mat to keep out the sun. The traveller enjoys entire privacy as regards the people on his own kelek, for he gives orders that nobody is to come abaft his gable. At the end of his little house, and projecting astern of the raft, is a tiny bath-room protected from public gaze by cloth walls. The kitchen is forward of the gable and out of sight. Thus the kelek combines all the advantages of a modern mansion—living-room, kitchen, sanitary arrangements, abundant light and air, and panoramic scenery that is an eternal feast for the eye.

The procuring of all these delights was easily managed, for an ex-padre of one of the numerous churches of Diarbekir agreed to arrange the whole business for me out of pure love. He hired space on a kelek for £6, and instructed a carpenter to build my hut at a cost of £4. When I jibbed at the price of the hut he swore that at the end of the voyage the materials would sell for two to three-fifths of the original price. One must take a clergyman's word, however wide he may open his mouth. Eventually I sold my hut for 6s. instead of the £2 promised. Then I heard that the padre had been worsted to the extent of nearly fifty per cent in the bargain for accommodation on the kelek. So next time I want a kelek I'll procure it through a tinker or a tailor, or through somebody with a more practical knowledge of the value of money.

We sailed one morning at ten o'clock, with the temperature over a hundred in the shade. June in Mesopotamia is like summer in Hades, and fit for none to travel in but salamanders, corpses, and journalists. But heat may be corrected by a minimum of clothes and a maximum of cold water. The Tigris came straight from the snows of the Taurus, and its turgid flood was like ice compared with the fire of the air. For a man who couldn't put on his own socks, or tie the buttons of his waistcoat, or hold a rifle, and doubled up, moreover, with a chronic lumbago, that first plunge overboard into the boiling river was rather a venture. The kelekjis said I need have no fears, and the two soldiers supplied by the Turkish authorities to guard my person declared the river quite safe, though none of them cared enough for cold water to give me a lead. I looked for a long time before I leaped, thinking the while that though a man may forget how to sing, or dance, or pray, he can never forget how to swim, and then I shut my eyes and jumped. The existence of this volume proves that I didn't drown ; indeed I found myself a much better man in the water than on dry land. For my faith I was magnificently rewarded, and though I am not partial to the use of adjectives, I will say of that first swim in the brimming Tigris that it was absolutely and completely glorious. All the miseries and horrors of the eight days' drive in the burning heat, all the aches and bruises from the eternal bumping, all the foolish brooding cares and anxieties engendered by many months of sickness and inactivity, were washed away by the cool, quick-flowing, laughing water. Swept along by the same current in which floated the raft, I could swim away from it or round it,

could dive again and again from its quivering deck,
could beat the water with my limbs until it foamed
and effervesced; and most delightful of all, I could
float on my back and gaze into the blue depths above,
and listen the while with submerged ears to the eternal
rustling of the little stones beneath as the stream
scurried over its gravelly bed.

There was mild adventure too. Every now and then
the narrow bed of the river expanded, and the running
water spread itself out over wide flats, where it rippled
and tumbled and sparkled over stones and sand. Where
there had been deep water there was now shallow, and
swimming became impossible. I was caught in such
a place when nearly a hundred yards away from my
floating house. The stream ran about five knots, and
the depth was no more than a foot. I lay flat on my
back and skimmed lightly along with an occasional
scrape on the sand. My progress was delightful until
the water shallowed still more, and the bottom changed
from sand to pebbles. Then I was rattled along over
the smooth stones at an alarming pace, and no efforts
that I could make saved an important part of my
anatomy from a series of gorgeous, tooth - loosening
thumps. I stood up to walk, but could make no
speed over the stones with my tender feet. The kelek
flew farther and farther away. The kelekjis had little
control over their craft in the shallow water, for it too
was rubbing along the bottom at a terrific pace. Then
I lay down again, thinking it better to be bumped
where I had been salted in early youth, than to be
left naked in a foreign land. Suddenly the water
deepened, and then I swam frantically after the kelek.
Just as I caught her up, the river shallowed again, but
this time I had a hold which I was determined not to
lose. I tried to jump aboard, but the jagged projecting

poles of the framework made throwing oneself forward most difficult. The pace was so great that no sooner had I lifted a foot than the kelek slipped away from it, and with my weak hands I could not help the situation. And so I was hurried forward, the hot sun above scorching my skin, the stones underneath mangling the soles of my feet; incapable of being assisted, and with no time to weep. A deepening of the water resulted in rescue from a ridiculous and uncomfortable position, and I was lifted aboard more dead than alive, and with an appetite that knew no bounds. What cloud is without a silver lining?

Our kelekjis numbered two—one the captain, who rowed and cursed the crew, the other the crew, who poled the vessel out of danger and suffered the cursing, like mariners before the mast all over the world. The soldiers were also two, and armed with Martini rifles and enough cartridges for a battle. They were obliging fellows, and held their weapons for me while I aimed at birds and pulled the trigger. The only drawback to this form of sport was that my shoulder bore the kick. One soldier was always on watch, while the other slept. When we anchored and I went ashore, one of them always accompanied me, with tunic buttoned, belts and bandoliers buckled up, and rifle at the shoulder. I asked the reason of so much caution, when it appeared that Constantinople had decreed that if one hair of my head was injured my guards would be done to death. Would that they might have shut the stable door before the horse escaped.

Our first day's voyage lay through comparatively uninteresting country, with a distant view of snow-capped mountains in the east. The river twisted and wriggled about in an utterly disconcerting manner, between banks that were sometimes low and covered with grass and wild flowers, sometimes high and wooded. A charming progress, but not exciting, except for such episodes as related above, and one other recurring scene which kept one's interest alive. Earlier in this volume I mentioned that when crossing the Kurd Dagh I was vouchsafed several opportunities of noting certain domestic customs of the Kurdish women. Then, I had but fleeting glances, but now, thanks to the silent progression of the kelek, and to a pair of powerful binoculars, I was able to make closer and more extended observation of tableaux vivants more graceful and unaffected than anything to be seen in the glare of the footlights.

Imagine the raft slipping quietly along in the current, close to the high and broken bank, the oarsman dozing at his post, all the others asleep in the heat. We whisk round a little cape and come full upon a tiny bay with sandy shore, where, within a few yards, are disporting themselves a bathing party of women and children. They are so astonished at our sudden apparition that they just stand transfixed as we first catch sight of them, and remain so until we are swept out of sight. One soft rounded figure with glistening russet skin will be standing knee-deep in the water, with her back to the river and her hands dipped to splash a little flock of crowing infants. She delays the splashing and just turns her head to see us pass. Another full-blown rose perhaps stands in an attitude of languid amusement watching the play, her feet in the water, arms thrown up, and hands behind her head—Psyche to the very life. Half-grown girls running about like fawns suddenly halt on one foot and stare at us with their big round brown eyes. In rear will be pairs of squatting

figures, one braiding the other's hair, the other watching the process in a little flashing mirror. For background there are the boiling pots, the grey old women
busily washing, and a great patch of garments spread
out to dry, bright scarlet on the deep green of luxuri-
ant undergrowth, dark blue on the silver sand. Grouped
here and there is the fascinating variety of corn-
coloured, golden, peach - pink, creamy, glowing skin,
covering figures postured in every attitude of grace
and abandonment, with never a rag to hide the curved
and swelling lines.

Clouds of white on the shore far ahead turn out to
be flocks of sheep resting at the water's edge during
the heat of the day, guarded by slim brown boys,
mother-naked and unashamed. A little archipelago
of small black rocks, visible down the stream, proves,
as we sweep past them, to be the snouts of a herd of
buffaloes, that for coolness have sunk their bodies up
to the eyes in the blessed river. Clusters of meek red
cattle stand fetlock-deep in the shallows, and great
storks pace the islands, or stand on one leg with folded
neck and rested beak, dreaming of the chicks that are
being reared in the bulrushes, chicks that will some
day rival their parents in length of limb and dignity
of manner. And every now and then a gay bathing
party, sometimes seen far ahead, again appearing suddenly and spinning past, as if the river bank were a
countryside through which we raced on a noiseless,
smooth-running, railway train. Slowly turning round
and round in the current, with sometimes a clumsy
lunge of the great oars to keep her off the bank, our
strange craft floats swiftly through the burning air,
without effort or sound or movement from within.

As evening approaches there comes a great change

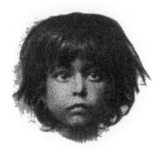

A little Kurd Girl.

in the temperature. The fury goes out of the sun, a cool breeze springs up, and the pleasantest place on the kelek is a perch on a bale of goods from which one can see the soft pearly haze in the north and south, the clear-cut mountains in the east, and the flooding gold of the setting sun. Just as night is about to fall we glide quietly to shore and draw up before a broad beach of smooth sand. The crew wades to land with a great rope of twisted twigs, a stake is driven into the sand, and we are made fast for the night. One of the soldiers is sent off to an adjacent village to search for eggs and milk, the other accompanies me for a little walk. When we return we find the beach that we had left deserted alive with busy shouting figures. These are the officers, crews, and passengers of a large fleet of keleks that had hastily been put in commission when it was noised abroad that a man with a hat, a flag, and a brace of soldiers was putting to sea. The hatted foreigner in himself is a host in Turkey, especially when escorted by minions of the Government. All the passengers and merchandise for down-stream that had been waiting for weeks at Diarbekir for safe convoy were hurriedly embarked, and there was much rejoicing when the fleet caught us up, and was able to anchor under the shadow of my flag — a weak imitation of the Union Jack, composed of a white handkerchief and an old red tie sewn diagonally.

There was much reason for this anxiety in regard to company, for the next hundred miles of the voyage took us slap through the mountains of south-western Kurdistan, a region where everybody is a robber according to his ability. The aghas of each tribe levy blackmail on all who pass through their country, the

little people kill and murder whenever they dare.
Usually, however, the foreigner with the hat, escorted
by gendarmes, is not molested, though it has often
happened that he has been stopped and invited to
make a handsome present. In the gorges through
which the Tigris flows at this point there are many
cave-dwelling Kurds, Arabs, and Yezidis of the lowest
type, near whose villages no kelek is safe, however
carefully guarded. These people live in such inaccessible places that the Turks have practically no
control over them. Were it not that the river
races through the gorges at a terrific pace, making
the stopping of keleks impossible, nobody would
venture to penetrate so dangerous a neighbourhood.
Even as we passed through, a company of Turkish
soldiers was engaged in rooting out wrongdoers, with
little success the kelekjis told us.

After dinner Shuckri set up my camp-bed, and we
found it just fitted exactly into the after-part of my
house. Insects and moths gathered round the candles
by the million, so we rigged the mosquito-net to the
roof, and inside it I smoked and read, to the great
annoyance of my attackers. During dinner ten
thousand mosquitoes had bitten my ankles, and before
turning in for the night I sat on the edge of the kelek
and dangled my legs in the water to allay the irrita-
tion. How black and cool it was, curling about my
burning feet like swathes of softest velvet, hissing
gently past the swollen skins, lapping with contented
little gurgles upon the friendly beach. There were
the camp fires on the shore, surrounded by singers
and talkers. In the kelek next to mine a hookah
bubbled intermittently, the rising and falling glow
darkly showing the silent figures seated around it.

The starry vault above, the black moving river, the heavenly air, the barbaric people in the flickering lights—there was nothing left even to pray for on that first delightful night, afloat on the bosom of the great motherly Tigris.

CHAPTER XVI.

RISKS OF THE VOYAGE.

ABOUT a hundred miles below Diarbekir the Tigris receives the Batman Su, a tributary flowing from a snow-clad spur of the Taurus, lying far to the north. Thereafter the river plunges into a gorge that traverses the waterless limestone plateau of Tur Abdin, part of the system anciently known as Mount Masius. Below the junction with the Batman Su there is a complete change of scenery. Where we had hitherto swept along a comparatively level plain we now raced between gigantic barren rocks that towered high above on either hand. The piercing of this obstacle in its path has been hard work for the river, and in following the line of least resistance it flows in a series of loops that turn back one upon another until one's sense of direction is completely paralysed. Progress here is full of excitement, for we spin along at from six to ten miles an hour, with seldom a view ahead of more than two thousand yards. In front there often seems to be nothing but an impenetrable curtain of rock, upon which our frail craft must hurl itself to destruction. While yet the heart beats wildly in anticipation of some desperate happening, the gorge is suddenly seen to wind its way to one side, forcing the stream in tumbling

In the Gorges of the Tigris.

rapids abruptly to change its course. At such places the kelekjis struggle madly at the sweeps in the endeavour to keep the clumsy raft in the middle of the current. At the edges of the stream there are eddies and whirlpools raised by projecting and sunken rocks. To be dashed on one of these means almost certain shipwreck to the kelek, loss of the cargo, and danger to the lives aboard, for only the strongest swimmers would have a chance in the boiling flood.

While the river flowed in the level country below Diarbekir the water gradually warmed as it felt the rays of the sun when passing over broad shallows and the slower reaches, and I was equal to a couple of hours at a time of swimming, floating, and clinging to the kelek. But with the advent of the chill waters of the Batman Su, the temperature fell far below the pleasant point, and all I could do was to dive in and get hauled out almost in the same breath. Wrapped up in a couple of towels I sat on a bale all day, watching the scenery and taking a dip when the water looked safe. Where it was rough and broken the kelekjis said I must get out, and out I got, for my days for tempting Providence are over. To be in the boiling water with a firm hold of the raft was rare fun, but it was quite awesome to feel one's legs swept hither and thither by undercurrents. What I dreaded was being sucked under. All sorts of fierce things seemed to be happening beneath the surface. We would be slipping along fast, but peacefully, when suddenly beside the kelek there would rise up with a sullen rush a thick gout of water that made the river churn furiously, where before it had flowed quietly. Breakers ahead were continual, and always the signal for frantic rowing by the kelekjis. Sometimes they would call sharply to the zaptieh on watch, and that sleepy individual would dart to their aid with an alacrity that proved him alive to danger.

We passed old castles perched high above, curious little villages hidden between crevices in the rocks, and several places where were inaccessible cave-dwellings, now apparently deserted, whether ancient or modern I could not tell. At one place where the kelekjis showed great timidity there were crowds of naked boys in the water, and women and children on the shore, who yelled and shouted impudently at us. The kelekjis made me put on my cap, and both the zaptiehs stood up to show their manly forms, their rifles, and the rows of cartridges that adorned belts and shoulder-straps. As we swept past I quite expected to hear the whistle of a bullet, for these wild people, even when they have no intention of robbing or killing, frequently amuse themselves by taking pot-shots at travellers, to see how near they can go without hitting—a precarious business for the potted, for the weapons of the potters can by no stretch of imagination be termed precise. These people are too poor to possess anything but ancient flint-locks.

Hassan-Keif, where we arrived in the evening, is surely one of the strange places of the earth. The gorge of the river opens somewhat to accommodate a great oval hollow. The high precipice overlooking the left bank forms the eastern side of the hollow, its face literally honeycombed with cave-dwellings connected with each other by internal staircases. On the opposite side of the hollow, half a mile to the west of the river, is a high ridge of rock overlooking the pleasant wooded space below. This ridge also presents a continuous frontage of arches and openings into the caves beyond. Groups of white-clad Arabs sat in the

Face of a Precipice honeycom ed with Cave-dwellings.

arches, smoking and gazing into space. One little crowd surrounded a man who was trying a rifle—apparently so, though he might as well have been shooting at his neighbour for all I know to the contrary. Firing from the mouth of a huge cave gives some curious sound results, quite different from those of rifles fired in the open. A loud crack is followed by a dull muffled roar, as if sound were belched instead of spat out. Then a double echo reverberates across from cliff to cliff, the cracks overtaking each other in their haste, the roar merging into a solemn boom that lasts long after the cracks have ceased to repeat one another.

Hassan - Keif was important in ancient times as Saphe, and here are the remains of a magnificent Roman bridge and the ruins of a city. The piers of the bridge are nearly a hundred feet high, enormously massive, each seemingly a citadel in itself. How they were ever joined together is a mystery, for the two principal ones are a hundred yards apart, with no suggestion that they ever supported an arch. On the top of a very curious square spur of rock projecting from the western bank is an old castle, and in the bay inside, terrace upon terrace of tiny dwellings half built of stone, half hewn from the solid rock. A strange place is Hassan-Keif, and a wicked. The caves on the eastern side of the river are inhabited by Yezedis, with an evil reputation as thieves and murderers. The village on the western side was recently Christian, but is now mostly Kurd. There are still thirteen Armenian families, the remnant of those who were cut off in the massacres, or who have migrated to less lawless parts. Their pastor and schoolmaster, sent out by the American missionaries at Mardin, came to see me. He could speak a little English, and told me miserable tales of the treatment to which his little flock was subjected. They lived in continual fear of their lives, with no chance of emerging from poverty, for everything worth having was immediately taken from them by Moslem neighbours so soon as acquired.

Some thirty miles below Hassan-Keif the tributary Bohtan Su joins the Tigris and adds materially to its volume. A few miles from the junction is the ford where the Ten Thousand on their splendid march to the Black Sea crossed the Bohtan Su, the supposed Centrites of history. Hereafter the swollen Tigris enters a magnificent gorge over fifty miles in length, and at many points little more than a hundred feet wide. At such places the stream rushes along with terrifying fury, in waves that make the kelek heave like a boat at sea. Here mistakes by the kelekjis meet with instant retribution, and tales of complete wreckage and loss of life are associated with various points in the series of rapids. The current now and then runs at a pace that seemed to me to equal the speed of the rapids of Niagara, the slope down which the river rushes being plainly visible to the eye. Fortunately the tendency of a heavy mass like a kelek is to float in the main current, and comparatively small exertion is needed to keep it there. At the same time its great weight and unwieldiness in the water make it extremely difficult of management, and the strength of a couple of men has but small influence on its course. Wind is one of the chief obstacles to navigation, especially of a kelek carrying a house with roof and walls acting like sails.

We were to sample this factor in rafting in a manner not altogether pleasant. While racing down the gorge, past precipices of infinite grandeur, one of them clothed with green from top to bottom, and throwing

Keleks entering the Gorges below Hassan-Keif.

Remains of a magnificent Roman Bridge.

off a waterfall that began 400 feet up in a thin spout
and ended in a white cloud of spray, we were struck
by a squall rushing down from a gash in the hills.
At the moment we were making for one of the worst
places in the river, where huge rocks fallen from the
heights above sit in the narrow bed and deflect the
stream in bulging torrents from side to side of the
gorge. Heavy overfalls, raised by the wind blowing
against the current, caused the kelek to rock wildly,
and for a moment I thought we had no earthly chance
of holding together. I stood outside the house, in the
scantiest attire, ready for whatever might happen.
The system of binding skins and poles together, however, gives great elasticity, and we weathered the
waves, but only to be caught by the wind and driven
slap on the rocks, fortunately just below the danger
point. Wherever the racing stream impinges upon
projecting rock there is, luckily, a thick cushion of
escaping water that deflects most floating things
before they strike the obstacle that banks up the
cushion. This was our salvation, for though one corner of the raft struck the shore with a heavy smash,
half the force of the shock was absorbed. But the
scrape along the bank had resulted in the damage of
many skins, and loud was the hissing that escaped from
their torn sides. In a few seconds about thirty were
deflated, and our displacement reduced so that one
corner of the kelek was under water. In this semi-
sinking condition we regained the current and were
swept along, the kelekjis and zaptiehs pulling like mad
and looking for a haven where damages might be
repaired. They made a shot at the lee of a small
peninsula, one of the men dived overboard with the
rope, and every effort was made aboard to force her
into the eddying current. But without success. The

rope was torn from the hands of the unfortunate boatman, who had just managed to make the shore, and the kelek flew onward, leaving him stranded. Shorthanded, there was nothing to be done but to make desperate efforts to keep in the stream and to avoid the danger points that followed one after the other. The man left behind would be all right, for there were eight keleks following, and he would surely manage to get aboard one of them.

While I was wondering what was going to happen next, another kelek, a small one lightly laden, was thrust close up to us by the current, and its captain, a sporting old Moslem with a grey beard, offered the loan of his assistant to our captain, who was almost completely exhausted. The new man made a daredevil rush at us across the intervening space of foaming water, and climbed aboard. A few minutes later our opportunity came, and we managed to draw up at a stretch of sand about a hundred yards long. Four other keleks succeeded in making the same place, all in need of repair. Three others swept past at a terrific pace, having failed to make the eddy. One kelek was missing altogether, to the great anxiety of the little knot of excited boatmen who were discussing our escape. For nearly a quarter of an hour we watched for signs of wreckage in the swirling stream, but were then relieved to observe the missing raft come racing down to us. When successfully manœuvred alongside, she was received with loud shouts of congratulation, and was found to be practically undamaged. At the place where the squall had struck us she became entangled in a great whirlpool, in which, before the crew were permitted to extricate her, she made many gyrations on her own centre in honour of the local Jinns.

Then there followed the labour of repairs, a process requiring little strength but deep lungs. The skins are of goat, very light and thin, much tenderer than the mussack of our friend the Indian bheestie. When ripped up they are thrown away, or kept for leisured repair, but a small puncture is ingeniously and quickly mended. The skin is loosened from its fastenings, and blown up that the leakage may be located. A flat double-flanged button of wood, like a large but low shirt-stud, is placed on the hole and pulled through the neck. A string is now tied tightly round the button between the flanges, isolating the leakage and leaving the button where the hole had been, when the mend is passed back through the neck. A skin will stand this neat and effective method of repair many times over, and it is quite common to see one showing a dozen of the buttons.

The mending of the skins and their blowing up like balloons was duly completed while we halted for the night. Apparently the raft was none the worse of the rough handling it had received, and before daybreak we were once more afloat. Sunrise was a wonderful function. We cast off while the sky far above held but the merest promise of day. In the semi-darkness the cliffs on either hand seemed of measureless height, their ragged tops dim in the twilight above, their feet wrapped in sombre shadow. The black waters of the river filled the gorge from side to side, their dull thunder humming ceaselessly in the ear, except where a rock stood in the way and raised a harsh roar of rage that might have been the noise of artillery furiously driven over broken ground. We glided into the mysterious flood and were soon hurtling forward on its boiling and foam-streaked surface. Before long came the light of day, shining athwart the double line of precipices that flanked the river. Some of it came down to us, forming a gloaming that was hardly less eerie than the former darkness. Colours tipped the peaks and pinnacles above, and reflected light gradually pierced the dimness below. When the sky attained its fulness of blue, day penetrated the gorge and showed us the way we went. An hour later we were out of the canyon and floating swiftly between low hills that were fast dwindling down into the Mesopotamian plain.

Where there was a broad opening in the hills, and people on the eastern shore, the oarsman slewed the raft into an eddy and we grounded softly on the sandy bank. When I stepped off and essayed to climb the low ascent from the water's edge there sprang from under each of my feet as I walked a spray of straw-coloured insects. The dried-up vegetation was alive with them, never a square yard that did not contain its hundreds. In these helpless hopping creatures, from half an inch to two inches in length, I recognised the dread curse of many lands, the all-devouring, devastating locust. Here were the brutes by the million million, eating greedily of every growing thing, and turning smiling country into howling wilderness. But at this particular spot the locust had been too late. A Yezidi tribe had gathered in a plentiful harvest of yellow wheat, which was now garnered in stacks of sheaves, or already threshed into great pyramids. The plague of locusts could now do little harm, and the people were busily preparing the corn for transport down the river.

Here we saw a small crowd of people gathered about a prostrate figure. I went up to see what interested them, and was told it was the body of a man picked out of the river a few minutes before we arrived. They

A Kurdish Village on the Tigris.

The murdered Yezidi.

uncovered the head, and I saw that a large bullet had
entered below the eye and come out behind the
temple, carrying away with it a piece of the skull, a
wound that must have caused instant death. The
uncovering of the head was the signal for two women,
the dead man's wife and sister, to break out into loud
lamentations that were woful to hear. It appeared
that earlier in the morning the man had walked up the
river to another encampment, and on the way had
passed a field belonging to Kurds. Seeing a lot of
birds feeding in the corn he had made a noise to
frighten them away, and had then been rudely asked
by the owners of the field why he did so. He explained, and for his trouble was shot on the spot,
apparently out of pure wantonness, and his body
thrown into the river. Other Yezidis had seen the
outrage and had run down-stream to warn the relatives, who were thus able to catch the corpse as it
floated past them. An armed follower of the local
Kurdish Agha was now taking charge of the body for
the purposes of an investigation. I asked what the
punishment would be, and was told that the murdered
man was only a Yezidi, while the murderers were
Kurds who could do no wrong towards such scum.
Perhaps the Agha would order a small payment to the
wife. Nobody except the unfortunate relatives thought
anything of the matter.

Having left a bale of goods with the Yezidis, we
cast off and continued our voyage down-stream, soon
reaching the small town of Jezire ibn Omar, one of the
most evil places in all the Turkish Empire. Here is a
sort of no-man's-land, where Arabs and Kurds of different organisations lord it over hapless Christians, Jews,
and Yezidis. Robbery and murder are mere pastimes
for those strong enough to indulge in them, and retri-

bution by the law is practically unknown, for the Turk
either cannot or does not want to enforce obedience.
Immediately outside the town was camped the headquarters of the Sheikh of the Tai, an important
Bedouin tribe settled in northern Mesopotamia since
the Arab conquest. The Tai furnish a contingent of
Hamidieh, a species of irregular soldier, armed by the
Turkish Government and paid by nobody. The logic
of the situation is that if the Government won't pay
the Hamidieh, the Hamidieh must pay themselves as
best they can, a fact that the Turk recognises by non-
interference in organised robbery and blackmail within
more or less understood limits. One of the exemptions
is the foreigner, another the Turk himself, and another
the dues of the Public Debt Administration. But
none of the three is ever really safe, for the wild
Kurd or Arab does not care a pin for authority, and
when the impulse moves him he will satisfy his lust for
blood and plunder with very little thought of consequences.

Our two gendarmes were very much alert as we
passed the great Tai encampment. There were several
hundreds of brown hair tents spread in orderly lines
parallel with the river. In one very large tent with
open sides I could see through the glasses about two
hundred Arabs taking their ease, smoking, drinking
coffee, and doubtless discussing local politics. I half
expected to have a shot across our bows, and to hear
an order to come ashore. But the zaptiehs sat up
prominently and we swept by unmolested, followed by
the now greatly augmented fleet of keleks that sailed
under my protection. A few miles lower down we
passed a Kurdish bathing party, which seemed to
number no less than a hundred and fifty women and

children, all naked, and enjoying themselves immensely. This was our last view of the nude, for thereafter the washers and bathers were Arabs, who are as particular about hiding their bodies as they are their faces.

We were now in the plains, floating peaceably away from the mountains we had just traversed. We did not travel nearly so fast as heretofore, while the scenery became uninteresting and monotonous, there being nothing to see but endless lines of sandy bank and distant stretches of level ground. The temperature of the river, however, was perfect, and I spent hours in it, with appalling effect on my lumbago. The heat was now terrific, and there was no comfort to be obtained except in the water. We were invaded, too, by a fly that bore all the innocent appearance of the house variety, but who was armed with a spear that projected from his nose. Having settled quietly on one's bare skin, or upon some part lightly protected, this villainous insect would place the point of his spear on the spot selected, and give several fierce wriggles with his head. The spear thus forced from behind would suddenly penetrate with a jerk deep into the flesh of the victim, who would forthwith leap up with a loud curse and slap violently at the place involved. But the slap was always too late in my case, and the flies who tormented me invariably lived to torment me again. Nothing but recourse to the shelter of the mosquito-net gave me relief from these ruthless attacks. Once I was recumbent on my bed under the net the desperate heat usually induced a weary and troubled sleep, from which wakefulness was little removed.

So we were floating along when, as in a dream, I heard the clear ringing report of a rifle. No sooner

realised than I was up and out to see what the matter
was. The kelekjis were wildly excited, the zaptiehs
were standing to their arms, and my Armenian servant
was waving his revolver. The long string of keleks
behind us was alive with shouting and gesticulating
figures, and it was some moments before I could discover what the commotion was all about. Hamidieh
were the cause of it anyway, although I could see
never a sign of them near. But it soon came out
that the hindmost of the keleks, the one captained
by the old man who had succoured us when we were
nearly shipwrecked in the gorges, had been fired at
by Arabs hidden in the bank, and forced to go ashore.
When I heard who had been stopped I was all for
halting and going back with the zaptiehs to effect a
rescue. But none of the kelekjis wanted to stop, nor
was either of the zaptiehs keen on going back. Very
bad men were these Tai Hamidieh, who thought no
more of shooting a man than of shooting a sparrow;
besides, there were a dozen of them. Apparently our
fleet had been observed at Jezire, but was allowed to
pass, as the place was too public for an outrage. But
there had been nothing to prevent a party riding
across country and intercepting us at a bend of the
river, where the eye of the Turkish Government could
not see, and where the responsibility could not be laid
at the door of the Sheikh of the Tai. To attempt
rescue was really a hopeless business, for there were
only my two armed gendarmes against the dozen
Arabs who had been seen, with who knows how
many more in the neighbourhood. So there was
nothing to be done but to continue the voyage
with due melancholy, praying the while that the
grey hairs of the old kelekji might protect him from
anything more serious than robbery. Sure enough

he turned up at our anchorage for the night, very
late, very woe-begone, and much in need of sympathy.
He had been kicked and cuffed for not coming more
quickly ashore to be robbed, and all the goods on his
kelek coveted by the Arabs had been confiscated.
The poor old fellow was thankful to have escaped
with his life.

The bend on the river where this robbery took place
is notorious from one end of the Tigris to the other.
There is here a big loop in the course of the river,
so that in case of an order to halt being disregarded
at the entrance to the loop, it can be enforced by
heavy fire when craft float down towards the outlet.
Thus eighteen months before, Baron le Grand, the
French Consul at Mosul, and a Norwegian Colonel,
when making a kelek voyage down the Tigris, were
ordered to stop by a party of Hamidieh. They took
no notice of the order, and were subjected to a slight
fire, out of the range of which the swift stream soon
carried them. But warned by the kelekjis of the turn
in the river, they made a barricade of their baggage,
and prepared for attack as they returned on the lower
side of the loop. They saw about twenty horsemen
gallop across the neck of land and take up a position on
the bank awaiting their arrival. The travellers had five
rifles between them, and the result was a brisk fusilade
in which nobody on the kelek was hit, but wherein
the Baron is prepared to swear that he winged one
of the attackers. Arabs being abominable cowards,
they seldom leave cover when there is a chance of
being shot, and in this instance they lay so low that
the party on the kelek had very few fair shots. So
nervous were the Arabs rendered by the determined
defence that they could not even shoot straight, and
although the kelek was within a range of between

O

one and two hundred yards for a full minute, they not only missed the people on board, but hardly hit the kelek itself. One reads a great deal about the chivalry of the Arab of the desert, but the truth is that he is mostly a low-down thief, possessed only of that kind of courage which expands when there is no danger, and evaporates before a show of strength.

To detail the endless incidents and scenes that recur to the voyageur by kelek would be unfair to the reader, pleasantly and amusingly though they may linger in the recollection of those who have tried this fascinating method of travel. Passing quickly down the Tigris, then, we find ourselves on the fifth day out from Diarbekir anchored near Eski Mosul, and within a few hours' sail of that Mosul where muslin first was manufactured, where Jonah grew his gourd, a town built almost on the ruins of ancient Nineveh. Eski Mosul, besides being the site of ruins of former greatness, has one small and melancholy claim to notice, for here a poor Frenchman, engaged in walking round the world, disappeared from mortal ken. With the wisdom usually displayed by gentry engaged in Titanic tasks, this unfortunate man took kelek from Diarbekir in order to save his legs, there being nobody for several hundred miles to say whether he walked, or flew, or floated. But being a conscientious fellow he left the kelek at Eski Mosul, with the object of arriving footsore and tired at Mosul, and with local knowledge of the road to lay before a sympathetic and helpful Consul. Alas, that virtue should meet with such a reward, for the unhappy man struck out on foot from Eski Mosul, and never arrived at Mosul, though the distance is no more than twenty miles. Arab robbers got him, and not a sign of him was ever found, despite all the efforts of the local authorities, backed by the

wrath of the French Consul. This is one of many
stories I have heard of the peculiarities of travel in
these regions, of beatings, of robberies, of murders,
and of disappearances. The marvel is that travellers
are still found willing to brave the risks—perhaps if
all of them knew the risks they would not be so brave.
At the same time one must be careful not to leave a
false impression of what the risks really are. My
own adventure in Mesopotamia would hardly have
occurred if I had been armed, or had had an escort.
On the other hand, a missionary and his wife, though
escorted by two gendarmes, were held up a year ago
near the Euphrates, and literally stripped of everything they possessed, their escort standing by help-
lessly. Then the French Consul and the Norwegian
Colonel had an escort of four gendarmes, and had to
fight for their lives. Within the year, however,
several parties, including ladies, passed through the
same country without molestation. Properly escorted,
there is little danger to life it would seem, though
there is never any immunity from robbery. Altogether it is a journey to make, in these days when
travel has become prosaic, for one novelty succeeds
another in endless succession, while the places visited
are of interest second to none in the world.

CHAPTER XVII.

MOSUL.

OF all the cities in the Turkish Empire, perhaps Mosul is the one that has been least touched by Western civilisation. Built on ground that once was a suburb of Nineveh, Mosul stands on the western bank of the Tigris, looking across at the mounds which are all that remain of the glories of the capital of ancient Assyria. Nineveh has a history that stretches throughout a period nearly 2000 years long, ending with the fall of the empire of Sennacherib in B.C. 626-608. From that time until Layard with reverent hands unveiled the palaces of Assurbanipal and Sennacherib, and unearthed the literary chamber containing the famous Deluge tablets, the ruins of Nineveh, for two thousand five hundred long years, have slept undisturbed. Mosul itself is continually mentioned in all history since the Arab conquest, suffering pillage at the hands of the ruthless Tamerlane, siege by Nadir Shah, and a host of other vicissitudes. To-day it is the least accessible spot in the dominions of the Sultan.

The town is surrounded by a half-ruined wall, built in modern times as a protection against the Shammar Arabs. The houses are large, dark, and mysterious, constructed to enable the inhabitants to escape in

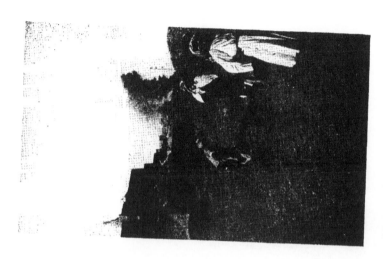

Winnowing corn under the shadow of Jonah's Tomb at Nineveh.

The Walls of Mosul, overlooking the Tigris.

some degree the terrible heat of summer. Serdabs, or underground chambers, offer some relief in temperature, and in these dark refuges the people who can afford it hide by day, to emerge in the comparative cool of evening with hopes of a breeze that at night on the house-top will help them to a spell of wholesome sleep. Humanity shares these house-tops with innumerable storks, who build their ragged nests on the highest and most dangerous places, and rear their young to an utter disregard of the laws of gravity. The stork is a curious bird in other matters besides appearance, for, so far as I was able to discover, he has no voice at all; certainly in eight days' acquaintance with four different families I never heard father, mother, or child, sing, whistle, scream, or twitter. Yet the stork has a language in which he can express his inmost thoughts. How he does it the uninitiated could surely never guess, for the method is unique and employed by no other living creature, fish, flesh, or fowl. I first became aware of it in the very early morning, before the sun had properly topped the eastern mountains. Four great preposterous specimens of the species stood on a wall beside the roof where I slept, and I dimly realised that they were performing their morning toilet. Their great wings were flapping, their long necks twisted hither and thither, and their huge pointed beaks poked and scratched and ruffled with the utmost diligence. Their lordships took no notice of me, prone on my bed a few yards away, and I was content to imagine myself in dreamland, with these strange creatures as figments of subconscious imagination. But a loud noise like some one rattling a stick in a wooden bucket partially waked me, and made me curse the early rising of my host's cook. Then somebody else with another bucket made a similar noise in a different key, and I wondered what in the world could they be doing to the buckets. Then it dawned upon me that half the population of Mosul must be rattling buckets, for the sound came from far and near, faint or loud according to distance, and in a hundred different keys. It was too early in the morning to exert intelligence, and I was content for the moment to suppose this quaint, not unmusical clatter to be perhaps the voice of some kind of patent prayer-wheel. Then came a loud rattle close to my ear. Within nine feet of me stood a solemn stork, his toilet over, his attitude a graceful balance on one leg. The noise came straight from his quivering beak, the hollow upper and lower halves of which he was clapping together with incredible rapidity. And that is how the stork expresses himself, in love and in anger, in pleasure and in distress. Truly there is more in the world than even Munchausen ever dreamed of.

Mosul is a place of some difficulty for the residents. Prices of every mortal thing are dearer almost than anywhere else in Turkey. Water is procured only from the Tigris, and every drop required must be carried therefrom in skins upon donkeys. A couple of pounds per month is a very ordinary expenditure on this essential, and provides but a scanty bath, the water of which thereafter is not thrown away; but is carefully lavished on a few potted plants that adorn the courtyard. Security of person is never assured, and individuals highly protected are at any moment liable to feel a knife between their ribs. When missionaries go to Mosul with the full consent of the Turkish Government, they find that neither love nor money will enable them to rent or build a house. When I was at Mosul a Jewish school, of which the master had been imported from Paris, was opened, and shut within

The Bridge of Boats at Mosul.

A future Winner of the Arab Derby.

a few days by arbitrary order of the authorities. To go out at night is to place one's life in jeopardy. To walk across the bridge in broad daylight is a danger owing to the frailty of the structure. The bridge is a wonderful affair, and yields an income of some thousands of pounds annually to the contractor who farms it from the Government. Three hundred yards of it is solid masonry, and the remaining 150 yards a wooden platform laid upon a row of crazy boats. Where the bridge of boats abuts the shore at one end, and the stone bridge at the other, are the points of danger, for owing to the height of the river when I was there the joinings were at a slope of forty-five degrees, and consisted of narrow gangways up which people, sheep, cattle, donkeys, mules, horses, and camels had to scramble. No wonder there were many fallings into the water—dangerous water too, for it coursed like a cataract between the boats, and swirled and boiled in fierce eddies and whirlpools below the bridge. One poor zaptieh, with rifle slung and bandoliers strapped round his chest, was walking across, when his horse slipped at the ascent to the boat part of the bridge, and both fell into the water. The horse was rescued but the man was drowned. Life has small value in Mosul, however, and nobody bothered to mend the huge holes in the bridge or to make its passage less precarious.

The fact was that the Vali, or Governor-General, of the province was a bad man and cared nothing for his charge, but only to sweat the populace as best he might. Being a full brother of Turkey's arch-traitor and robber, the notorious Syrian, Isset Pasha, chief of the Yildiz camarilla, no evil of the Vali could reach Constantinople, and he was able to work his wicked and foolish will with impunity. Yet the wicked do not always prosper, of which an amusing incident that happened while I was at Mosul is proof. His Excellency's carriage, containing one of his wives, his gold-mounted sword, much decorative uniform, and several bucketfuls of jewellery, was stopped by Arabs a few hours away from Mosul, and every blessed thing taken but the wife and the skimpiest of her garments—the wife was well entered into the sere and yellow leaf else she too would have been taken. No less than sixteen zaptiehs stood by inactive while this dastardly deed was being done. Mosul was delighted, for the news travelled like lightning, gathering magnitude as it went, even to the violation of the lady. The Vali made a brave show when condoled with, for he declared that the only thing stolen had been a silk handkerchief, since returned by the sheikh of the Arabs, with the head of the man who took it inside. How glad everybody said they were that the stories current were so exaggerated, and how they all laughed in their sleeves at the great man's discomfiture. Truly the hand of Allah is visible in all things !

Most of what I heard about Mosul I learnt while reposing on the flat of my back, for in my instance the hand of Allah had indeed been heavy. I had neither the strength nor the will to put one foot in front of the other. In our courtyard the temperature was 110° F. in the shade, and there were no punkahs, no ice, and no breeze. Nevertheless I meant to see Nineveh before I died. I nursed my strength for six days, and then got ˙ myself hoisted on the back of a horse. A friendly resident accompanied me to show me round. We wandered among the mounds for an hour, seeing bits of ancient wall, scraps of writing, broken statuary, potsherds, and other relics of past habitation, where now the

jackal and the raven make their home. Layard and
other excavators have blocked up the entrances to the
galleries that expose the palaces of the kings, and
there is practically nothing to be seen. One of the
famous Assyrian bulls, of which there are specimens
in the British Museum, we looked for in vain, though a
few months before it had lain in the sand seemingly
protected by its formidable appearance and ponderous
bulk. But we afterwards heard that what any museum
in Europe would have given thousands of pounds for,
had been ignominiously sold by the Vali for a few pieces
of silver, to be broken, burnt, and powdered into lime
by the masons of the city. Turkish law now forbids
the export of archæological valuables, and there was no
other way by which this greedy and ruthless official
could profit by so precious a relic of the past.

Half a mile from the mounds that cover the palaces
of Assurbanipal and Sennacherib is the mound known
to the Arabs as Nebi Yunus, or the Tomb of Jonah.
That the prophet should be buried near the city that
he turned to righteousness is proof of the story of Holy
Script. But there are some inconsistencies in the Bible
narrative which the higher critics may think worthy of
explanation. When Jonah fled from the presence of
the Lord he took ship from Joppa and paid fare to
Tarshish, which, though now unapproachable from the
sea, was in ancient times, as explained in another
chapter, a great inland port attainable by a navigable
river. On the way arose the storm which caused the
mariners to pitch Jonah overboard. Being swallowed
by a great fish—the Old Testament says nothing about
a whale, which everybody knows is too small in the
throat for a man to pass—Jonah prayed from its belly,
and after three days and three nights was duly vomited
out upon dry land. That dry land presumably was some

part of the eastern shore of the Mediterranean. But later in the Bible narrative it is stated that Jonah took three days to journey to Nineveh, though the distance from the nearest point of the Mediterranean coast is 400 miles, a distance impossible of accomplishment in so short a time.   There is the hypothesis that the great fish carried Jonah past the Straits of Gibraltar, round the Cape of Good Hope, into the Persian Gulf, and up the Tigris to within a hundred miles of Nineveh, and there spued him forth.   But it must have been a clever fish to swim 20,000 miles with a man in its belly in three days and three nights, the time of Jonah's unpleasant imprisonment.   The fish, however, according to the Scriptures, had been specially prepared, doped perhaps, as they call it in America, and there is no knowing what its powers might have been.

The visit to Nineveh nerved me for another effort on the following morning, this time to an institution of something more than academic interest, being no less than the stables of Haji Ali bin Talib, the famous importer into India of Arab horses.   Mosul is one of the great buying centres for India, and from here the horses are marched in droves for twelve days to Baghdad, where they are shipped in the Lynch steamers to Bussorah, and then transhipped to the Gulf boats for Bombay.   The Haji was absent, but his son received me with distinction, and I delighted my soul once more with Hindustani, though my host spoke tolerable English.   I expressed the wish to see the horses and to take a few photographs, and was assured that the place was my very own to do with as I pleased. I inspected about fifty animals, all in the pink of condition, and apparently as happy as crickets, despite the prospect of travel and the permanent departure from their desert homes.   Perhaps if they knew how the

Chaldean Women at Mosul.

A Cheerful Giver.

heavy-handed subalterns and boxwallahs of Ind were likely to instil into their simple minds the principles of polo, they might have looked less bright. But fortunately for us both the future is hidden from horse-kind as well as from mankind. I was interested to note that the stable arrangements were as neat and as clean as anything to be found in India.

When it came to photographing I was told not to take the beasts standing in line, but to wait patiently. The Arab always keeps his best hidden away from sight, and will only produce it under great temptation. The bait I employed was the promise of reproduction in a book that would be read all over the world, and make the horses famous before they had even left their native land. The Arab understands the uses of advertisement, and indeed of anything that tends to cause a gravitation of money towards his pocket. Two beautiful colts were brought from an inner courtyard, and I snapped them in not very successful attitudes. They are exquisite creatures all the same, and their proud owner declared that one would be the very finest ever imported into India. This cup and that cup were already at his mercy, and Master Talib expected to get so many rupees for him that it would be necessary to charter a ship to bring them home. May their future be gladness!

Then we retired behind the shade of a lofty house, and I was given the place of honour in a row of patriarchal Arabs, who sat cross-legged on carpets spread along a raised platform. Up and down before them were walked, trotted, and cantered horses brought for sale to the famous dealer. My opinion was asked about several of the animals shown, and I said I disliked the hocks of one, the shoulder of another, and found a third too light below the knee. They hailed me with respect, for it was evident that I was deeply educated in the horse-culture that is the pride of the dweller in the desert. What I condemned was sent away with contumely, though I afterwards observed that the syces went no farther than the nearest corner. But these friends of the great Haji were the personification of courtesy, and would no more allow that I talked rot than they would allow me to pull their beards. We drank coffee and smoked cigarettes, and discussed horse until my poor back was broken entirely. Then I shot at the Haji's son the question—did he remember a particular animal brought to India by his father about fourteen years before? He rolled the name mentioned round his mind for a minute or two, and then, to my great delight, responded with enthusiasm—a flea-bitten grey, fast as the wind, with a head that had been kissed by Allah and all the Prophets! The very same, I almost wept, for the flea-bitten grey in the long-past irresponsible days of yore had been the very apple of my eye, the pride of my youth, and the constant replenisher of my purse. How many times had he not carried me first past the post, sometimes twice in the same day, over any distance you liked to ask him— with his spun-glass tail of shimmering white streaming behind, tiny ears cocked straight to Heaven, great eyes blood-red with excitement and the fury of galloping! What unexpected memories were waked by the thought of that big-hearted, little-bodied horse, upon whom I had had so many a joyous ride! His indignation when I tried him at polo, his astonishment when asked to follow a dirty pig — he, a pure-bred, delicate-nosed Mussulman — and how he climbed a tree in protest when I vainly endeavoured to persuade him to lead tandem! Here, near Mosul, had been his early home, for he had sprung from the loins of a well-known

stallion of the adjacent desert, and had been brought
to these very stables when a fiery frolicsome colt. And
now he is old and stricken in years, and somewhat
slower on those beautiful clean legs that are still the
marvel of all who behold them. It is years since I
have seen him, but I hear of him often, and know
that the fire in his eye is undimmed. Good oats and
plenty of them will keep a horse well and happy; and
this well-beloved, never-forgotten friend, I am glad to
think, is in hands that grudge nothing that the soul
of horse can desire.

CHAPTER XVIII.

LOCUSTS, SHARKS, AND ROBBERS.

ARRIVAL at Mosul marked the end of the voyage so far as the Diarbekir kelek was concerned. Our kelekjis were now far from their own country, and were much concerned to think of their return journey through a region given up to Shaitan. Within an hour of reaching Mosul the kelek was dismantled, the bales disembarked, my £4 house lifted bodily on to the bank, the poplar poles untied from the skins, and the skins themselves, deflated, laid on the ground in a slimy heap. In a day they would be dry, and then two donkeys would carry the lot back to Diarbekir. To the zaptiehs I presented three golden Turkish pounds wherewith they could buy them asses to ride homeward, and plenty of food by the way. Having returned to the place whence they came they would sell the asses and find themselves each worth a clear pound, not a bad result considering that they were drawing pay and rations all the while. There is no obligation to make any payment to the escort provided by the Government, but as being sent away from home generally entails expenses on the men which they can never recover, the custom has arisen to make them a daily allowance of ten piastres, or two francs. Under ordinary circumstances this pays them very well, and when they encounter a lordly globe-trotter who doubles or even trebles the usual fee, there is deep satisfaction.

Departure from Mosul entailed the chartering of another kelek, and I might pitch my camp on a very large one of 800 skins, carrying wheat, or have a small one of 100 skins all to myself. The former took double the time to reach Baghdad, but cost only half as much money as the other. Being now a confirmed vale-tudinarian I flinched from the slower voyage in the desperate heat of summer, and paid the larger sum for an express kelek guaranteed to travel day and night without ceasing. The skins were speedily affixed to the pole framework, and my house tied on top. Then we were ready, and having spent ten days at Mosul hovering on the brink of the grave, I was glad to leave it while the vital spark within me was yet aglow. We hoped to make Baghdad on the fifth day. It is no great catch getting to Baghdad in the sultry month of July, but it was civili-sation of a sort, and where, moreover, they dealt with local conditions after the Indian fashion, which knows how to make the best of warm weather.

To the robust traveller the voyage from Mosul to Baghdad offers various attractions, for there are many places on the way worthy of visit. First come the sulphur baths of Hammam Ali, and in their neighbour-hood a petroleum field from which great things are expected. The Turks have set up some machinery and have attempted the manufacture of kerosine. So far, owing to want of experience, they have not succeeded in producing oil that burns well, but that difficulty will soon be got over. About twenty-five miles below Mosul lie the ruins of ancient Nimrud, where Layard discov-ered the vast palaces of Sargon, Assurnasirpal, Shal-manezer, Esarhaddon, and other worthies, who in

Assyrian times chastised the Jews for the good of their morals. Not far from Nimrud is the place where the Ten Thousand crossed the Zab, an important tributary of the Tigris. At Shergat, a few hours farther down stream, are the mounds of ancient Asshur, where a German archæological expedition has been settled for some years, making extensive and scientific excavations. A day inland from Shergat are the remarkable ruins of Hatrae. There are the interesting towns of Tekrit, Samara, and Kasimin to be passed, each with its attractions in the shape of ancient ruins or comparatively modern mosques of curious and marvellous construction. Every inch of the ground is classic, and redolent of Chaldean, Assyrian, and Parthian among the more ancient civilisations, and of Roman, Persian, and Arab among the later.

At Shergat I plucked up courage and paid the Germans a visit, being received with much kindness and courtesy by the three young enthusiasts who are conducting the excavations. They have built an excellent house, convenient in every respect for residence, storage of archæological valuables, and for scientific work. They take meteorological observations, study the country and people, and generally make use of their opportunities in the thorough and business-like manner characteristic of German enterprise. They keep up health and spirits in this place of exile by unremitting attention to work, relieved by regular hours for rest and recreation, the latter mainly shooting, and swimming in the river. The evidences of method and system in all that was done at Shergat, and the utter absence of haphazard either in work or play, were impressive. Having had former opportunities of observing the systematic methods of the German, in relation to subjects widely different from archæology, I was interested to note that the national genius for organisation, product doubtless of scientific education, was capable of application to things academic as well as material. One wonders, perhaps, whether great devotion to detail may not tend to lower that power of imagination which must initiate everything great, and if the studious, methodical, industrious German does not sometimes miss the essential in his pursuit of the concrete. Whether or not the German suffers from the defects of his qualities, it remains that wherever we encounter him, in the domains of politics or commerce, science or scholarship, he is a formidable antagonist, all the more formidable because he is entirely worthy of respect. It seems a pity that at home it should be the fashion to decry Germany and to suspect all her motives, to dislike the individual and to scorn his methods, for that would seem but to indicate the envy of conscious inferiority. Why not admit that by every natural law Germany is entitled to work out her own national salvation, whether at our expense or somebody else's, if she can. Having looked the essential fact in the face, we can then take measures in self-defence in the degree and with the calmness the situation demands. To rage vainly against the rival who is cutting into our business, and looking longingly at possessions which we have not always administered with consistent wisdom, is not the way to preserve our position in the world. The danger to our Empire does not lie without the Empire, but within it—a truism perhaps, but one that cannot be too often reiterated.

The point at which the Germans have centred their archæological activity is one of great interest, for it has turned out that the mounds cover the remains

P

of Asshur, the earliest capital of that Assyrian Empire
that sprang from the loins of Babylon, and eventually
brought its progenitor to the ground.   A long cylinder
of Tiglath Pileser I., the great Assyrian conqueror, is
one of the principal finds, while the fact that upon
the long-covered remains of Asshur there has been
found the remains of a Parthian city, itself covered
by sand for over 2000 years, adds greatly to the
interest of the investigations.   The mounds are of
greater height than those of Nineveh, and were long
known to travellers, though the nature of their contents was not divined.   But a slight change in the
course of the Tigris resulted in the cutting of a new
bank by the river, and the exposure of ancient
walls constructed of the well-known hard-burnt
bricks of the Babylonian and Assyrian periods.   In
bringing the kelek to shore we ran considerable risk
from damage by an old wall now submerged, and
behind which the water unfortunately is cutting its
way.   These indications of former importance, together
with the magnitude of the mounds, decided the Germans to prosecute their investigations at Shergat,
with results that have proved highly satisfactory.

I was taken over all the excavations, which consist
of a tunnel into a projecting mound, and the entire
removal of the *débris* overlying an area of several acres.
The latter process has resulted in the laying bare of
the foundations, floors, and lower walls of many houses
of the old city.   These are in perfect preservation
in many cases, and show the exact arrangements of
rooms, and frequently the purposes to which they were
devoted.   Every house had its place for the dead—
the poorer a scooped-out hollow fitted with a lid,
the richer subterranean chambers entered by heavy
wooden doors.   Winding lanes between the houses,

tiny channels for running water, stables for horses, sanitary accommodation, and a host of other matters having their modern equivalents, were observable. The excavations seemed to bring before one the domestic life of these ancient people — the fact that they were human and not monster, as their warlike and bloody history sometimes suggests—and gave to one's conception of them a reality that all the winged bulls and baked inscriptions of the museums can never give. The builders of Asshur had an advantage over the Babylonians, for they were able to employ stone where the others were forced to use brick. But the brick crops up at many points, showing how strong was the Babylonian influence, and how difficult it must have been for the early Assyrians to depart from established custom. The labour entailed in these excavations is tremendous, and would have been impossible of accomplishment were it not for the employment of light railways and patent trucks which carry away the *débris*—early instalments of the Baghdad Railway, quoth my guide, with a humorous glance at my British countenance. A great deal has been done at Shergat, but there still remains work that will take years to complete. Unluckily the most promising point in the whole area of the mounds is occupied by a Turkish guardhouse and its enclosure. This spot of course is sacred, and cannot be touched. Perhaps with the slow but sure progress of enlightenment in Turkey, a day may come when the authorities will view with more favour the process of research. The recent establishment of a Museum of Antiquities at Constantinople, and the promulgation of an Irade forbidding the removal from the country of antiquarian treasures, suggests that the desirable interest is being awakened.

Below Shergat the heat was very great, and if it were not for the cool waters of the river I must have been burnt up completely. I spent hours in it, floating or swimming or clinging to the kelek. Once I got the kelekji to loosen a skin and hand it over to my tender mercies, having in my mind ancient experience with mussacks in an Indian swimming-bath. Throwing the inflated skin a few feet away from the raft, I mounted a sack of wheat, and from that point of vantage sprang forth, meaning to grip the skin between my legs and ride it in the water as one might ride a horse, a trick at which I had once been expert. But the Mesopotamian mussack is a frail thing compared with the Indian one, and the result of my leap was a loud report and a slimy empty bag clinging round my waist. Another one was got ready, and this time I was cautious, hoping to slip across it by strategy rather than by force. But my reward was only a long melancholy combination of wail and whistle, which once more left me with the slimy and undesirable empty skin. I gave up trying to ride cock-horse. The people of the country, however, make great use of the skins, and one of the quaintest things to be seen on the Tigris is the process by which an individual crosses from one side to the other. Desirous of reaching the opposite bank, he walks up-stream to a point from which he calculates to make his destination, and there prepares. He begins by blowing up two skins and tying them together. Next he strips naked and packs his clothes either on the top of his head or upon the diminutive raft. All is now ready, and our friend, rifle in hand, wades into the water, pushing the skins before him. When up to his middle he halts and proceeds to mount. With the tenderest care he lays his stomach across the nearest mussack and spreads his elbows over the one beyond, both hands tightly grasping the rifle. He carefully feels the position by lifting his feet off the ground, makes any adjustment necessary, and then turns on the steam, which consists of furiously paddling with the legs after the manner of a frog. All his body is out of water, and two-thirds of his legs, half submerged, trail behind. In order to force the legs down to get sufficient grip of the water, it is necessary somewhat to raise the hinder parts, which, in propelling the lower limbs, are violently agitated. The result is effective, though highly ludicrous, which does not matter much in a country where a sense of humour is not common. When such an one passes close to the kelek it is most fascinating to observe the curious motions, to note the rapt expression on his face, and to realise the delicacy of the position, which forbids any movement of the body, or even the head—indeed the eyes are only turned with the greatest caution. The cause of all the anxiety of course is the rifle, to wet which would be a great misfortune.

At Tekrit, the birthplace of Salah‑ed‑din, the chivalrous Saladin of the Crusades, I had to limit the scope of my aquatic performances on account of sharks, which are said to penetrate up-stream to this point from the Persian Gulf in the hot season. It was hot sure enough, and I was in mortal fear of having a leg nipped off,—with both hands badly damaged I could not afford to sacrifice any more limbs. My tri-daily dip was a hurried business, and the lightning manner in which I dived, twisted back in the water, and regained the shelter of the kelek, would make the fortune of any music‑hall artist who could emulate it. Clinging to the raft, I never ceased beating the water with my legs, this being the time‑honoured method of frightening a shark. Occasionally I ventured forth, forgetful for the moment of the risk, always to return in haste, frightened to death because something had touched me below the surface. For a galvanic shock I commend the experience of having a tiny fish rub up against one's legs in water known to be frequented by sharks. The ensuing shudder is electric to the highest degree.

Deprived of the opportunity of unrestrained disport in the river, I spent the day in the lightest possible attire, waging war with the afore - described flies, and with myriads of locusts which leapt aboard in battalions whenever we touched shore. For hundreds of miles along the banks of the river the country was alive with them, mostly arrived too late to ruin this year's harvest, but constituting a serious danger to the agricultural prospects of next year, for the brutes breed furiously, and for each one now there would be a hundred twelve months hence. They lay their eggs in holes in the ground, out of which as many as three hundred young ones are said to come in the fulness of time. In thickly populated countries, where a visitation of locusts means starvation to the inhabitants, soldiers are employed to destroy the larvæ, while on individuals is imposed a poll-tax payable in bushels of the same. These endeavours to extirpate the vipers are useful if undertaken on a sufficiently large scale, but the only effective cure is a flood, which destroys the seed. Curiously enough the arrival of the locust, which spells devastation in settled regions, is welcomed by nomads in the desert with much joy. Great numbers of the visitors are roasted and powdered, the flour resulting therefrom being regarded as a fine food by the Arabs, one part equally nourishing to two of barley-flour.

Locusts attain considerable size, and the Germans at Shergat showed me some that were fully four inches in length, with legs like lobsters. Brutes like this can bite a man's finger to the bone, and are highly unpleasant customers. A friend, with whose moral character I am insufficiently acquainted, tells me that in Beluchistan there was a well-authenticated case of a woman who put her baby down in a field while she went to assist the beaters in an endeavour to disperse a flight of locusts. When she returned an hour or two later there was nothing left of the baby but the bones. The creatures that took possession of my kelek, however, were not so formidable, though they made themselves extremely objectionable. I never quite realised why women entertain such a terror of mice, until several locusts got up the legs of my pyjamas.

Near Samara we passed the ancient coast-line that marks the boundary of Mesopotamia proper, and entered upon the immense plain of alluvium which constituted the wealth of Chaldea, more commonly known in these days as Babylonia. For a distance of nearly four hundred miles to the Persian Gulf, and for a breadth of some hundred and fifty miles between the Persian mountains in the east and the edge of the Arabian plateau in the west, there lies a region unadorned by hills, without a single excrescence above the general level that is not the handiwork of man. The drop to the sea in this great distance is only 130 feet. The soil, except where temporarily ruined by the accumulation of water and salt, equals the richest to be found in any part of the world. Here flourished the ancient irrigation system that exceeded in magnitude anything existing in the present day, and by the science of its methods and the perfection of its arrangements excites the admiration of the modern experts who have studied it. Of all the millions of acres that once were densely populated and highly cultivated, there is now not five per cent inhabited. Only along the banks of the two great rivers, and beside what remains of the ancient canals, is there a narrow strip of cultivation which abundant irrigation renders prolific in the highest degree. Hereafter both sides of the Tigris are thickly occupied by erections designed to hoist the water from the river to the level of the surrounding land. The system is simple, consisting of a projecting framework supporting axles. On these axles run ropes attached to great bags of skin, which are dipped in the stream, hoisted up, and relieved of their loads of water, which thereupon runs down a canal to do its work in the fields. The motive power is furnished by horses, donkeys, and cattle, which march up and down a slope, harnessed to the ropes that hoist the laden skins in the manner well known in various parts of the East. This process in proper season goes on day and night without ceasing, and the creaking and skirling and wailing of the ungreased wheels of these clumsy wooden contrivances is one of the weirdest noises to which it has ever been my lot to listen. In the night, when all is dark, as the raft floats silently along upon the black water, their unearthly sounds thrill one through with horror and fear, for they tell of torture, of murder, of the agonies of the everlastingly damned.

Our last night on the river was not quite uneventful. The horrid water-wheels were stilled, and we were floating quietly down within a few feet of the bank, which loomed high and black above us, when the silence was suddenly broken by a deep resonant voice which asked who we were and where we were going.

Irrigation Works in Mesopotamia.

" . . . *the creaking and skirling and wailing wheels* . . ."

I was awake at the time, and wondered at the commotion that ensued. My servant jumped up and
stretched out his hand for the revolver that hung
from a nail beside him. I could hear the zaptiehs
rattling the bolts of their rifles as they loaded, while
the kelekji woke up and began rowing madly away
from the shore. The suspense for a time was intense,
for from the darkness under the bank we momentarily
expected a rifle to flame forth. But the robber, for it
was one of this kidney without doubt, was probably
deterred by the number of voices and the activity on
board, for we heard nothing more, and were quickly
swept away from the spot whence had come that
suspicious and imperious inquiry. This is the way
of robbers in the night when they cannot see their
quarry. A question results in movement, and by the
sounds the robber can judge of the risks of venturing
an attack.

The remainder of the night passed without incident,
and in the morning we found ourselves entering a new
region where riverside villas and a busy boat traffic
indicated the neighbourhood of a populous city. Our
long and fascinating kelek voyage is over at last,
and we float past the gilded dome and minarets of
the mosque at Kasimin, between groves of date-palms
and orange-trees, down to Baghdad itself, with its

". . . shrines of fretted gold,
High-walled gardens, green and old."

CHAPTER XIX.

BAGHDAD AND IRRIGATION.

BAGHDAD is a magic word, as the place itself was magic in the days of long ago. But the wonder of it has long departed, and the Baghdad of the present is but a suggestion of the glory of the past. The ruins of a few mosques, an old gateway, the tombs of queens and prophets, hint at ancient grandeur where now reigns the commonplace. Yet Baghdad has its charms for the traveller. The narrow streets, the quaint houses, the iron-bound doors giving glimpses of shady court-yards and splashing fountains, are redolent of the East and all that it means to those unsatisfied souls who adore the picturesque and ache continually for touches of imagery in a world of materialities. Memory and imagination, too, are faithful genii easily summoned, and they will conjure for you from the pages of the Nights the most gorgeous palaces, the most impregnable castles, and the most beautiful gardens, all alive with running water and singing birds, coloured like a dream, and languorous with the smell of roses.

But the city of Haroun al Rashid is no more. That grandson of Genghiz with the ill-omened name, Hulagu, smashed it, and Timur the Tartar struck again when its head was in the dust, and Shahs and Sultans hammered at it without ceasing until its greatness died completely away. So the Baghdad of to-day is of mushroom growth and mean appearance, remarkable only as the capital of a remote province of the Turkish Empire, where Trade is greater than Tradition, and foreign Consuls are above the names of the Caliphs. Truly, Ichabod is writ large below the history of Baghdad.

Official British connection with Baghdad commenced in the days of Napoleon, when French activity in Egypt and Syria was expected to lead up to the invasion of India. To act as a link in a chain of overland communication between India and Europe, and to report upon French intrigue in the country, the East India Company appointed a Resident at Baghdad, which appointment was duly approved by the Sultan at the beginning of last century. War between ourselves and Turkey followed soon after, and British residents at Baghdad and Bussorah suffered injury and insult, the outcome of which was an undertaking by the Pasha of Baghdad which established British right to high honour, security, and instant compensation for injury. Ten years later, however, the Resident was actually besieged in his own house, and forced to leave the country. These proceedings cost the Pasha his head, and the British position became firmer than ever, a sepoy guard and a river gunboat thereafter being included in the establishment of the Residency. Hitherto our representative at Baghdad had been under the Bombay Government, but in 1834 the post was transferred to the Government of India, and vested with Consular powers by the British Government in 1841. It was not until 1880, when our official connection had lasted seventy-seven years, when we had created a large trade at Baghdad, when we had changed the road thereto through the Persian Gulf from a haunt of pirates to a parade for nursery-maids, that our example was followed by other foreign nations. In that year Russia, to whose nostrils the advance into Central Asia had brought the smell of warm water, established a Consulate, and thereafter Consuls followed like sheep from France, Germany, Austria, Italy, the United States, Holland, Denmark, Norway and Sweden, Belgium, and Switzerland, all of whom grudge us our trade, our sepoys, our gunboat, and deny to our Resident his official title, conferred in 1798 and approved by the Sultan since 1802.

The reason for which is not far to seek. The commerce of Baghdad with abroad has an annual average value of £2,500,000, of which nearly 90 per cent is British and Indian, an advantage which no efforts on the part of our numerous rivals seem materially to reduce. Imports form two-thirds of the total, and the only item of importance which we do not monopolise is sugar, which we have long given up manufacturing for export. The principal import is piece goods, a trade so firmly established that it is difficult to see how our position can be assailed. The importers are three British firms and a number of Jewish ones, all represented by agents in Manchester, who understand the requirements of the market, and who by reason of local standing and long connection obtain credit and financial facilities which they could not obtain elsewhere without long probation. Lest the above figures convey a false impression of the purchasing powers of Baghdad, it should be stated that something like a third of the total represents goods in transit to and from Persia viâ Khanikin, four to six days' journey by caravan. This route taps an important district of western Persia, of which Kermanshah is the distributing centre. Persian buyers deal with the direct importers at Baghdad, but arrange that their goods paying Turkish custom duties shall be subject to refund thereof, less 1 per cent, when crossing the border. The total annual quantity crossing the Persian border is said to amount to 100,000 loads outwards and 20,000 inwards, carried on camels, horses, mules, and donkeys, an aggregate of about 12,000 tons altogether. These figures in relation to the Baghdad - Khanikin trade are interesting, for, together with those relating to the pilgrim traffic, said to average 200,000 persons annually, they constitute an important factor in the prospects of the lower sections of the Baghdad Railway.

Leaving consideration of commercial affairs for inclusion in remarks on the Gulf trade in general, I now turn to an aspect of these regions in which Baghdad as the modern capital is the principal point of interest. I refer, of course, to irrigation, which made Babylonia great, and might again conceivably lead to the regeneration of a land hopelessly fallen from former civilisation. The system of canalisation which once watered this country is said to be without parallel in modern times, both on account of its magnitude and on account of the area affected. Ancient historians are unanimous about the fertility of the soil, Herodotus declaring that grain commonly returned 200-fold to the sower. Pliny says that wheat was cut twice and that a third growth afforded good feeding for sheep. The country was studded with a vast number of cities, and fruit and nut trees grew wild. There is no indication that the rainfall was regarded as an important factor of the agricultural conditions, though there is evidence to suggest that it once was greater than it is to-day. The present mean for figures since 1888 is 8·34 inches per annum, with a maximum of 22·31 inches in 1894, and a minimum of 1·47 in 1901, variations which indicate that water is capable of proving a curse as well as a blessing, and which, if of continual recurrence, would render agriculture impossible. Archæologists have shown that water was the greatest enemy to the permanence of the great platforms on which were constructed the fortresses, palaces, and temples of Babylon. Reference is made to long, heavy winter rains and their effect upon crude and even burnt brick. To protect the loosely constructed mounds from permeation with moisture, the builders contrived an artful and admirably executed system of drainage tunnels, which poured the collected water into the plain out of mouths beautifully constructed in the shape of arched vaults. These arrangements suggest more rain than falls in present times. Then, both among Babylonian and Assyrian remains, there are many sculptures, reliefs, and inscriptions to show that hunting of wild beasts in dense jungles was a form of sport constantly indulged in by ancient kings, in places where to-day exist no jungle, but only utterly unwatered desert. Highly cultivated areas dotted with trees must surely have been subject to meteorological conditions different from those of to-day, when the same areas are howling wilderness. In all probability the summer crops of the Babylonians were irrigated by the spring floods in the rivers, while rain supplied moisture for the winter crops when the rivers were low.

The question is whether the conditions that obtained in ancient times are susceptible of being reproduced. The decline of the rainfall, if that has taken place, and there would seem to be little doubt on the point, is not important apparently, for if Egypt is any criterion a country may flourish exceedingly without rain, so long

Baghdad, showing the floods beyond the western bank.

c c c c c c c

c 2004, XXX

as moisture is provided in some other manner. Here the Tigris and Euphrates furnish the needful water, and in a degree which experts declare is equivalent to that supplied to the ancient system, and sufficient at any rate to irrigate millions of acres. The Euphrates and Tigris in the latitude of Baghdad have average discharges of 1200 and 1500 cubic metres respectively per second, with maximums of 2500 and 4000, and minimums of 300 and 250 respectively. These calculations have been made by Sir William Willcocks, who claims for them only approximate accuracy, and will enable irrigationists to form their own opinion of the value of the volume available. With this enormous supply it is obvious that whether or not Mesopotamia is suffering from the desiccation that is surely and visibly spreading in Central Asia, there is enough water to irrigate immense areas of land, and to recreate, in some degree, a new Chaldea, under Turkey or anybody else upon whom the task may devolve.

Of this prospect Sir William Willcocks writes with all the enthusiasm of the expert who perceives suitable soil for the exercise of his beneficent art. As Sir William expressly leaves politics completely out of his calculations, it would not be fair to say that he has neglected considerations which make his dream difficult of realisation. But his ideas in regard to the regeneration of this country by irrigation, conjointly with the inauguration of railway communications in the shape of the Baghdad scheme, have obtained wide currency, and are apt to lead to unduly optimistic conclusions, for the very reason that he has debarred himself from any but the one view of his subject. Given certain conditions, the irrigation of Mesopotamia would indeed be a profitable venture, but under existing conditions, and with finance dependent upon politics, as it is to-day, particularly with regard to Turkey, it is hard to see how Sir William Willcocks' fascinating picture of a restored Chaldea can be given reality. Not because of the physical difficulties, for one accepts without question the great Egyptian irrigationist's opinion that they are easily surmountable, but because it is difficult of belief, among other things—

(1) that Turkey could procure the restoration by herself;

(2) that she would allow another country to step in and do it;

(3) that any other country would undertake the expenditure involved unless the political control were vested in herself; and

(4) that in a region so sparsely inhabited the population necessary to cultivate the reclaimed land could be found.

Into the details of Sir William Willcocks' remarkable scheme I am not competent to enter. From cursory examination of the country he has been able to map it out into districts, each requiring different treatment, and its own separate system of canals, according to levels. Before anything can be done he insists on the devotion of two years to accurate survey of the country and study of the conditions. He is convinced that then the scheme which he formulates on general lines will prove to be practicable. This scheme involves the reclamation of 2,800,000 acres at a cost of £21,000,000. It deals only with the richest and the most accessible parts of the deltas of the Tigris and the Euphrates, some 4000 square miles in the neighbourhood of Baghdad. The land thus reclaimed he estimates would be worth £60,000,000. After deduction of working expenses from the rent received from occupiers, there would be an annual balance of about £4,000,000, or nearly 20 per cent on the capital involved.

These figures are open to criticism, for they are based on the assumption that an unlimited supply of labour is available. Estimates of population in Turkey are always difficult, and in this far distant portion of the Empire they are still more difficult owing to the number of nomads and the existence of a large floating population in the shape of pilgrims. Apart from these two classes of the community, the inhabitants are all engaged in easy and profitable agriculture on the banks of the rivers and the remnants of the ancient canals. These latter are not to be lightly attracted to coolie work. Some of the nomad tribes are poor, but they are poor not because they have no opportunity of bettering their position, but because they are too indolent to labour, preferring to move about with flocks upon which they can exist without exertion. The pilgrims that crowd the holy cities of Kerbela and Nejef frequently stay for a year in the country, mostly living on the money they have been saving for years to enable them to make the pilgrimage. This floating population is always on the look-out to make a little money, but it is not usually of the class nor of the age from which coolie labour can be expected. In fact, it may be said that there are no people in these regions poor enough to do coolie labour who are not poor from deliberate choice, for land and water in plenty are available for anybody with energy to work. There are, of course, in the towns a certain number of men who correspond to our navvy class, but in a country where there are no public works or industry these are limited in number, and their absorption in a great irrigation project would merely upset local conditions and raise the rate of wages. Poor Arabs from Arabia would come in for the sake of earning a little ready money, but it is doubtful if they would care to stick to the work. Persians and Kurds from the mountains would also be attracted, but they again would not like hard manual labour in a climate that is not conducive to energy. On the whole it would seem that there is very little labour available, and that the necessary amount could not be attracted except by much higher rates of wages than are now prevalent. As Sir William Willcocks' scheme of reclamation entails an expenditure on works of £21,000,000, practically every penny of which would be required for labour, it is obvious that an under-estimation of 50 per cent, or even 25 per cent, for wages would make all the difference in the result. To obtain all the labour required, the probability is that the rise would be 100 per cent, or double existing rates.

Other aspects of the case suggest remark. Rich country, highly irrigated, requires a very dense population. The land is here, the water is waiting, and it might be, under Allah, that the money and the political situation which would make the scheme feasible would be forthcoming. But where are the two or three million of inhabitants to come from? They do not exist at present; and while Arabia and Persia would furnish a quota, it remains that climatic considerations will always deter immigration to a region that is difficult of residence except to those who are accustomed to similar conditions. Examine the meteorological tables attached to Sir William Willcocks' report, and note the torrid character of the country for six months out of the twelve. The people capable of doing hard manual labour in such a region are not to be found in great numbers in the Turkish Empire. To suppose that they can be brought from India, where already the everlasting agricultural problem begins to arise in the irrigation districts, and where every industry is starved for lack of labour, is to be ignorant of the conditions of life in India.

Then to compare results in Egypt and India with those attainable in Mesopotâmia is surely misleading. Egypt is perfectly placed with regard to the markets of the world ; India itself is an immense market, exporting only surpluses. But here, where there is no industry, no large garrison, and no absorption by famine, the value of the reclaimed land would be entirely dependent upon foreign demand for its produce. The prices paid for wheat or cotton in Egypt, whence transport to market is low, are very different from those that would rule in Mesopotamia, where produce would be handicapped by land or river transport charges in addition to heavy marine freights. It is easy to rear fowls, but another matter to get the eggs to market. In Egypt, too, the high value of irrigated land is due greatly to the quantity and to the fine quality of the cotton grown. Sir William Willcocks is of opinion that the conditions in the neighbourhood of Baghdad are favourable for the growth of cotton, though it would seem unlikely that the heat would permit of the slow maturity which is essential to production of the higher grades. But cotton cultivation entails labour out of all proportion to that required for the cultivation of cereals, and if the foregoing remarks in regard to population correctly state the conditions, the area devoted to the growth of cotton is bound to be strictly limited. With low prices for the product of their labour, mostly cereals, settlers could pay but low rents to the proprietors of their land, who would thus have to be content with a small return for the capital spent on irrigation. Sir William Willcocks has, of course, made some allowance both for this and for higher labour rates than presently obtain. But has he made sufficient allowance? Add 50 per cent to his estimates for work, and take 50 per cent off his values upon the land after reclamation, and the attractiveness of the scheme as an investment disappears.

India throughout the last fifty years has spent some £40,000,000 on irrigation, upon which she now receives a dividend of 7 per cent per annum. This return upon capital expenditure by no means indicates the full measure of the benefits derived, for in addition to large prospective returns on works about to become productive, there has to be counted the gains in the shape of revenue augmentation, increased trade, employment of labour, and so forth, all of which act and react upon each other to the infinite advantage of the State. But this result has been attained under conditions very different from those prevailing in Mesopotamia. The unlimited agricultural population of India has been drawn upon for settlers; labour, owing to famine and to the low standard of living, is cheaper in India than anywhere else in the world; and in India there are twenty rivers as big as the Tigris and the Euphrates from which immeasurable water is available. Yet Sir William Willcocks estimates for his project a success infinitely greater, in proportion to its size, than has been attained by irrigation in India. What irrigation can do for a country all the world knows, and no one has a greater right to speak upon the subject than the enthusiastic and talented engineer who has been so largely responsible for the evolution of Egyptian irrigation. But the Mesopotamian problem presents many idiosyncrasies, and is not to be solved in a day. Rather will the restoration of the Babylonian irrigation system be a very long and a very slow process, as the extension of irrigation has been slow and long drawn out in India; and for a beginning we must wait until the one country in the world competent to move in the ˆmatter is ready to commence operations. That country is Turkey herself, and none other.

Curiously enough, this beginning is almost an accomplished fact, for while I was in Constantinople last October (1907), the Turkish Government called for tenders to undertake the repair of a barrage, which, when completed, will have very important results. More curiously still, the Turks are supposed actually to have £100,000 in the Ottoman Bank waiting to be spent on this project. At the time of writing nobody had tendered, and no progress had been made, though a move in the near future is a certainty. The plan is to complete the existing barrage at the entrance of the Hindia Canal, which takes off the Euphrates near Babylon. At present practically the whole of the Euphrates deserts its own bed at this point, and flows down the Hindia Canal into a region of swamps and lakes that have gradually increased in recent years, and permanently flooded good ground previously cultivated in some degree and valuable as pasture land. The controlling of the water by a barrage should gradually have the effect of draining much of the marsh land fed by the canal, and will further divert into its true bed the river itself, which will make possible once more cultivation of banks that have been deserted since the stream took another course. This scheme is fraught with tremendous possibilities, for if successfully carried

out it will lead to further enterprise of a similar character, and set afoot a process of regeneration which, if
much slower than Sir William Willcocks predicts, may
result, a hundred years hence, in the new Chaldea that
he has presented to our imagination.[1]

---

[1] Since this chapter was written a very important step has been taken
by the Turkish Government, for they have actually engaged Sir William
Willcocks to go out to Mesopotamia to report upon the question of the
Hindia barrage, and upon the prospects of irrigation generally.

CHAPTER XX.

ON A LYNCH STEAMER.

How heavily does the flesh sometimes drag upon the spirit. When at Baghdad I had all the will in the world to visit the local sights, which include the ruins of Babylon and the holy cities of Kerbela and Nejef. A day's drive would have brought me to any one of them, and five days would have enabled me to have made a round tour that for interest has few equals in the world. Yet the miserable body chained me to Baghdad itself, and mostly to one house, and one room thereof. My own weakness on the one hand, and the all-consuming, soul-destroying heat on the other, absolutely defeated my honest aspiration to view the wonders of the land. Cellars by day and star-lit roofs by night just make life possible in Baghdad during the warm weather, and a northern wind that springs up in the evening gives sweltering humanity that gasps all the day a chance of breath in the night. But the northern wind was fast failing, and there was about to settle upon Baghdad that midsummer stillness from which there is no escape. I had no heart to face the fiery ordeal, and so I fled, fearing even to look over my shoulder lest calcination should overtake me, as happened to the poor lady of the Scriptures.

The way of going had its terrors as well as its charms,

for I was to journey by that bullet-riddled *Blosse Lynch*, which not long before had suffered attack at the hands of the Arabs, and killing and wounding of her passengers. A guard of thirty soldiers is small protection against a thousand or two of brigands, and where there had been no retribution for the first outrage, there might well occur a second. It was just a matter of temper. The Arabs had no grievance against the Lynch Company, but they had against the Turkish Government. They could get no redress from the local Turks, so they flogged the British steamboat and made Constantinople hear — the British Ambassador made Constantinople hear. After long delay local officials were about to hold a parley with the Arabs with a view to settlement of differences. The attack had succeeded in its object so far as to bring these grievances to the fore, and it had cost the Arabs nothing but powder and lead, for the Turks had not taken the field against them to avenge the insult to the British flag. The Arabs had pulled the lion's tail and taken no hurt. Another roar of the lion into the Sultan's ear at Constantinople might have further good effect, and a very loud roar would surely result from a second attack. If the Arab had any sense of humour he would certainly take another pull at the tail. Besides, on this voyage the *Blosse Lynch* carried a passenger who was well used to martyrdom in the cause of local politics. Another hole or two through him would not matter much, and would quicken things generally. To my disordered nerves the prospect was full of undesirable fascination, for escape from frying at Baghdad might merely result in roasting in the fire of Arab rebelliousness.

I boarded the *Blosse Lynch* at night and slept uneasily on the windless side of the deck, where mosqui-

A Devil's Elbow, and other scenes in the lower reaches of the Tigris.

toes and sand-flies held high revel at my expense. In the early dawn we cast off and commenced our 500-mile river voyage down to Bussorah. As we swept past the hospitable house where I had been entertained, I cast my eyes towards the roof, and there beheld the bare feet of my host and another visitor projecting over the parapet in the effort to catch all the winds that blew. They, good men, slept the heavy sleep of hard-worked Baghdadis, and I contrasted their state of blessed unconsciousness with my own nervous condition. But it was too late to go back, and before the morning was a quarter spent I found myself being shown the numerous marks of damage caused by the Arab attack, and having explained to me the defensive measures against a second bombardment. There seemed to me to be a good deal of nervousness aboard, and no small blame, for the vessel had certainly gone through a blood-curdling experience. For half an hour she had been subjected to a heavy and continuous fire from the banks of the river at ranges varying between 100 and 800 yards. Navigation was so difficult that it was imperative for the officer of the watch to remain on the bridge, where his white clothes made him a fine mark for bullets. Crew and passengers laid themselves flat on the deck that they might present to the fire as small a surface as possible. The ship was loaded to the hatches, so there was no burrowing under the water-line, while the deck itself afforded no cover. The casualties numbered three killed and five wounded. The affair had taken place some time before, but a repetition of it was possible at any moment.

Of scenery below Baghdad there is little, for on either side of the Tigris there stretches nothing but yellow limitless desert. The ruins of Seleucia, on the right bank, are barely discernible from the wilderness that surrounds them. This great Greek city, where once dwelt 500,000 people, is now utterly desolate. Not far below, on the opposite bank, lie the ruins of Ctesiphon, the capital of mighty Parthian kings. Here there still stands, a landmark for leagues around, the façade and a portion of the gigantic vaulted hall of an ancient palace. In the shadow of these ruins we have the modest tomb of Mahomet's barber, a place of much pilgrimage. One hundred miles from Baghdad, but over two hundred down-stream, owing to the incessant winding of the river, we come to Kut, a military post, to the south of which live the Beni Lam Arabs, who give all the trouble. Here the river sheers east, and flows towards the Persian mountains, of which we later obtain a fine view.

At Kut we take our guard on board, an officer and thirty picturesque ruffians, and thereafter sail in constant peril of attack. Sacks of wheat are ranged round the upper deck of the vessel, and form an effective protection against Martini fire, though not against small-bore bullets. The bridge is eighteen inches higher than the deck, and in full view of the banks, despite the barricade of sacks. For its protection a quantity of half-inch ship's plates have been provided, and these, ranged on end against the railings, make an impenetrable barrier, except for the rows of holes punched in them for riveting. On my pointing out this weakness in their defence the ship's officers faithfully promised me that in the event of an attack they would not stand in front of the holes—for I am fearful for others as well as for myself. On board were several rifles belonging to the ship, and one of these I annexed, together with a large iron bucket full of cartridges. I had struck up an acquaintance with a Persian passenger who could speak a little Hindustani, and this sporting old boy

this sporting old boy agreed to load for me . . ."

we sail in constant peril of attack."

agreed to load for me and place the rifle in position, so
long as he was not required to put his head above the
wheat. These warlike preparations completed, I felt
easier in mind, and ready to do or die as circumstances
demanded.

From the mountains of Kurdistan to Kut, a distance
by water of nearly 800 miles, the Tigris is a broad and
noble river, flowing within well-defined banks varying
between 300 and 500 yards apart. Entering its delta,
the speed of the water is reduced from six or seven to
three or four miles per hour. At Baghdad the difference between high and low water is about 18 feet, while
the depth of water at its lowest is never less than some
15 feet. These conditions continue to Kut, whereafter a
great change takes place in the dimensions of the river.
Where for several hundreds of miles the average breadth
has been 350 yards, the stream now gradually dwindles
until at the narrows near Kaleh Saleh it is no more
than 50 yards wide, with a depth at low water of no
more than 3 feet. Where there had been a trough
capable of accommodating an enormous rise of water
there are now no banks at all, the river flowing flush
with the adjoining land, which itself is water-logged
except when the stream is at its very lowest.

This extraordinary change is easily explained. At
Kut an ancient canal takes off and flows across towards
the Euphrates, more than 100 miles away. This canal
in the time of Haroun al Rashid was the Tigris itself,
the present bed having practically no existence. But
going further back, to the time of Alexander, it seems
that the Hai Canal was then a canal only, and that
the Tigris flowed almost exactly in the bed it occupies
now. These curious diversions indicate what must
happen farther down-stream, where the height of the
banks is greatly lowered and the trough shallows to

a quarter of its previous depth. Half the river goes off into the Hud Canal, which empties itself into a great region of marsh and swamp to the east. Reduced to a breadth of 100 yards, the Tigris now breaches its right bank at many places and overflows to the west, forming swamps and marshes that correspond to those bordering the eastern bank. With a trough totally incapable of dealing with its volume in time of flood, the Tigris simply spreads its waters over the desert, a mere remnant of itself continuing to meander aimlessly southwards along a ditch that is hardly worthy of the name of river. Here are several devil's-elbows that are extremely hard of negotiation. The river at one of these places doubles on itself almost completely, the breadth at the turn being no more than 50 yards. Round this corner has to pass a vessel nearly 300 feet long. The task is accomplished by jamming her bow into one bank and her stern into the other. There being only a few inches of water under her keel, the stream finds itself completely blocked, and can only proceed by pushing the obstruction forward. The moment her nose clears the elbow she then shoots free. The banks all the way for 500 miles are composed of stoneless mud, else such tactics would be out of the question. Depth in these regions, too, is always a problem. At flood-time it is possible to load a steamer up to a four-foot draft, but at low water two and a half feet is the maximum safe draft. Even then it frequently happens that a vessel grounds and cannot be got off without lightening, an expensive and laborious process. Lower down, however, conditions change again, and near the junction with the Euphrates the Tigris once more becomes a respectable river, in breadth about 150 yards, and of ample depth. The loss of water takes place at various points in a section about 150 miles

Country-boats on the Tigris.

long, but the recovery happens all at once, for the swamps on either bank, covering thousands of square miles, suddenly tail off towards the Tigris and empty their waters back into the stream whence they originally came. The loss on the way, owing to absorption and evaporation, has been enormous, and the lower river is never again anything more than a fraction of what it was at Baghdad.

We took our soldiers on board at the point where this process of depletion begins. The danger zone occurred where the river is only 100 yards broad, and where not only continual turns make navigation difficult, but also a series of loops enables an enemy to deliver an attack and then run across country and resume firing as a ship again winds its way down towards them. We had the mitigated pleasure of seeing armed parties of Arab horsemen moving about. There were two troops quite close to the river bank, each about fourteen strong, and riding along in extended order. It looked at first as if they were manœuvring against each other and about to collide. In a former voyage the ship's officers had actually seen fighting under similar circumstances, so we watched with intense interest, wondering whether we were to witness a fight or to be the victims of an attack. There would be no warning in any case, for the Arab only fires when there is little chance of being struck himself. The recent attack had been commenced by a volley out of a perfectly innocent-looking fringe of grass on the river's edge, where trenches had been prepared. Nothing happened this time, however, and we afterwards heard that the parties we observed were on their way to Kut to attend a conference of the local tribes on the one hand and the Government officials on the other. That they thought it necessary to move in separate bodies, each extended, when proceeding to a peaceful parley, speaks volumes for the disturbed condition of the country and the suspicion in which each tribe holds its neighbour.[1]

Our progress down the narrower part of the river was extremely interesting, for we were continually passing within a few yards of temporary villages placed at the water's edge. The huts were mostly built of straw, with open sides, and the occupants of each, whether smoking or sleeping or working, could be clearly seen. These riverine Arabs are a villainous lot in appearance, very dark-coloured, dirty, and ragged. In the heat of the summer they settle on the banks of the river for the sake of coolness and the fish that teem in it. When the floods are over and the water subsides from the higher ground they spread over the country with their flocks. Laziness is their chief characteristic, and robbery their favourite diversion. As our boat swept by these camps we were greeted by loud yells on the part of the women and children. The men looked as if they would like to murder us, their usual expression to friend or foe. It appeared to me as if from such places a dangerous attack might easily emanate, but I was assured that with soldiers on board, who might shoot the women and children, we were perfectly safe from the men.

The company of which the *Blosse Lynch* is the property might here be appropriately mentioned. Its name, curiously enough, is the Euphrates Valley Steam Navigation Company, though, so far as I am aware, it has confined its attention entirely to the Tigris river. It will be known to those interested in this part of the world that in 1834 the Turks granted

[1] A month after the writer passed down the Tigris, navigation was temporarily suspended owing to the threatening attitude of the Arabs.

Turkish Guard on a Lynch Steamer.

Some of the Passengers.

a firman to our Government for the navigation of the
Euphrates by two steamers. In 1835 the famous
Chesney Expedition landed at the mouth of the
Orontes, near Antioch, and after infinite labour transported the steamers *Euphrates* and *Tigris* in pieces
across the desert to the Euphrates, where they were
put in the water near Birejik. The *Tigris* was lost
under distressing circumstances when making the
voyage down the river, but the *Euphrates* after a
passage of extraordinary interest reached the Persian
Gulf, a feat of navigation that from all accounts
would now appear to be impossible. With the
expedition bringing these two boats came a young
officer called Lynch, who shortly afterwards dropped
into command of the flotilla of Indian Marine gunboats
guarding British interests at the head of the Persian
Gulf. Lynch formed a high opinion of the country,
and advised two of his brothers to come out and
commence trading. This they did, and in some way
or another appear to have inherited the concession
which gave to the British Government the rights of
navigation under the firman of 1834. They were
successful, and in 1860, desirous of forming a company, they asked the Turkish Government for confirmation of their navigation rights. This was accorded, the existing company was formed, and two
steamers were brought out by the newly opened
Suez Canal.

So far the firman and all succeeding documents
related to rights of navigation on the Euphrates, and
said nothing whatever about the Tigris, on which alone
the Lynch steamers had hitherto traded. In 1875 the
company asked for permission to bring out a third boat
to act as reserve to the other two, which could never
undergo repair without disorganising the mail service

to Baghdad. This was granted, but still without reference to the fact that the steamer was obviously designed for traffic on the Tigris. A few years ago there was a further successful application to the Turkish Government for permission for the steamers to tow lighters. Then in 1907, when the British Government found itself in possession of the leverage conferred by the Turkish desire to increase the Customs duties, the long - desired permission was obtained to employ three boats continually instead of two. But still there was no reference to the Tigris, and to this day, so far as I have been able to discover, the Lynch Company navigates one river on the strength of a firman that refers to another river, which firman, moreover, was never granted to the Lynches at all, but to the British Government. A truly Turkish situation, but one which need cause the shareholders no anxiety, for although their rights seem far from founded on a rock, their long-established position on the Tigris, frequently the subject of tacit acknowledgment by the Turkish Government, could not now be decently disputed. The British Government, too, having concerned itself in obtaining permission for the third boat, would appear to have committed itself to the defence of the Lynch rights, in case they are ever assailed.

Immediately below the narrows, and at the point where the Tigris suddenly regains part of its former dignity, stands the Tomb of Ezra, a place much visited by Jewish pilgrims. Hereabout, Chaldean scholars declare, runs the coast-line of the Persian Gulf as it was in 4000 B.C. The present coast of the Gulf is still about 100 miles distant as the crow flies, but as the advance of the land at the outflow of the combined rivers Tigris, Euphrates, and Karun is some

A Bazaar in Bussorah.

Ezra's Tomb—a place of pilgrimage for Jews.

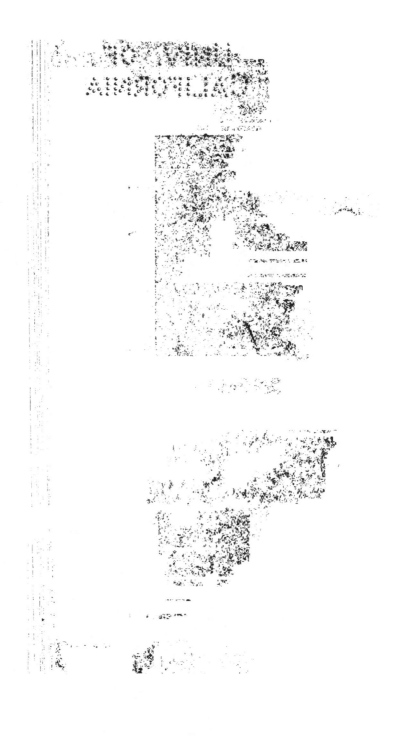

80 feet per annum, it is not difficult to believe in this enormous conquest over the sea. Hereabouts also the Tigris begins to feel the effect of the tide. Not far below we come to Gurna, where we are joined by the Euphrates, the combined streams thereafter being known as the Shat-el'-Arab. Our steamer is now once more in a great river which from a width of 300 yards below Gurna gradually widens out, until at Bussorah, 40 miles down-stream, it flows between banks a full half-mile apart. Bussorah ends the voyage, which has taken sixty hours, and I leave the *Blosse Lynch* with a very pleasant recollection of the comfort on board, and the interesting scenes which we passed through. Of the heat I have said nothing, but in fact it was very great and very trying, for July is not the best time of the year for travelling in this part of the world. In late autumn, winter, or early spring, however, the voyage up or down the Tigris is one of the pleasantest experiences open to the traveller, and one to be heartily commended.

R

CHAPTER XXI.

BUSSORAH AND THE BAR.

BUSSORAH has various claims upon public forbearance. It is the place where the dates come from ; it will surely be the terminus of the Baghdad Railway, in so far as it is possible for a railway to have an end whose beginnings are almost imperceptible, and whose middle nobody believes in ; and its European inhabitants only remain alive during the day through a perception of the humour of their situation, and by night through the agency of the prayers of their despairing relatives—for Bussorah has the most malarial air, the most choleraic water, and the most infernal climate of any spot in the world outside Tophet. So says the careworn but cheery little community that struggles through existence on the banks of the Shat-el-Arab. Theirs is a sad case, only less sad, perhaps, than that of the officers and crew of a little man-o'-war who in summer sail up to Bussorah to escape (?) the heat of the Persian Gulf. But I struck Bussorah at a bad time, when the weather was at its worst, and when I myself had one foot and four toes in the grave. July, August, and September are months in which poor humanity exists by sheer mental effort alone, and when there is no hope for a fainting spirit. But in October comes a change, for the desperate heat begins to merge into a pleasant warmth. November is cool, and in December people sit by the fireside and almost hanker for the summer, for the air is cold and raw. In March there is no more thought of fires, in April begins the hot breath of summer, May and June are bearable, and then once more comes round the humid, enervating, suffocating heat of July. To the young and healthy Briton Bussorah has its charms, for here, between the intervals of work, there is the finest snipe-shooting in the world, plenty tennis, cricket, and golf, and a club where each member loves his neighbour as himself. But no knights of rueful countenance need come to Bussorah. It is a place for optimists only.

Bussorah has no niche in ancient history, for when the Chaldeans were at their cuneiforms and astrology, the spot whereon it now stands was fathoms deep under the salt sea. The Shat-el-Arab did not exist in those days, and the Tigris and Euphrates separately poured their waters into the Persian Gulf. Sinbad the Sailor and contemporary worthies are among the first to hint at Bussorah's existence, and thereafter its name is indissolubly connected with the dates which delight the Oriental world. Great Britain stepped into Bussorah in the year 1764, by virtue of a Turkish firman granting permission for the posting of a consul, with the right to have a military guard, to beat drums, to celebrate the king's birthday in the most public manner, and to purchase male and female slaves free of duty. The sultan of those days was a man of feeling.

Bussorah has a trade which fluctuates in value between £3,000,000 and £4,000,000 annually, the greater part of it represented by goods in transit to and from Baghdad. Of the local exports dates weighing some 60,000 tons are worth £500,000, and wheat and barley anything between £250,000 and £1,000,000, according

to season. The number of date-trees at Bussorah and
in the immediate neighbourhood is said to be no fewer
than 8,000,000, all lining the river to a depth of three
miles, beyond which on either hand the country is
desert.   Cereals come from the banks of both rivers,
and in considerable quantity down the Hai Canal,
mentioned already as taking off the Tigris at Kut and
joining the Euphrates after a course of 150 miles.   The
banks of this and other remnants of the ancient canal
system are highly cultivated as a rule, but seldom to a
depth of more than a few hundred yards.

Of the total trade it is difficult to say exactly how
much is British and how much foreign, for the consular
reports do not analyse the figures.   But a fair idea of
the relative proportions may be derived from consultation of the shipping returns, which show that of a total
steamer tonnage of 237,000 tons in 1907, 88 per cent
were British bottoms, 7 per cent German, and 3 per
cent Russian.   The German steamers brought sugar,
coffee, matches, petroleum, &c , to the value of £168,000,
all from the Continent, and took away goods to the
value of £153,000.   As the British steamers chiefly
carry cargo to and from the United Kingdom and
India, it would seem clear enough that importations
represent British manufactures almost entirely, with
the one important exception of French sugar picked
up at Marseilles.   This may be regarded as all the
more certain from the fact that for the year under
examination, 1907, outward freight has been 27s. 6d.
to 35s. from the United Kingdom, and only 20s. to
22s. from the Continent.   In these circumstances it
hardly seems possible for anything more than chance
parcels of foreign goods, such as Austrian transhipped
at Port Said, to have found their way out to the Gulf
in British steamers.   The British percentage of the

tonnage does not really represent the relative quantity
of freight carried, for while British ships arrive comparatively full, both German and Russian ships come
and go comparatively empty.

This remarkable difference in freights is to be
accounted for by the fact that three North of England
companies practically monopolise the shipping trade
of Bussorah with Europe, and are consequently in a
position to make their own rates. Combination between these companies to maintain rates, and to fight
intruders, if necessary, has prevented competition, particularly as the Gulf trade has certain peculiarities
which are not convenient to legislate for except by
those who prosecute it regularly. The recent advent
of a German line, therefore, has been a positive benefit
to British trade rather than a loss, for it has forced the
combine slightly to lower rates, and to make concessions to exporters whom they had previously treated
with scant regard. The German line has carried nothing
British heretofore, though it might very easily begin to
do so if the British lines continue to hold their heads
too high. The single Russian boat which visits Bussorah
four times a year brings petroleum and wood from the
Black Sea, and takes away anything she can get for
the Red Sea and for Levantine ports. Both she and
the German boats trade with Bussorah at a heavy loss.

Inland from Bussorah there is but one means of
transport for produce and merchandise, and that is by
water, for there are practically no roads, what there
are being frequently impassable owing to floods and
always dangerous from robbers. Native boats work
up and down the Shat-el-Arab, Tigris, and Euphrates
in considerable numbers, but at a very slow pace up-
stream, owing to the speed of the currents and to the
absence of any prevailing wind, such as in the case of

the Nile makes upward navigation so easy.   The
Euphrates is navigable after a fashion for about one
hundred and fifty miles beyond its confluence with
the Tigris, whereafter it becomes a mere ditch, owing
to the fact that the whole of its volume leaves the
river bed near Babylon, and for a distance of nearly
two hundred miles traverses the Hindia Canal, and
a succession of lakes and swamps, before rejoining
its proper course.   The Tigris is navigable for river
boats up to a point about one hundred miles up-
stream from Baghdad, beyond which only down-stream
raft traffic is practicable.   Some of the old canals
and some of the small rivers joining the main waterways are navigable by light boats for short distances.
During flood-time within the deltas of the two great
rivers it is said to be possible to go cross-country in
almost any direction in small boats, for everywhere
exist the remains of old irrigation works containing
the few inches of water necessary.

The great bulk of the Mesopotamian trade is of
necessity carried on the Tigris by steamers, against
which the native boats seldom come into competition.
I have already explained the difficulties of navigation
on the Tigris owing to the narrowness of the river, the
severity of the turns, and particularly because of the
depth, which for months together is so small that boats
cannot be loaded to draw more than $2\frac{1}{2}$ feet.   A recent
traveller to these parts, optimistically inclined, wrote
that he looked forward to the day when 1000-ton boats
drawing 6 feet, as per Irrawady river, will freely navi-
gate the Euphrates to the far north, and the Tigris
to Diarbekir.   If he can continue to look forward, after
reading my observations on the subject, he must indeed
be a hardy sceptic, impossible of conversion.   The fact
is that the companies engaged on this river traffic do

about all that it is possible to do, and there would seem to be very little room for improvement either in their methods or in the class of boats employed.

These companies are the Lynch, of which I have already written, and the Hamidieh, owned by the Civil List. The latter was once known as the Oman Company, and, like most things of any value in the Turkish Empire possible of appropriation, was commandeered by the Sultan. Despite its ownership the Hamidieh Company is wonderfully well run, and does rather more than half of the steamer-carrying on the river, with a fleet of boats that has recently been augmented to eight. The Lynch Company has now three boats running, instead of two as formerly, and carries about three-eighths of the total. Several of the Hamidieh boats are small and old, while the newest one has not yet begun work, which accounts in some degree for the company not carrying a share proportionate to the size of the fleet. But the proportion is bound to increase, for there is no limit to the number of boats it may employ, while its rivals are strictly confined to three. Freight by the Sultan's line is uniformly about 10 per cent lower than by the Lynch, a difference that is compensated for by quicker and more efficient handling of goods by the latter. The Lynch line is certainly the favourite both for merchandise and with pilgrims, and would speedily outdo the other if the field were free. The Turk is no match for the European at business, nor does he compare with him in the handling of steamers.

The Lynch Company is in rather a curious position. While the two companies are on excellent terms, rendering each other mutual assistance in time of need — though the Turks stick in the mud far the more frequently — it remains that the Sultan's boats are being steadily increased, and that in time sheer force of numbers will give them the power to drive their rivals off the river. To do so would cost the Turks a lot of money, for the Lynch Company would not succumb without a struggle. There is no denying that the British Company has been a highly profitable concern in the past, but with this ever-rising competition profits are decreasing, while prospects for the future are not of the brightest. It may be that the Turks will be content to go slow and share the traffic in proportion to numbers, rather than run at a loss for several years in order to crush the Lynch line. Whatever may happen, it seems fair enough that the latter should endeavour to make hay while the sun shines, though the consequence is inflated prices for transport on British goods. The effect of competition in the shipping of the Gulf has been to lower rates, and the same thing on the Tigris would have a similar effect, thus decreasing the transport handicap on British trade. But if lowering rates would make it easier for us it would also make it easier for our rivals, and leave things pretty much as before, except that the Lynch shareholders would make a smaller profit, and British manufacturers a trifle more. Whether it would be better to have the Tigris opened, which would materially lower transport rates and slightly quicken British trade, or to keep it closed, to the benefit of a small British Company, is an economic problem I do not offer to solve. It would seem, however, that if the Baghdad Railway ever comes to Bussorah, it will tend to prevent the monopolists on the Tigris from charging fancy freights in time of bumper harvests, as they are wont to do, in imitation of people in all other walks of life when they get the chance, from parsons down to cabmen.

At the same time it is fair to recognise that while freights on the Tigris appear high, they are not so profitable as might appear. The smallest examination of the expenses and receipts of the Lynch steamers will show that there is no possibility nowadays of their earning usurious dividends. To begin with, each boat is manned by six European officers, whose expenses are paid back and fore to England, on a three-year agreement. These officers are necessarily paid on a higher scale than is usual, and are an expensive luxury. It is their efficiency which enables the company to charge higher freights than the rival company, and still to retain their share of the traffic. Besides the officers, each steamer carries supercargo, pilots, quartermasters, and crew, numbering over thirty, and paid from £6 to £1 per month. Every voyage 75 tons of coal is burned, at a cost of 40s. per ton. Repairs are a continual item in the economy of a shipping line, expensive European management is an essential, insurance is heavy, dues of all sorts are payable, backshish to make things work smoothly an ever-recurring necessity.

Against these expenses, earnings are limited in various ways. The carrying of the mails, for which the Lynch Company receives £1000 per annum from the Indian Government, necessitates a regular service of steamers, running according to schedule and not in accordance with the requirements of traffic. The normal time occupied in making the double journey between Baghdad and Bussorah is eight days. But owing to the mail arrangements each of two steamers can make the trip once a fortnight only, with the result that one day at Bussorah and five days at Baghdad are always lost. This occurs equally when freights are high or low. When full cargo offers at

Baghdad boats must wait the full five days, and when there is nothing offering at Bussorah they must sail empty because of the mails. Then when the river is high the utmost that can be carried is 450 tons, including cargo in the steamer itself and on the single barge which it is possible to tow lashed alongside. This gives a draught of 4 feet, for which water is seldom available in the river. At low water draught must be reduced to $2\frac{1}{2}$ feet, which only allows of a cargo of 200 tons. It often happens, too, that boats go up and down half empty, for since the increase of the Hamidieh fleet and the adding of one to the Lynch boats there is none of the accumulation of cargo which used to be such a dire handicap on the Baghdad trade. In fact, if it were not for the probability that the Lynch steamers now stand in the company's books at nothing, owing to writing down for depreciation, their privileges would not be worth much. In any case the fat years are past, and the lean ones are coming.

The writer already referred to, who has advanced such optimistic views in regard to the potentialities of navigation on the Mesopotamian rivers, passes severe strictures on the trade facilities of Bussorah, declaring that he leaves the place depressed by the melancholy spectacle of wasted opportunities. He dreams of enormous sheds, miles of wharves, and huge lighters for the handling of trade, where now none exist. But the fact is that none of these facilities would give advantages anywhere proportionate to their cost. It has to be remembered what kind of country surrounds Bussorah, and how trade transport is affected by the conditions. The town itself does not lie on the river, but is two miles from it, and is reached by a creek along which the traffic goes in boats. Creeks by the hundred intersect the land in every direction, affording the

Bits of the Bussorah Creek.

cheapest and most convenient mode of transport.
Collection of up-country produce and distribution of
imports are effected by boat, for roads there are none,
where indeed they must be superfluous. The consequence is that much of the transhipment is done direct
between country boats and the ocean-going steamers,
and by small lighters which can enter the Bussorah
creek. Where the river steamers carry only from
200 to 450 tons, to be collected perhaps from half a
dozen vessels lying at anchor, huge lighters would be
out of place, as wharfage of great extent would be a
superfluity under the circumstances.

Having reached Bussorah alive, I thought it well to
tempt Providence no further, much as I should have
liked to retrace my steps to Baghdad, and to return
therefrom to Syria *viâ* the Euphrates valley, on to Constantinople by way of Asia Minor and the Black Sea.
But these roads are for strong men in the cool season,
not for broken-down invalids in the depth of summer.
The taking of a passage by sea was an ignominious
surrender to circumstances over which I had no control,
and the memory of it spoilt the luxurious voyage down
the Persian Gulf in one of the charmingly officered and
well - found steamers of the British India Company.
Bussorah is a bad place to get away from, for one must
take either the expensive mail route *viâ* Karachi and
Bombay, or a homeward - bound tramp, and die of
scurvy on the road. One tramp agent whom I approached on the subject of a passage to Suez said he
couldn't give me a ticket for less than 25 guineas. To
this offer I made no response, and the next anxious
inquirer was told 22 guineas, again with no takers.
Yet a third aspirant for departure from Bussorah
applied, and was quoted 20 guineas. Still no takers,
and that tramp sailed empty of passengers, though if

the agent had not been greedy he could have had all three for 45 guineas, quite a sufficient price, considering the accommodation, the speed, and the feeding, which last, I am told, is truly rural. Anyhow, the three of us met on the mail-boat and duly set sail one misty morning at the end of July.

The Shat-el-Arab below Bussorah is not interesting until one comes to Mohammerah, where the cannon of the Sheikh boom out a salute of two guns to the mail flag The ship returns the compliment in a manner that completely mystifies its passengers, but which seems to satisfy the Sheikh. As we approach His Highness's palace, a plug is taken out of a hole in the flat wooden rail of the ship's upper deck, and a small brown paper parcel put in its place. The officer of the watch then pulls a string, and lo! there is a loud report. While one is thinking that this must be the meanest possible way of firing a salute, and wondering where the second shot is to come from, there occurs another loud report far up in the air— a shell, if you please, from the hole in the rail! If flying machines ever evolve themselves into vessels of offence, doubtless our battleships will learn to defend themselves on the same principle, and employ their funnels for the purpose.

The Sheikh of Mohammerah is an important personage in this part of the world, for he controls powerful tribes in the neighbourhood, is married to a Persian Princess, and has a small navy for the maintenance of his prestige. The navy is not very big, consisting, in fact, of no more than a single steam-yacht. But it answers the purpose, for no other grandee in the Persian Gulf has a larger fleet. The Sheikh's yacht lies at anchor near a very fine palace recently erected, and as we sailed past her we were

interested to observe another vessel lying alongside of
her. This we discovered to be the navy of another
power in the Gulf, the Sheikh of Koweit, a very important man in his own estimation since there has
arisen the talk about making his capital the terminus
of the Baghdad Railway. That talk, however, is beginning to die away, and the hope in the mind of
the Sheikh begins to fade. So he amuses himself
by tripping anchor every now and then and running
across to see his old crony, the Sheikh of Mohammerah.
When their conversation does not run upon Paradise,
and houris, and the delights of the future that is
not so far off in the case of one of them, these two
little potentates discuss politics with a vigour said to
be extremely refreshing by those who have heard
them at it. Both used to have a wholesome respect
for the British flag, and still have, in a far-off manner,
as for something that was once great but is now
declined. Russia bulks largely in their minds, for
they think the Agreement is just a dodge to cover
secret machinations. Germany is a grievance, for
she has raised hopes that have not been fulfilled.
The constitutional movement in Persia is not deemed
worth breath, where the supply is somewhat limited,
and both portly gentlemen dismiss this subject with
a spit. They are much amused by the Arab attacks
upon the Lynch boats on the Tigris, and regard it
as sure evidence of the decline of British power
that we don't settle the matter without reference to
the Turks. The gun-running through Beluchistan is
another source of amusement, for while we are em-
ploying columns on land and warships at sea to put a
stop to it, British vessels are bringing the rifles out
to Muscat and discharging them into native boats
under the eyes of the British Resident. Another

thing that tickles them to death is the way the Persians have fooled us on the Karun river, the which is too well-known a story to repeat.

The Karun river performs an important duty in these regions, for it has a great deal to do with the gradual retreat of the sea before the advance of the land, a process operating at the head of the Persian Gulf with astonishing rapidity. The great Mesopotamian rivers, on nearing the sea, have already flowed through their deltas for distances of several hundreds of miles, and have to a great extent lost the silt which they brought down in suspension from the mountains in the north. The Karun, on the other hand, is a short river, and at its junction with the Shat-el-Arab at Mohammerah its course over plain has been no more than a single hundred miles. Rising in the Persian mountains, less than 200 miles distant, it rushes down their western slopes with great rapidity, carrying in its swollen flood a tremendous amount of matter, which has no time to settle during the short passage, with the result that a dirty and muddy river joins the comparatively clean water of the Shat-el-Arab. But Mohammerah is still some fifty miles from the sea, and subject to a tidal rise and fall of nearly ten feet. The consequence is that for nearly half of each day the flood from the Karun river is thrust up the Shat-el-Arab, and into the numerous creeks and backwaters that are characteristic of that river throughout its length. Thus, instead of being totally lost in the sea, somewhere about half of the silt of the Karun is beneficially employed, and helps to make possible that splendid harvest of dates for which Bussorah and its neighbourhood is famous.

Forty miles below Mohammerah we anchor for half an hour to exchange mails with the lonely telegraph station at Fao, and then steam into the open sea and cross the famous bar that encumbers the entrance to the Shat-el-Arab. This bar is said to do much to complicate the question of the Baghdad Railway, for its existence is thought to hamper trade with Bussorah, and has suggested the advisability of choosing another port as a terminus. The selection of Koweit as an alternative imported into the scheme a political element not involved in the case of Bussorah, for Bussorah is Turkish soil; while Koweit, though suzerainty is claimed over it by the Sultan, is in reality an independent protectorate owing its independence to British intervention. Nothing relating to foreign affairs can very well be done by the Sheikh of Koweit without British approval, and so important a matter as the establishment in his territory of the terminus of a German railway, having its genesis at Constantinople, gave us a direct concern in the scheme which we could not have claimed were the railway confined to purely Turkish ground. The reason for the selection of Koweit on the part of the Germans is difficult to fathom, for, as I shall proceed to show, there can be no possible doubt that Bussorah is the natural terminus of any railway to be constructed to these parts. Only a grotesquely exaggerated idea of the commercial future of the line could have suggested the necessity of an open port on the Gulf, when there already existed a river port equal to all requirements; or, as is far more probable, a political motive must have prompted the inclusion into the scheme of a point recognisedly within the sphere of British interests. Whether the selection of Koweit was a cunning endeavour to involve us in the scheme, or whether it is meant as a preliminary step to an ultimate claim of important commercial interests in the Gulf, I do not venture to say. Probably both objects were in view, for in the negotiations which took place between the German syndicate holding the concession and a committee of English bankers, before the signing of the Convention of 1903, British capital was invited to participate in exchange for the good offices of the British Government in the matter of the terminus at Koweit; while the persistent endeavours of German shipping and German traders, working at a heavy loss, to establish themselves in the Persian Gulf have since been a feature of trade in these regions.

It seems easy enough to establish the view that there is no necessity to look beyond Bussorah for a terminus to the Baghdad Railway. Leaving out of consideration that extension to Koweit entails a hundred miles of construction in pure desert and expensive harbour works at Koweit itself, it will be found that Bussorah offers all the necessary facilities to whatever volume of trade is likely to grow out of the institution of railway communication in Mesopotamia within the next fifty years. Were the re-creation of Chaldea by irrigation a possibility of the morrow, that opinion might require modification, but in view of the conditions described in the previous chapter neither irrigation nor railways would appear to have any chance of materially augmenting the resources of this country in the immediate future. A railway will, of course, stimulate trade and add an immediate percentage to its volume. But it will in no wise alter, except at a very slow rate, the productive power of the country, which is the ultimate basis of commercial exchange. With all the merchandise that in our time will ever pass up and down the Baghdad Railway from and to Bussorah the shipping facilities of Bussorah are ample to deal.

The difficulties of the bar at the mouth of the Shat-

Bussorah—the Koweit Gate.

el-Arab have been much exaggerated, and while it is
no doubt a handicap to shipping, it is not by any
means so much so as is generally supposed. The bar
lies some ten miles off the entrance to the river, and
the low-lying shore is invisible from a steamer's deck.
The troublesome part of the bar is about $2\frac{1}{2}$ miles
in width, and here at low water in spring-tides there
is no more than ten feet of water. But at high tide
there is twenty feet, and with a strong southerly wind
as much as twenty-five feet of water. Owing to the
liability to minor changes in the bed of the channel,
however, these greater depths cannot be counted upon,
and no vessel drawing more than eighteen feet ever
essays the passage even in the most favourable circumstances. A strong northerly wind of course reduces
the depth on the bar to a very low figure.

But a depth of eighteen feet recurring at regular
intervals gives a very fair opportunity to shipping, and
vessels of 3000 and 4000 tons burthen of suitable construction can slip across the bar at high tide without
difficulty. There are certain types of vessels having
accommodation for 9/10,000 tons, which with a load of
5000 tons draw only sixteen feet, so that it would
seem as if the bar offered little difficulty to really large
boats. In practice it is found that vessels sail from
and to Bussorah with 4000 tons aboard, taking in or
discharging the balance of their cargoes outside the bar.
Lightering no doubt is an expensive business, but so
too is the payment of harbour dues. It is, of course,
much more convenient to sail into a dock and discharge
at a wharf; but the difference in expense is not great,
for if lighters entail extra handling of freight the facilities offered by docks that may have cost millions of
pounds must also be paid for. The main advantage
provided by extensive harbour works is the capacity

S

for speedy handling of cargo. That at Bussorah is a matter of comparatively small importance, for a week or two either way in the Persian Gulf counts no more than as many half-hours in other parts of the world. Moreover, the Bussorah system of loading and unloading cargo, as already explained, is peculiarly suited to local conditions. Every ounce of produce that leaves Bussorah reaches it either by the small steamers trading on the Tigris or by country boats from the rivers, canals, and creeks that intersect the country. Every ton of importations likewise is despatched to its destination by water. Harbour works at Koweit would mean much transference of goods from boats to train all the way down from Baghdad to Bussorah, handling out of the train, housing in sheds, and reloading for export. But vessels lying at anchor at Bussorah are approached on both sides by swarms of country craft, and are loaded up with a minimum of trans-shipment. For the handling of an enormous volume of trade within the limited space offered by the majority of great centres, there is no doubt that docks, wharfs, and the latest contrivances are essential to commercial activity. But at Bussorah trade is strictly limited, and will remain so for many years; while the waterway is one of the finest in the world, and capable of containing every ship afloat that could cross the bar, inside of which there is ample depth.

It would seem, therefore, that the establishment of a terminus at Koweit, entailing additional construction and outlay in the perfecting of the harbour, would be an expense utterly out of proportion to the benefits to be derived, and that the Baghdad Railway will effectively and satisfactorily connect with deep-sea shipping when it has reached Bussorah. One hears now and

The Bussorah Creek.

Bridge over the Creek at Bussorah.

again of vessels sticking on the bar at Bussorah, and
it is not very long ago that a large Russian steamer
spent thirteen melancholy days on its affectionate mud.
But such misfortunes are usually due to ignorance of
the conditions, or to optimistic shippers who take undue
chances. The British India mail-boats never stick, because they cannot afford to run risks. They, however,
have an advantage over the ordinary tramp steamer,
for they have greater power and can force their way
through the three feet of semi-liquid mud that always
overlies the bar, where the heavier and less powerful
cargo steamer is helpless. In comparison with the
difficulties of approaching other well-known river ports,
those of the mouth of the Shat-el-Arab are small. I
shall long remember spending ten days on the bar of
the Peiho, a few miles off the Taku Forts, in company
with half a dozen other vessels, and in weather miser-
ably cold. This sort of thing is of common occurrence
off Taku, although the trade of the Peiho is much
bigger than that of the Shat-el-Arab. Vessels crossing the Peiho bar are never of more than 3000 tons
burthen, I think, and half their cargoes have always to
be lightered before crossing, in an open roadstead liable
to heavy storms that seldom have a parallel in the
Persian Gulf. Ordinary lighters are used for the trade
of the Chinese river, while off the Shat-el-Arab cargo
is transhipped into small steamers of a size equal to
those which regularly trade between Tientsin, Taku,
and Chinese ports in the south. Large steamers going
up the Elbe have to be lightered of several thousand
tons at more than one point before they can sail the
hundred miles up to Hamburg, one of the three biggest
ports in the world. In comparison with the difficulties
of the entrance to and the navigation of the Peiho,

those handicapping the approach to the Shat-el-Arab
are insignificant, and the actual situation undoubtedly
is that Bussorah is entirely sufficient as a terminal
port for the Baghdad Railway, and that even the
dredging of the bar, a difficult and expensive business,
would seem unnecessary while the volume of trade is
what it is now or can become for many a long day.

CHAPTER XXII.

ROUTE OF THE BAGHDAD RAILWAY.

HAVING brought the Baghdad Railway to Bussorah, and decided that it shall go no farther, it would now seem appropriate to cast a retrospective eye across the country I have travelled, and to endeavour to give a more comprehensive view of a scheme hitherto discussed only in detail, as the progress of my journey suggested. Then while I have been on the road, a very important development of the Baghdad Railway question has taken place, for at the end of May it was suddenly sprung upon the world that the Germans had cajoled the Turks into appropriating revenue for guarantees upon a further extension of the line. It is freely stated by Germans in Turkey—for there is no shame attached to bribery in the land of the Sultan—that the arrangement was arrived at by the expenditure of very large sums of money in the shape of backshish to highly-placed officials in the Palace. When we are informed that the Imperial Irade provides for the construction of four more sections, a distance of 800 kilometres, or nearly half-way to Baghdad from the present railhead, it will be seen that the Baghdad Railway is still a very live issue, and the project much nearer realisation than when the Convention of 1903 provoked such a storm of criticism in England.

Any review of the route of the Baghdad Railway necessarily includes the Anatolian line, for the latter forms an important link in the chain of communication that is designed to connect Constantinople with the Persian Gulf. Of a total distance between the Turkish capital and Bussorah, following the route of lines constructed and projected, of some 3200 kilometres, the Anatolian Railway is responsible for 759 kilometres. In chapter ii. I have touched upon the physical characteristics of the country traversed, but further observations are necessary if a correct idea of the capacity of the line is to be conveyed. From Constantinople the Anatolian Railway runs south-east along the bluff shore of the Sea of Marmora, following the line of least resistance, with little regard to curves or gradients. This part of the railway was originally built to give access to a favourite shooting-box of Sultan Abdul Aziz, and was not designed for either fast or heavy traffic. In order to avoid expense the line climbed where it should have gone through cuttings, and turned round corners where it should have inexorably tunnelled. Ballasting, embanking, and such-like were originally of the inferior quality appropriate to such a track, but have since been considerably improved to meet the requirements of growing traffic.

Having passed the hilly region of the Marmora littoral the line next enters the plain of Ismid, where it has an easy passage to the foot of the mountains that border the central plateau of Asia Minor. The transit of these mountains, however, and the attainment of the plateau, entail stern climbing, for throughout a total distance of 148 kilometres there is a rise of 2600 feet, giving a general gradient of 1 in 180. The ascent is from terrace to terrace, the climbs from

one to the other giving severe gradients, as, for instance, the rise of 1024 feet in the ten miles between
Biledjik and Karakeuy, equal to 1 in 50. The steeper
ascents are accomplished through deep dark gorges
of great beauty, which, delightful though their transit
may be to the traveller, are a heavy handicap on speed,
while their narrowness absolutely prohibits any change
of alignment which would permit of improved running
—presuming the observation of reasonable economy.

The plateau having been reached, the Anatolian
Railway henceforth runs along practically level plain
to Konia, where any speed might be attained provided
the permanent way were sufficiently ballasted, though
it is doubtful if the rails are heavy enough to stand
prolonged hard usage. The following time-table will
show what the one eastward mail and passenger train
at present running does throughout its journey :—

	Distance.	Gross time.	Speed, inclusive of stoppages.	Speed, exclusive of stoppages.
	Kilometres.	hrs. min.	m.p.h.	m.p.h.
Haidar-Pasha (Constan-tinople) to Eski Shehr,	313	13 35	14½	18
Eski Shehr—Konia, . .	445	15 0	18½	21
Konia—Boulgourlou (Baghdad Railway), .	199	5 50	21½	26

Notes.—No trains allowed to run at night.
    Regulations provide that engine-drivers shall exceed these speeds when
    necessary up to an average maximum of 25 per cent.

This does not look like great confidence on the part
of the administration in the powers of the line. While
economy is responsible in some degree for the slow
speeds maintained, it is obvious that the alignment of
the earlier portions of the road really necessitates
careful travelling. On the plateau it is possible to
go faster, but the weakness of the permanent way,

constructed though it is without curves and upon
level ground, is evident from the speed limit imposed
by the regulations.   Article 37 of the Convention
provides for a sum of £320,000 to be expended
upon the Anatolian Railway in alterations that will
permit of the express traffic stipulated for in the
Cahier des Charges (Article 30).   But it is very
difficult to see how so small a sum can pay for im-
provements that will allow of material enhancement
of speed.   It is instructive to note the thriftiness of
the concessionaires in this connection, for the article
recording the agreement of the Anatolian Company to
spend the above sum of money in improving their
property also stipulates for an annuity from the
Turkish Government to cover interest on the sum
expended, at the rate of 4·375 per cent per annum.

Coming to section one of the Baghdad Railway
itself a marked difference is found in the quality of
the line.   The rails are heavier, the ballasting is good,
there are neither grades nor curves, and there can be
no doubt that here a fair speed can be attained.
The present gross speed of $21\frac{1}{2}$ miles per hour is
ample for existing traffic, but is not a criterion of the
capacity of the line.   Beyond section one, however,
comes the crossing of the Taurus, discussed at length
in chapter iv., and here, for a distance of over 100
miles, when section two has been constructed, only a
very slow rate of speed can be anticipated.   For fifty
miles along the Cilician plain quick speed can.be again
attained, until a brief check is imposed by the extremely difficult transit of the Giaour Dagh.   The Kurd
Dagh is a lesser obstacle, and thereafter the railway
emerges upon plain throughout which, right down to
Bussorah, there is nothing to prevent the maintenance of express speeds.

Having bridged the Sihun (ancient Sarus) and the Jihun (Pyramus), the two considerable rivers of the Cilician plain, no further streams of importance are encountered until the Euphrates is reached. Here a very long and expensive bridge will be required, notes in regard to which will be found at page 129. After the passage of the Euphrates there is a gradual rise of 600 feet in the next ten miles to the east, then after a slight descent a level run across the thickly populated strip of plain known as Serouj, whereafter a region of low limestone hills gives access to Haran. Beyond the plain of Haran begins desert inhabited by nomads, where only the villages of Ras el-Ain, Nisibin, and about two other small hamlets, occur in the distance of 250 miles to Mosul.

Having reached Mosul, lying at a height above the sea of 800 feet, the railway now follows the right bank of the Tigris as far as Baghdad, encountering no obstacles on the way, and needing only a few minor bridges. A short distance north of Baghdad the line leaves upper Mesopotamia and enters the alluvial deltas of the Tigris and Euphrates. At Baghdad the two great rivers have converged until they are separated only by about forty miles. Here the railway will leave the bank of the Tigris and strike south-west, encountering the Euphrates at Mussaiyib, where a big bridge will be required. Thence to Kerbela and Nedjef, places of Shiah pilgrimage, through a series of swamps it will run parallel with, and sometimes touching, the Euphrates to Bussorah. While construction from the Euphrates in the far north to the ancient coast line near Baghdad will be on the cheapest possible scale, there now follow regions that present considerable difficulty. Baghdad and its neighbourhood, lying in the alluvial portion of Mesopotamia, is

liable to heavy floods which remain on the ground
sometimes for as long as two years. Where such
floods follow in successive years the land becomes
permanently bogged; and on the western banks of
the Euphrates, right in the track of the railway, are
thousands of square miles of swamp, in great part a
consequence of that divergence of the water of the
Euphrates into the blind alley of the Hindia Canal,
referred to at page 245. The transit of this swampy
country for a distance of at least 200 miles will require
heavy embanking that will not only be expensive to
build but expensive to maintain, for the subsoil is
soft as butter. The terrific heat of summer will
prevent the binding of the earthwork by vegetation,
and will render the surface so friable that showers
of rain in winter will materially assist the hot winds
of summer and autumn in a continual process of dis-
integration. The construction of rubble embankments
will hardly be possible, for there is not a single pebble
to be found in the alluvium, and no stone or rock to
be obtained nearer than the debouchure into the
delta, 200 kilometres distant from Nedjef, where the
swampiest region commences. So much does this
feature of the conditions appear a difficulty that one
is prompted to suggest that if the Baghdad Railway
ever reaches Baghdad, it may pay the Company to
halt there altogether. Not because the original construction will fail to give them a large profit, but
because the subsequent upkeep—for which there is no
provision by the Turkish Government, except in so
far as the annuity for running expenses provides it
—must prove a heavy drain upon their resources.
Even where the country is not morass the same
difficulty crops up in another form, for everywhere in
the neighbourhood of the rivers there are creeks and

old canal channels that must be crossed. These are
dry at low water, but heavily flushed in the spring
of each year. Their bridging will be a difficulty.
Stone must be transported from a long distance, and
will be continually subsiding. Wooden beams are
equally difficult to procure, and they would soon be
spoilt by the heat. Iron ·is expensive, and must in
any case have masonry supports. The small bridges
and culverts required to span obstacles of this description are not costly, but where there will be a
great number of them in constant need of repair
the question of upkeep becomes important.

Having passed the so-called Sea of Nedjef, and
threaded the intricacies of a great region of swamps
to the south, the railway will run close to the
Euphrates for nearly a hundred miles, and then cut
across country *via* Zobeir to Bussorah, which lies rather
less that 10 feet above the level of the sea. From
Mosul, 500 miles to the north, there occurs a descent
of 800 feet, and in that distance, so far as I know, it
will not be necessary to deviate from the general level
by more than perhaps 50 feet at one or two points.
Of the distance from Mosul, 400 miles consist of deltaic
alluvium, and in this long portion of the line the drop
will be no more than 110 feet, a fact that effectively
illustrates the extraordinary flatness of lower Mesopotamia, which in this respect has no rival in the world.
It further suggests that whatever route may be selected
along the alluvial plain, the railway will always be
liable to assault on the part of one or other of the
two great rivers, prone as they are, like other rivers
in similar regions, perversely to seek new courses.

Turning to the economic aspect of the country
traversed by the Baghdad Railway, one finds abundant food for reflection. Again including the Anatolian

Railway in my purview, one can but say of it that it has proved, and will prove for many years to come, an exceedingly expensive luxury to the Turkish Government. We hear a great deal about the agricultural development that has taken place since its inauguration, and that the increase of revenue in the districts through which it passes amply compensates the Government for the expenditure upon guarantees. I cannot believe that it has. For a variety of reasons certain districts on the plateau, chief among them Konia, have shown a remarkable advance in prosperity, and consequently in the tithes that are the principal source of revenue in agricultural regions. The Konia plain is peculiarly adapted for the production of cereals, and where very little grew before the arrival of the railway, there is now a large harvest which finds a market at the coast. The railway has done so much for Konia undoubtedly, but not unaided. Konia and the neighbourhood has been the scene of a considerable immigration experiment which has cost the Government a lot of money, and conferred no great gain on the immigrants, for the bulk of them would give their ears to return to the country whence they came. But, as mentioned at page 29, they are completely tied to the land of their adoption, and cannot move. They must till the soil to get bread, and in so doing they enhance the revenue, and create a small demand for importations which confers some meed of prosperity upon the merchants of Konia. There has further been a considerable gravitation of Anatolian peasantry to the railway country, a process that merely enriches one district at the expense of others. Nothing alters the fact that the Anatolian system costs the Turkish Government £180,000 per annum in guarantees, and that there has been no material diminution in its liability in this respect during the last few years. The reason of this lack of progress is that the sources of emigration are more or less dried up, and that the Anatolian peasantry do not care to any great extent to exchange a less prosperous existence in more attractive parts of the country for the dull monotony of the lonely treeless plain through which the railway runs. The huddled mud villages that are responsible for much of the cultivation to be seen from the railway are bare and miserable-looking in the extreme, and calculated to give all but the hardiest traveller a fit of the blues. The difficulty in Anatolia is population, which is of the most meagre, and must always remain so, it would seem, for there is no natural increase among the Mussulman subjects of the Sultan, and never will be until some revolution is wrought in their dispositions and in their manner of life. Then, whatever of progress has been made by the Anatolian Railway has occurred principally in the portions of the line adjoining Constantinople. Local trains running to Haidar-Pasha station do a large traffic, and the thickly populated plain of Ismid gives rise to a great trade. Cut the first 100 miles off the railway, and you would have a busy and prosperous line entirely justifying its existence. As for the ascent to the plateau, and the two long legs of line to Angora and Konia, there are to be found on them only a few points where any real development has taken place, a development procured at the expense of creating hundreds of miles of railway across country that is economically blank, and that must remain blank until changes occur that are inconceivable for generations. There is no question of the richness of the country, or of the fertility of the soil. It would, I believe, be well within the truth to say that the Anatolian plateau generally is capable of

supporting a population ten times as great as it now
carries. The trouble is to find the population.

In regard to the first section of the Baghdad Railway,
these remarks apply with double force, for the country
traversed is still more desolate than that through
which the plateau sections of the Anatolian Railway
run. The largest town on the route is Eregli, containing some 5000 inhabitants, besides which there are
only a few insignificant villages scattered along the
line. The poverty of the land and the expense of
the railway are well contrasted in the following table,
showing the working for three of the four complete
years during which the line has been open to traffic :—

	1905.	1906.	1907.
Gross receipts for the section of 200 kilometres	£12,920	£10,960	£13,844
Total guarantees paid on the section	111,080	113,040	110,120
The gross receipts represent the following percentages on the capitalised value of the guarantees .	·425	·360	·455

A return of a good deal less than ½ per cent to be set
off against the state loan and the annuity for working
expenses, together equivalent to a capital liability of
over £3,000,000 sterling, does not look like remuner-
ative investment on the part of the Turkish Government, nor can one see what causes can operate
materially to enhance the return in the near future.

Coming now to that part of the Baghdad Railway
which is still in the air, we find that practically the
whole of section two will be constructed in the Taurus
Mountains, to which I have made extended reference
in chapter iv. Between Boulgourlou station and the

town of Adana there is to be found only the merest
handful of inhabitants, and hardly enough cultivable
ground to keep them in bread.   The whole of the
section will be unproductive throughout all time, unless
there should be discovered minerals in paying quantity,
of which there is no indication at present.   Beyond
Adana, on the other hand, the line will tap the wealth
of the upper Cilician plain, and it is quite on the cards
that half of section three—that portion between Adana
and Osmanieh—will in the near future earn returns
equivalent to a fair dividend on the expenditure involved.   Beyond Osmanieh there are the Giaour and
Kurd Daghs to be crossed, the former totally unproductive, the latter inhabited in a minor degree.   Between the two ranges, however, there is the magnificent
valley described at page 102, and here there might very
well be entrained for Mersina some of the large numbers
of cattle at present marched to Alexandretta for export
to Egypt.   The valley has immense agricultural potentialities, which are little likely to be realised while the
population problem dominates the future of the country.

Emerging at Killis the railway leaves mountains
altogether and immediately enters upon a rich, rolling,
down-like plain of red loam, where are planted thousands
of olive-trees.   Between Killis and the Euphrates there
has been a steady increase of population within the last
few years, due to the tactics of the Civil List Depart-
ment, which has begged, bought, and stolen property
hereabouts with consistent energy in recent years.
The land thus acquired is offered at low rents to
settlers, who, by virtue of their occupancy of the
Sultan's property, are free of all taxation and exempt
from military service.   They are, moreover, secure from
exactions by any Government officials whatsoever, and
enjoy a degree of protection and security attained by

few people in this land, where the capacity for extor-
tion is only limited by the ability to pay.   Wherever
this process of acquiring land for the Sultan has been
going on—and it has been going on to a scandalous
extent in the north of Syria, as well as in many other
parts of the country—there follows a steady influx of
settlers anxious to avail themselves of the opportunity
to farm under safe auspices.   They are mostly Kurds
and Turkomans, who have hitherto led a semi-nomadic
life in the mountainous regions to the north, and whose
transformation into respectable tillers of the soil represents a distinct economic gain to the State.   Curious
that out of a system which entails the most ruthless
robberies upon Turkish landowners, and which deprives
the Government of recruits for the army and taxes
which are its just due, there should come any good
at all.

Between Killis and the Euphrates then we have a
country of which a considerable part is cultivated, and
wherein an increasing population will welcome a railway.   Beyond the Euphrates there lies a belt of low
hills at present destitute of population, but in the
hollows of which there might well exist a great deal of
cultivation.   Twenty miles east of the river the railway will enter the tail-end of the rich plain of Serouj,
where no fewer than 45,000 people inhabit some 350
villages.   Another belt of low hills, in which a considerable degree of cultivation is possible, and the railway strikes another fertile district.   Cuinet, in his
Gazetteer of Turkey, states that in the plain of
Haran there are 253 villages, with a population of
31,000 people.   Cuinet is not to be relied upon in
regard to this part of the country, but it is possible
that his figures were once correct, for there is no
doubt that within comparatively recent times this

region carried a greater population than it does now. Present local estimate puts the population of the plain at 16,000, and the difference in the figures might easily be accounted for by depopulation consequent on insecurity. Tribal warfare in northern Mesopotamia has been almost continuous for many years, and as Haran lies on the border of the fighting country it has always been the prey of raiders. Nothing is more probable than that there has been a large decrease in the inhabitants within recent times, while a further probability is that the remarkable increase of area under cultivation in the Killis-Aleppo-Euphrates district is in part a consequence of a transference of population from the disturbed regions in the east to this recently settled district west of the Euphrates.

The popular idea in regard to the country immediately east of the Euphrates is that it is a desert region, sparsely inhabited, and promising no profit to a railway. On the contrary, the first hundred miles east of the Euphrates is in parts extremely rich, supporting, within a few miles on either side of the projected route of the railway, a population of 60,000 settled, though by no means industrious people. From Haran it is planned to build a branch to Urfa, a course that I believe will prove unnecessary, for the following reason. Urfa lies at the mouth of an opening in the northern mountains, through which filtrates into the plain below the water of a large catchment area. Some of the water runs through the town in the shape of a small river, which in rainy weather is a roaring torrent, but in summer a mere trickle. The bulk of the water, however, flows underground in a gravelly strata, and throughout the plain of Haran, thirty or forty miles long, and varying between two and five miles wide, may always be

found by digging a few feet below the surface. Urfa,
at the head of the water-supply, beautifully situated
among the foothills, easy of defence in olden times, and
on the ancient trade-route between the southern slopes
of the Taurus and the Mediterranean, is the focus of
the wealth of the plain of Haran. But when a railway passes through the southern end of the plain,
produce for export will gravitate towards the railway-
station and not towards the blind alley in the north,
with the result that Urfa will speedily decline in importance. Of these two plains, Serouj and Haran—
the latter particularly, for the other is already pretty
well developed—one can only say that they are extremely rich and might support a much larger population than they do now. The advent of the railway will
here signalise an immediate increase of production for
export, with a corresponding demand for imports,
conferring prosperity both on the people and the
railway.

East of Haran, however, for a distance of several
hundred miles on the route of the railway, the conditions, which so far present considerable inducements to
a railway, change entirely, and no longer offer any
attraction from a commercial point of view. Where
we have found a comparatively thickly populated
country, whose proximity to the Mediterranean coast
gives opportunity for a profitable export and import
trade, henceforward the railway passes through regions
inhabited by roving nomads who hate agriculture, and
where the points of settlement are few and far between,
and very far, moreover, from an outlet to the sea. So
far as I have been able to ascertain, there is no
particular change in the character of the country
east of Haran, and though, owing to the adventure
described in chapter xi., I got no farther than ten

miles past that place, I saw enough, in conjunction
with what was told me by a party of archæologists,
to indicate that while the ground is now desert it
was once thickly populated.   Immediately beyond
Haran the rolling hills contain large flat valleys
covered in the middle of winter with thick herbage,
and are interspersed with˟ the tels or mounds that
indicate ancient habitation.   These conditions, I am
assured on competent authority, are maintained along
the route of the railway, through Ras el-Ain, Helif,
and Nisibin, until within a day's march of the Tigris at
Mosul, on the right bank of which, in this latitude, it
would seem there is a strip of sandy waste of not much
promise.   With this exception, however, the character
of the soil compares favourably with that of the region
wherein is situated the fertile districts of Serouj and
Haran, and there is abundant evidence in the shape of
ancient remains to show that the land actually was at
one time highly cultivated.   The trouble here, as in
the section of the Baghdad Railway already built, is
the lack of population, and the prospect for many years
to come of there being neither export nor import trade
to feed a railway.

So far the route of the railway has traversed a region
in which there is a considerable rainfall, and into which
flows much of the drainage of the southern slopes of
the Taurus.   The two great rivers are responsible, of
course, for the principal part of the water collected in
the mountains to the north, but between them there
are large districts, like Serouj, Haran, and others, very
lightly populated, which either get the benefit of some
of this water as it passes through on its way to the
Euphrates, or which absorb it altogether either above or
below ground.   Wells at almost any point in the flats
will furnish water a few feet below the surface, while

in the presently desolate region west of Mosul it is clear that the ancient inhabitants practised irrigation to employ water that would otherwise have flowed to one of the two rivers. Such regions are potentially of considerable agricultural value, owing to the fact that they are blessed with a rainfall that alone is sufficient for the growth of cereals. Any conservation of water above ground, or pumping arrangements for raising to the surface water that is abundant below, would of course add greatly to that value, and make possible crops of other kinds, and in seasons of the year when there is no rain.

At Mosul the railway will turn south and follow the right bank of the Tigris to Baghdad, a distance of some 300 miles. The change of direction marks a change in conditions, for the farther south one goes the less becomes the rainfall, while the mountain drainage disappears altogether. Between Mosul and Baghdad, curiously enough, the Tigris receives, so far as I am aware, not a single tributary, great or small, from the country beyond its right bank. To the west of the river there are no mountains to precipitate moisture, with the result that the meagre rainfall is absorbed by the thirsty flat desert upon which it falls. Cultivation on the right bank there is practically none, and without irrigation from the river there never can be any of much account. This long portion of the railway, so far as the right bank of the Tigris is concerned, will therefore run through country that will never contribute anything to its support. Not that the land, if irrigated, would prove unproductive, but because irrigational enterprise in these regions must always be conducted in the alluvial tracts that give the greater return. The country to the left of the river, however, differs in that it is comparatively well watered by the drainage from the Persian mountains in the east. Between Mosul and Baghdad four large and important streams flow into the Tigris, and materially add to its bulk, and water on their way regions that are desert now simply because there are no people to cultivate them. The littoral of the left bank receives no more rain than falls on that of the right bank, and irrigation would here be essential to a development of agriculture. But eastward, at the foothills of the mountains that give rise to the four rivers mentioned—the Zab, Lesser Zab, Adhem, and Diyala—there is considerable population and a large amount of cultivation. With this long strip of country it is anticipated that the railway will do a considerable trade by road and water.

On arrival in the alluvial delta of the two rivers, which commences some sixty miles north of Baghdad, the railway finds itself in country of a totally new character. Having already dilated upon the potential wealth of Babylonia in the chapter on Baghdad, it is unnecessary to do more than reiterate the opinion that if politics permitted, and population existed, and money were forthcoming, the country around Baghdad might easily be transformed into a modern Garden of Eden. As there is no prospect of a conjunction of these three conditions, or of the appearance of any one of them in present times, it is not much use discussing the Baghdad Railway in relation to a re-created Chaldea. It suffices to say here, putting aside for the present the subject of the trade which has its centre at Baghdad, that the course of the railway after its second passage of the Euphrates lies through country where the population is extremely thin—with the exception of the holy cities of Kerbela and Nedjef, whose wealth is due to the generosity of pilgrims and not to agricultural surroundings, and the date country north of Bussorah, which the railway avoids—and devoted chiefly to the herding of flocks, an occupation that furnishes its followers with little to despatch by a railway and less money to buy foreign goods. Having left Nedjef behind, the Baghdad Railway finds itself, in fact, in regions from which little can be expected in the shape of freights, either inward or outward. Arrived at Bussorah, the line, to all intents and purposes, as demonstrated in chapter xxi., has reached the sea, and fulfilled the ambitious design of its progenitors by linking the Mediterranean with the Persian, Gulf.

As conclusion to this chapter, it may not be amiss to draw attention to the fact that no better line of advance which involved the eastern route through Mesopotamia could very well have been selected. It has been suggested that instead of taking the railway across the desert region—not all desert, as I have shown—east of the Euphrates, and down the desolate right bank of the Tigris, it would have been better to have drawn an alignment through Aintab, Urfa, Suverek, Diarbekir, and Jezire to Mosul; and thence on the left bank of the Tigris through the towns of Erbul, Kerkuk, and Khanikin to Baghdad. These towns are certainly the centres of existing population, but most of them are so for the same reason as Urfa is the focus of the wealth of the plain of Haran. Each of them stands in a position favourable for defence and for residence at the source of the water-supply which fertilises a tract below. The basis of the prosperity of these towns is the cultivated plains which depend from them. Tap the plains with a railway and you get the milk out of the cocoa-nuts, and can afford to throw the empty husks away. Then all of these towns are surrounded by mountains which would be extremely difficult and expensive of negotiation to a railway. To get away from Diarbekir, for instance, would necessitate the transit of that hundred miles of the mountains of south-west Kurdistan which the Tigris tears through in such picturesque fashion. To touch at Erbul and Kerkuk would mean crossing a series of high parallel ridges projected by the main range of the Persian mountains, and the bridging of the numerous tributaries that flow westward to the Tigris, as well as the very expensive double bridging of the Tigris itself. By adopting the alignment planned, the railway escapes mountains entirely and rivers almost entirely. The plan of sending out feeders *up* plains to the towns, avoiding bridging and the climbing of lateral ridges, is obviously the better policy—policy, perhaps, which in some cases it may prove unnecessary to carry out at all. Then a railway involved in the line Aintab-Diarbekir would tap little else than the towns upon its route. But bring it straight across the plains of northern Mesopotamia and the possibilities are greatly increased, for there are enormous stretches of ground capable of cultivation on either hand. In the hills there is permanent poverty, in the plains potential wealth.

CHAPTER XXIII.

THE POPULATION QUESTION.

THE preceding chapter touches so frequently upon the question of population, and the subject is so important in relation to the Baghdad Railway, that it would seem necessary to endeavour to make some sort of explanation of the belief within me that the future of railway enterprise in Turkey is almost entirely dominated by this one grand factor. The same, of course, might be said of almost any country, for the institution of communications, whether by land or sea, can have no other object than that of fulfilling the requirements of mankind. Man and railways have a trick of reacting upon each other, to their mutual benefit. We have become so accustomed to observe the amazing success of the process in various parts of the world, that we are apt to lose sight of the fact that there is little intrinsic merit in the conjunction, and that if certain elements are not favourable man may be brought to a railway, or a railway brought to man, without there ensuing any material gain in prosperity. These elements are two: natural resources in the country experimented upon, and the power in man to multiply himself. In America and Canada exist conditions ideal to railway enterprise, for there the ages have expended themselves in fertilising the soil, while the nations of the world have combined to send their surplus people to gather the wealth lying fallow. Building a railway across the American continent is like driving a shaft into a mountain of solid gold. Persia, on the contrary, presents conditions exactly antithetical, for here nature is at her worst, and man least prolific. Building a railway across Persia would be like setting a man to walk the plank. Turkey comes midway between these two sets of conditions, for she has the resources but not the men.

Nor can one see from where the men might spring. There is nothing in Turkey to attract a stream of immigration. No Europeans, not even Germans, desire to become tillers of the soil in Turkey, and Turkey does not want Asiatics of alien race and creed to repopulate her territories. If she did, why should they come, when other parts of the world offer greater advantages. If the population of Turkey is to undergo any material increase, the increase must come from within. The railway is the great vitaliser of modern times, and one wonders if railways can revitalise what was once one of the richest and most populous parts of the world, but which has now become—Turkey. To put railways where they cannot achieve the process of vitalisation is sheer waste of energy, and it would seem as if construction on so great a scale as that of the Baghdad Railway means nothing else.

Turkey holds a large population, but its distribution is unfortunate from a railway point of view. Leaving European Turkey, by far the most thickly populated part of the Empire, out of consideration, it is found that the only points of real density occur on the coasts. Most excellently is this illustrated in the chart reproduced by the courtesy of the Delegates of the University Press from Mr D. G. Hogarth's learned

volume *The Nearer East*. Inhabitants to the extent
of over seventy to the square mile are found only
at Constantinople and its neighbourhood, in Crete,
on a short strip on the Black Sea coast, and at the
Beyrout-Tripoli section of the Syrian coast. I should
have thought that Mr Hogarth might have marked
another black corner in Cilicia, where I was told that
the population numbers some 350,000 in a comparatively restricted area. All these points, however, are
on the sea-shore, and offer no opportunity to railway
enterprise other than in the shape of local lines. Of
the second classification of between fifty and seventy
to the mile, the areas are again restricted to the Black
Sea coast around Trebizond, the Ægean coast inland
from Smyrna, and Cyprus. The Trebizond region offers
little scope to railway builders, while the Smyrna district is already tapped by the Aidin and Kassaba lines.
It may be used against me as an argument that the
fact of there being a well-populated area in the Smyrna
region is due to the district being the best served with
railways in all Turkey. On the other hand, it must be
remembered that Smyrna has always been the principal
port for the commerce of the interior of Asia Minor,
and the point upon which the principal trade routes
converged. The first railways in Turkey were laid down
from Smyrna, because the trade and the population
were there to begin with, and because the region is
the richest in Turkey. The Aidin railway has never
received a penny of guarantee from the Turkish Government, nor was the Kassaba line guaranteed until its
transfer from British to French hands. Both lines
were built with capital privately obtained on the
strength of the resources of the country they were
to tap and the existence of a large trade. Unques-

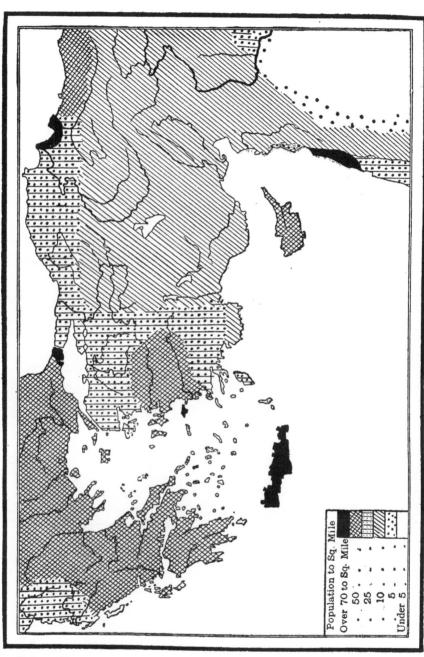

Population to Sq. Mile

Over 70 to Sq. Mile
50 ,, ,,
25 ,, ,,
10 ,, ,,
5 ,, ,,
Under 5

To face p. 298.

tionably both lines have done a great deal for the
development of the regions through which they pass;
but it must not be forgotten that a large degree of
prosperity already existed, which the railways came
to tap, not to make. Observe the result of railway
extension beyond the zone of population. Encouraged
by the success of the original Smyrna-Kassaba line, the
Turkish Government guaranteed a prolongation into
Anatolia. This was completed to Afium-Kara-Hissar
in 1897, and has since cost Turkey an average guarantee of £140,000 per annum. The Aidin concern, on
the other hand, has been going ahead step by step,
never building a mile of railway until the line in rear
showed signs of justifying its existence. Railways
certainly do bring population and prosperity, but by
very slow degrees, unless conditions are extremely
favourable. Conditions far away from the coast are
never favourable in Turkey.

Mr Hogarth's chart shows another classification of
between 25 and 50 people to the square mile. Such
areas are again confined to the littoral of the Black Sea
and to the western parts of Asia Minor, and offer limited
scope to railway enterprise. To Anatolia itself, Mr
Hogarth assigns a population of no more than between
10 and 25 to the square mile, and those to whom the
country is known will readily believe that the average
approximates much more closely to the smaller than to
the larger figure. Here it is where most of the mile-
age of the Anatolian railways lies, and where the first
section of the Baghdad Railway has its being. No
more effective demonstration of why these lines constitute a drain upon the Turkish exchequer can be
found than is furnished by Mr Hogarth's chart. The
limited population can only export and import in

limited quantity, and no more traffic will ever come to railways in such regions until the population is materially augmented.

An extension of Mr Hogarth's chart to the Persian Gulf would show a sad falling off, even from the unpromising conditions depicted in Asia Minor. With the exception of the slopes of the great mountain-system that dwindles into the plains of Mesopotamia, the population is to be measured mostly at the rate of about 5 to the mile. Baghdad and its neighbourhood aspires to the 10–25 classification, but on the other hand there is a great portion of the country lying between the two great rivers where the population is marked almost absolutely blank. It is this five-to-the-mile country which the Baghdad Railway will traverse for some two-thirds of its total length; and my contention is, that no richness in the soil will ever compensate for the lack of human beings to work upon it. One understands very well that the building of a railway through a thinly populated and insecure region will result in a gravitation of the inhabitants to the zone thus created, and henceforward providing protection and opportunity for profitable industry. But even that gravitation gives very limited prospects, and is attained, after all, at the expense of other regions. There is, too, as regards the route of the Baghdad Railway, the question of the disposition of the inhabitants. They are nearly all Arabs, to whom manual labour is as repulsive as it is to the unemployed of Trafalgar Square. At page 241 there will be found observations in regard to the possibility of obtaining labour for large irrigation works, which are entirely applicable to the general question of agricultural development along the route of the railway. Lower Mesopotamia contains millions of acres of land of unsurpassed fertility lying upon the very

banks of rivers and old canals. Arab tribes squat
upon these banks and dangle their feet in the water
when they might be working, to their own profit and
wealth. But they prefer to dangle their feet in the
water, trusting to the sale of the wool from their
flocks for money to buy the necessaries of life. They
prefer living in what we would call the deepest poverty
to doing any work whatever. To sleep, and smoke,
and contemplate, and fight when the spirit moves
them, is their only ambition in life, and they are not
to be stirred from these ideals in a hurry. This, in
fact, is the type evolved by the environment, and
railways are not going to cause any great evolution
in its representatives for many a generation.

Turkey, as we all know, has two main classes of population, Mohamedan and Christian, the former, so far as
Turkey in Asia is concerned, divisible principally into
Turk, Kurd, and Arab; the latter into Greek, Armenian,
and Syrian. Mohamedans, or Moslems, are everywhere,
the Turk in western and part of central Asia Minor,
the Kurd in part of central and in eastern Asia Minor,
and the Arab in Syria, Mesopotamia, and the southern
regions. Of the Christians, Greeks live only in the
coast regions of Asia Minor, any exceptions to this
rule being not worth mentioning. Syrians are rather
outside the scope of this volume. Armenians share
central and eastern Asia Minor with the Kurds. The
Turk, of course, is everywhere in an official capacity,
but as a tiller of the soil he is confined to that portion
of Asia Minor known as Anatolia. As porter, carriage-
driver, and in a few other capacities, he is to be found
in most of the coast towns. Except, however, as an
agriculturist in Anatolia, the Turk is not of particular
economic benefit to his country. Of the Kurds and
Arabs, it may be said that they do the least possible for

their own or their country's welfare. Greeks on the coast are not workers on the land to any great extent, their ambition always being a sedentary life. Syrians mostly earn a living by the sweat of the brow, in a country whose climatic conditions are favourable, and totally different from those of Mesopotamia. Armenians are really the most useful element of the population, for they are diligent farmers, expert craftsmen, capable shopkeepers, and, when education avails, they become skilled in the professions. It is just because the Armenians show both industry and intellectual power that the Turk is jealous of them, and took measures to crush them when comparatively trifling political intrigue gave an excuse.

These generalisations lead to a consideration of what is to be expected in the way of population on the route of the Baghdad Railway. Once the line leaves Anatolia it is finished with the Turkish cultivator, for he will never be induced to settle in Mesopotamia. The Syrian will never leave his own country for agriculture in another that offers severe climatic conditions. The Armenian will not lightly forsake his pleasant hill country for a low-lying environment unsuited to his constitution. There remains then for the Baghdad Railway in Mesopotamia only the Kurd and the Arab. The Kurd is much the more promising of the pair, for he is not so nomadic in instinct as the Arab, while in places he has shown a distinct inclination to settle and become a decent citizen.. At the same time the climate of Mesopotamia is equally against him as against the Armenian. Northern Mesopotamia, that part within sight of the slopes of the Taurus, might probably attract some Kurds, as it might some Armenians, if security were assured, as it would be on the line of the railway. But lower Mesopotamia, that part where irrigation may some day play a great part, is ground to which I believe it will always be impossible to draw any important mass of population from hill regions. Lower Mesopotamia, Chaldea, or Babylonia, whichever we like to call it, will therefore always depend upon the Arab for its development, for no other of the different classes of the population of Turkey will care about its climate. It would seem on the whole, therefore, that there is little likelihood of anything in the nature of a general gravitation of population to the country of the Baghdad Railway. Population already existing in the neighbourhood will surely tend to settle on the track of the line, and this alone must be the base of future development.

The question next arises—what can be expected from the existing inhabitants? Population in Turkey in Asia is steadily on the decline. Most authorities are agreed upon this, except, I believe, in regard to Syria. The most important factor in the decrease is the disappearance during the last fifteen years of some half a million of Armenians. Of these about half have been massacred, mostly during the atrocities of 1895 and 1896, but a good number since, in small numbers at a time, in isolated districts. The remainder have left the country. Turks from certain districts have left in large numbers, a fact proved by there being many thousands in New York,[1] and many thousands in Egypt and elsewhere. Military losses in the Yemen, too, have been very heavy in recent years. Greeks and Syrians have not emigrated to any great extent. It remains, however, that the tendency, despite a half-hearted scheme of immigration, has been for population to leave the country rather than to come to it. Of natural increase it would seem, too, as if there were

[1] There are 450,000 Turkish subjects in the United States.—*The Times,* 31st July 1908.

none, either among Moslems or Christians, unless perhaps a little in the case of the Greeks.

In support of this statement it is difficult to bring evidence that would pass in a court of law. But hearsay is generally worth something in a matter which is within general knowledge, and in confirmation of what is commonly said I am able to adduce the evidence of medical men settled in widely separated parts of the country. One European doctor, who is in charge of a hospital in a neighbourhood where the population is representative of three great divisions, Arab, Kurd, and Armenian, has for some time made a point of making certain inquiries from every woman with whom he comes in contact professionally. As something like fifty visit the hospital every day, and others are seen in their homes, the statistics thus compiled afford a fair basis upon which to generalise. His figures go to show that out of every ten children born to Moslem parents, Kurd or Arab, six die in childhood; out of every ten Armenian children born, five die in childhood. There is less evidence in regard to Syrians, but what there is shows that six out of every ten survive childhood. In regard to Turks, this particular doctor could offer no opinion, but other doctors with knowledge of them were of the opinion that quite six out of every ten of their children die in early youth. Christians, that is Armenians and Syrians, are far the more prolific, and families of six and eight are not uncommon. Doctors with knowledge of Greeks agree generally that these figures apply to them also. Moslem families are very much smaller, six being an exceptional number, and two being much more like the average. Families of official Turks are said to be the smallest of all.

The reason for this excessive death-rate among small

children is not far to seek. Accident and sheer neglect account for nearly all of it, for disease and inherited disability are minor causes. Whoever successfully runs the gauntlet of a Turkish upbringing, whether Christian or Moslem, must be hard as nails and possessed of a fine constitution. No weaklings survive, and owing to the fitness of parents, very few weaklings are brought into the world. Three forms of accident—falling into wells, toppling down stone stairs, and getting clothes alight from open charcoal fires—are the most fruitful causes of death. The utter absence of hygiene, and the utterly ridiculous treatment of childish ailments, are responsible for the remainder of the death-rate. Wherever one goes in Turkey the answer is always the same to account for the mortality among small children, accident and neglect, and nobody disputes that the proportion of deaths to births is rather more than half.

Curiously enough, polygamy is not responsible for large families, as one might suppose, and there are many harems in Turkey where the full complement of wives, and a further complement of females who are not wives, have not been able between them to produce a child at all. Nor does a single wife, which, after all, is the possession of the average respectable Moslem, always give a better result. This failure to propagate is usually a direct consequence of excessive sexual indulgence, and if this were a suitable place to discuss the subject, it would not be difficult perhaps to establish a connection between the state of physical and mental lassitude consequent on such indulgence, and the fatalism which is so characteristic of the Moslem. Prevention and abortion at various stages have recently become very popular among the more educated classes in Turkey, and in certain parts infanticide is said to be practised. Another important element has been introduced into the population question within comparatively recent years in the shape of syphilis, which has become extraordinarily prevalent. In one province no fewer than 30 per cent of the recruits examined for the army have been found to be suffering from this dread disease. The army is the medium through which it is spread, the disease being contracted by soldiers at the capital, than which no city in the world is more infected in this manner, and carried to the provinces by time-expired men. To combat the disease, Government dispensaries have been established all over the country, with what result I cannot say. Medical men say that syphilis is becoming very prevalent among the Arabs, who contract it in centres like Aleppo and Beyrout, and carry it inland.

The most important factor in the population question, however, is the death-rate among the children, for this affects all classes of the community, and is not to be combated except by a revolution in the life of the country. Hygiene is a product of a degree of civilisation from which Turkey is yet far removed, and the proper care of children is a consequence of a humanitarianism of which there is no present sign in the dominions of the Sultan. The small number of Christian families brought into the missionary fold hardly affects the question, and indeed there is no great improvement visible even where the missionary, by precept and example, has tried to imbue the people with Western notions of the treatment of children. Nothing but modern education carried into the humblest homes will ever modify this aspect of the social condition, and the possibility of enlightenment spreading to such an extent is not to be thought of at present in Turkey.

Turkish Coffee-shop.

One is therefore forced to the conclusion that very little natural increase can be expected in the immediate future from that portion of the population of Turkey which is settled, or is likely to settle, along the route of the Baghdad Railway, or in the regions served by the Anatolian lines. We know that in regions of natural wealth, accessible to open markets, settled conditions and enlightened government can work wonders. But enlightened government has not yet come to Mesopotamia, and will not come for a long time, for the double reason that the inhabitants are not ready for it, nor is Constantinople advanced enough to furnish it. Mesopotamia needs time, and in calculating what a railway may do for it it is essential to take into consideration the idiosyncrasies of the people, and the character of the country and climate, before jumping to the conclusion that railways will do here what they have done in other countries where the conditions are dissimilar.

CHAPTER XXIV.

IF it ever appeared that there was a definite prospect of the Baghdad Railway reaching Bussorah, certain questions of great importance to us would immediately become prominent. One of these would be the question of the carrying of the Indian mails, and another that of the future of British shipping in the Persian Gulf. The existing mail contract is a useful asset of our mercantile marine, and any transference of it to a railway, foreign or otherwise, would tend to lower our supremacy on the sea. Then it might be that a railway making a short cut to the head of the Persian Gulf would partially displace the British bottoms that now almost monopolise the transport of the trade of these regions. Involved in these two there would also be the question of the origin of the exports to the Persian Gulf. Where to-day nine out of ten ships entering the Gulf are British, carrying British goods in ratio to their number, a railway with all Europe for its base might effect an important alteration in the character of the trade. The mail subsidy would strengthen the resources of the railway, and react upon its powers of distribution. These powers would be exerted in favour of foreign goods. Every ton of foreign goods travelling by the railway would tend to displace a ton of British goods carried to the Gulf in British ships.

Whichever way we look at it, then, the prospect of a railway reaching the Persian Gulf is a matter of substantial interest to British commerce in general.

But it does not seem difficult to show that neither British trade nor British shipping need be affected to any material extent. In regard to the mails, there is no doubt that there would be a prospect of the contract going to the railway if it could show a substantially quicker service. However unfortunate the loss of the contract might be to our shipping, public opinion would demand the change if any serious expedition in the delivery of letters was to be derived from it. But the Baghdad Railway cannot hope to beat the present mail route for yet awhile. The P. and O. Company and the various railway companies are now under contract to carry the mails from London to Bombay in twelve days and eight hours. This time can be accelerated on land by a faster service of trains between Turin and Brindisi, a long-promised improvement, and by quicker steamers between Port Said and Bombay. When the P. and O. Company last tendered for the carrying of the mails, they specified four different schedules according to which they were prepared to run steamers. These schedules were on an ascending scale as regards speed and cost. The Government chose the slowest and the cheapest, that which gives sea-speeds of 16 and 16·1 knots, and is now responsible for delivery of mails in the time mentioned above. Clearly enough, then, the time by the sea route is susceptible of reduction, for not only did the P. and O. Company offer to provide a faster service than is now supplied, but they are on their own initiative continually building ships of enhanced power. The P. and O. Company, whatever its defects may be in the eyes of pessimistic Anglo-Indians, has step by step in the last twenty-five years reduced the time for transport of the mails by no less than seven days, and there can be no doubt that long before locomotives have begun to whistle in Mesopotamia, still further reductions will have been effected.

Now let us see what a potential Baghdad Railway might do to beat this timing. The following table has been compiled with some care, and shows what could be effected by the railway, in conjunction with existing facilities; what reduction in time is reasonably possible; and what net result is attainable by an all-round acceleration of speed. An allowance of forty-five kilometres per hour is made for the unconstructed portion of the line, the express speed stipulated for in Article 30 of the *Cahier des Charges* during the first five years after the line is fully open.

Between	Time now occupied.		Probable acceleration.		Net time for accelerated service.	
	days.	hours.	days.	hours.	days.	hours.
London — Constantinople, by Orient Express (*a*) .	3	0		—	3	0
Transit across Bosphorus from Oriental Railway's terminus to Haidar Pasha station (*b*) . . .	0	12	0	4	)	8
Haidar Pasha—Boulgourlou (*c*)	2	6	1	4	1	2
Boulgourlou—Bussorah (*d*)	2	2		—	2	2
Bussorah—Karachi—Bombay (*e*)	7	6	1	16	5	14
	15	2	3	0	12	2

(*a*) Present service is express except on the Oriental Railways, whose condition is such that they could not be rendered fit for express traffic without enormous expenditure.

(*b*) Linking up the termini is out of the question at present owing to the expense of bridging the Bosphorus.

(*c*) Stoppage for the night at Eski Shehr, and again at Konia, would disappear, in addition to which eight hours is allowed for increased speed on the Anatolian Railway.

(*d*) Allows for a speed, including stoppages, of forty-five kilometres per hour, for 2240 kilometres, the estimated distance of the route of the railway between the two points.

(*e*) Allows for a 16-knot service, and a reduction of distance by cutting out the Koweit call at present made by the British India steamers.

People acquainted with the conditions will agree, I think, that this estimate of the timing by the Persian Gulf route is a generous one, particularly in regard to the speed allowance between Boulgourlou and Bussorah. It allows for a very great improvement in running upon the Anatolian line, and for express traffic on the Baghdad Railway. There is also an allowance made for a much quicker steamship service from Bussorah to Bombay. The British India steamers are run under contract to carry mails between Karachi and Gulf ports at an average speed of about 13 knots. To increase that speed to 16 knots, as estimated for in the table, an entirely new set of steamers would have to be put on the run, at very great cost. Taking all things into consideration, it would seem clear enough that the most that could be expected from the Persian Gulf route in the earlier stages of the existence of the Baghdad Railway would be that it would equalise the Suez Canal route. The trifling difference of six hours between the estimate in the table, and the contract time for present delivery of mails, can at any moment be knocked off by the P. and O. Company, which Company, moreover, will have entered upon a new contract, giving quicker time, years before it is possible to get the Baghdad Railway even half - way to the Persian Gulf. Always, too, will the long sea-route be cheaper than the long land - route. The question of security also counts for something. The mails now pass through France, Switzerland, and Italy, where they are as safe as if they were in England. But the Persian Gulf route would entail transit of Austria, Hungary, the Balkan States, Asia Minor, and that part of Turkey in Asia where exist various incontrollable elements. On British steamers the mails have the benefit of the finest seamanship in the world, and the protection of the finest fleet in the world. And by British steamers the mails will assuredly continue to go, until something offers very much better than the Baghdad route can become, either in the near or the far distant future.

So, too, with the Indian passenger traffic, which is inalienable from the mail route. If there is to be no reduction in time, there will be no inducement for travellers to desert the sea-route. Ninety per cent of the people who travel between India and England do so with the object of escaping for a time from a bad climate, and of going home to recover lost strength. To such the double sea voyage is half the battle, and there will be but an insignificant majority who will care to exchange the fresh sea breezes for the hot and dusty land journey through Mesopotamia and Europe.

Coming to the question of the effect of a railway upon the carrying trade of the Persian Gulf, an understanding of the situation will again be arrived at most effectually by a comparison of prospective railway rates and existing steamer freights. Steamer freights as a rule are a very uncertain quantity, and their fluctuations are often the despair of shippers who have been at the business for years. But railway rates are usually fixed, and can be ascertained by consultation of a tariff which is always before the public, and liable to change only after due notice. So far as the Baghdad Railway is concerned, maximum rates are fixed by the *Cahier des Charges*, and a tariff once approved cannot be altered except with the concurrence of the Turkish Government. Herein lies an interesting safeguard. The Turks have limited the power to impose high rates, which might check—for instance—the import of British goods; and they have also limited the Baghdad Railway Company's power to lower rates indefinitely, which might be used—for instance—to stimulate the importation of German goods. For example, Indian indigo and Scotch whisky might be charged a stiff rate, while German beer and aniline dyes (a German product) might be rated lightly, to the advantage of German commerce. Preference to individuals is forbidden by Articles 24 and 25 of the *Cahier des Charges,* and there would seem to be no loophole for the administration of the railway to favour their own countrymen to the detriment of others—without the connivance of the Turkish officials whose business it is to audit the accounts. A most important point in the matter of rates is the fact that not only does the Turkish Government possess the power to prevent manipulation of rates, but they are interested in keeping them high, because, owing to the operation of the kilometric guarantee, deficiencies in the receipts have to be made good, up to the stipulated figure, out of their own pocket. On railways where traffic is elastic and capable of being stimulated by favourable rates, policy of this sort would be intolerable; but where, in the case of the Baghdad Railway, as everybody connected with it knows, whether Turk or German, there is no probability of it paying even working expenses for years to come, another policy is not unreasonable. If the railway collects freight charges of £10 on a truck-load of goods, the Government liability for guarantee is reduced by £10. If the railway collects only £5 the Government liability is £5 greater than in the other instance. What governs the situation are the facts that no concessions in rates can materially affect the traffic, and that it is best for the Government that the railway should charge the highest possible rates upon the given volume. This policy must also entirely meet the views of the Baghdad Railway Com-

pany, for where there is no hope of making their
line a commercial success, they must be content to live
upon their guarantees.   The higher the rates, the
smaller the traffic ; the smaller the traffic, the less the
expenses ; the less the expenses, the greater the profit
to the Company !   Could anything be more iniquitous ?

Yet herein lies some satisfaction from the British
trader's point of view, for if it is to the interest both of
the Turkish Government and the Baghdad Railway
that traffic shall be restricted, then there remains hope
for those British goods which at present have a position in Baghdad that may almost be called a monopoly.
The prospect is ridiculous, anomalous, impossible ; but
it exists.   The Sultan wants, or once thought he
wanted, the line built for strategic and administrative
purposes, for it would give him a grasp upon country
where his hold is now weak.   Once the line is built
the Sultan gets what he wants, and as the railway has
never been expected to be a commercial success, it
suits both parties, Government and Company, that it
should be run as cheaply as possible.   From which a
fair deduction is that tariffs on the future Baghdad
Railway will be kept high, and that they will remain
approximate to the maximum fixed by Article 21 of
the *Cahier des Charges.*   Any reductions with a view
to attracting traffic must immediately hit both the
Government and the Company, and though it may be
galling to the Company to have to sit and watch
the continuance of British trade and shipping within
the zone of their operations, it remains that their
own pockets are best served by not entering into
competition.

Taking, then, these maximum rates, the following
table shows the cost of carrying cotton and grain
between various representative points of the projected

railway. Mersina, in the earlier days of the Baghdad Railway, must be the port of entry for Mesopotamia, and has been selected for illustration instead of Constantinople, which is never likely to see any through traffic of importance.

Between	One ton manufactured cotton (a).	One truck-load (15 tons) cereals (b).
Mersina—Mosul, 940 kilometres . .	£6 17 0	£21 12 0
Mersina—Baghdad, 1420 kilometres . .	10 7 0	...
Mersina—Bussorah, 2120 kilometres .	15 9 0	...
Bussorah—Baghdad, 700 kilometres .	5 2 0	48 2 0
Bussorah—Mosul, 1180 kilometres . .	8 12 0	22 2 0

(a) Rate as per *Cahier des Charges* of 35 paras per ton per kilometre ; 20 paras = 1 penny.

(b) Complete trucks for distances over 900 kilometres, at 6 paras per ton per kilometre ; for less distances than 900 kiloms., 22 paras per ton per kilom.

With this table in front of us it is easy to calculate which will afford the cheaper transport rates, the railway or the sea route. A ton of cotton goods bound from England or Germany for Baghdad by the railway route costs for shipment to Mersina, at a moderate estimate, say, 15s. Add railway charges, £10, 7s., and the total comes to £11, 2s. The same ton of cotton shipped to Bussorah costs for freight, say, 30s., to which has to be added, say, another 30s. for transport in the Lynch steamers to Baghdad—total £3. In fact, the railway charges will be nearly *four times as great as those by the sea route !* Marine rates at the present moment would in reality cost no more than 47s., owing to freights being abnormally low, and a fair average rate would be somewhere between the two figures. In order to enter into competition with the steamers, then, the railway would have to be content with *a quarter* of those maximum rates which I have endeavoured to demonstrate are the rates which it will be to the interest of both Government and Company to maintain.

The Baghdad Railway has no better chance of beating the Tigris steamers, for they will take a ton of cotton from Bussorah to Baghdad for 30s., where the railway charges will be £5, 2s. With cereals from Baghdad to Bussorah the railway will be completely out of it with the steamers, for where the one will charge £48 for a truck-load, the other can carry an equivalent quantity for £9—though they have been known to charge as much as £30 when they got the chance. The root of the matter is, that railway haulage is fundamentally and unalterably more expensive than sea transport, and that when the two come into competition the latter must always win. It would be foolish to suppose that the Baghdad Railway, if ever built, would be governed by hard and fast lines which would prevent advantage being taken of circumstances that offered. It might pay the Company and the Turkish Government to throw certain self-imposed tariffs to the winds and to develop particular sections of the railway, while recognising that others are hopeless. But nothing can affect the main issues, which are that the railway cannot supplant steamship traffic to the Persian Gulf, and that it cannot, without loss to itself, defeat the steamers on the Tigris in the matter of carrying between Baghdad and Bussorah. It is only when traffic reaches a volume far in excess of what is either probable or possible within the near future that the railway will commence to have a look in. Meantime, so far as can be judged, the Baghdad Railway may be constructed and opened to traffic without there being any prospect of British trade or British shipping being a penny the worse, except in so far as we would be dealing with a country that was annually throwing into a bottomless pit a million of money that might otherwise have been spent on foreign manufactures.

CHAPTER XXV.

THE BAGHDAD RAILWAY QUESTION.

HAVING effected escape from the Persian Gulf I made a brief halt at Karachi, and there heard the first news of revolution in a country where I had spent nearly a year, and where it seemed unthinkable that the old order of things could really change. At Bombay the extraordinary intelligence was confirmed, ten days later in Cairo the marvel was an established thing; touching at Smyrna I found the people free, and in Constantinople itself one could hardly breathe for consciousness of the change.

The remarkable *coup* effected by the Young Turks, however, leaves the issues in regard to the Baghdad Railway where they were before. Whatever may be thought of the German scheme by the members of the new *régime*, it remains that the Convention is a document duly signed and sealed; that part of the railway has been built, and for several years has constituted a charge upon the revenues of the country; and that another large block of the line has been sanctioned, and the guarantees allocated in such a manner that the Turkish Government cannot alienate them. Nevertheless, recent occurrences are not without effect on the question of the Baghdad Railway, and the prospect that important modifications may ensue is of extreme interest.

Three countries are chiefly interested in the Baghdad Railway—Turkey, Germany, and Great Britain. Turkey, because she is making herself liable for an enormous capital sum and heavy annual payments; Germany, because she is embarking on an enterprise that entails huge profits, counterbalanced by the investment of much capital, and the placing of many eggs in the one basket; and we, because a great rival is penetrating into our commercial preserves, and establishing herself over against a possession which all the world envies us.

It needs no further demonstration that the railway will not pay while conditions are what they are, or what they promise to be for years to come. The German Technical Commission, sent in 1899 to survey the route of the line, was under no illusion as to the prospects. They estimated that after the railway was built, and a reasonable time allowed for development, the probable gross receipts would only average about two-thirds of the annuity for working expenses. Population is the grand factor, and that, if the arguments I have adduced are worth anything, cannot undergo material expansion in the immediate future. For Turkey, then, the Baghdad Railway must prove an Old Man of the Sea, doing far more to retard development than to accelerate it. All the benefits conferred by a railway, in the shape of construction expenditure to labourers, settlement of districts now insecure, increase of cultivation, and general stimulation of commerce, will be counterbalanced by the capital loss. The completed line will measure 2400 kilometres, or 12 sections, each entailing the issue of a State loan of 54,000,000 francs, or a total of £26,000,000. The

annual charges for interest and working expenses, after
making ample allowance for prospective receipts, will
be £1,200,000. It is quite inconceivable that the
advantages undeniably secured by railway enterprise
will compensate for this heavy and recurring expenditure. A milkman cannot afford to employ a powerful
motor-car for the distribution of his morning penny-
worths, not because the motor-car would not enable
him effectively to· accomplish his task, but because the
expense would be out of all proportion to the possible
gain. The railway would certainly achieve results.
But at what cost !

There are three British points of view—commercial,
political, and strategic. The first has already been
dealt with, and the conclusion arrived at that our Gulf
shipping has nothing to fear from railway competition,
and that our trade is unlikely to be affected by an
enterprise from which economic results are not expected. Whatever demand exists for British goods at
the present moment in Turkish Arabia will continue,
for the railway will afford to German, or other Continental goods, no easier access to that market than
they enjoyed before. The process of peaceful pene-
tration, of course, is not without effect, and German
railway officials, German engineers, and German contractors, will do something to popularise things and
ideas German. But not very much, for all the labour
on the railway will be native, all the foreigners employed in connection with its construction will have
their own "pidgin" to attend to, and it will always
be that the railway itself will not facilitate the bringing
out of goods which might be recommended.

Politically we can but look on the scheme with disfavour. A great enterprise organised by a rival Power
thrusting itself into territory that we have hitherto

regarded as our special preserve, could have but the effect of lowering our prestige and diminishing our influence. Until recent years the break-up of the Turkish Empire was looked upon as a distinct possibility, and while we have always regarded such an eventuality as calamitous, it none the less behoved us, principally for defensive reasons, to view the deltaic regions at the head of the Persian Gulf as territory in which the presence of other European Powers would be inimical to our interests. Lately Europe has been more optimistic about the cohesive powers of the Turkish Empire—or ought one to say, more optimistic about the power of Europe to maintain the cohesion?— and the probability of a break-up has diminished. To our very great satisfaction; for the head corner-stone of our policy in the Middle East is the maintenance of an independent, autonomous, prosperous Turkey, able to fight her own battles.

Strategically the railway touches us, for it opens out a new line of advance upon the Dependency that is our most valuable possession. Turkey herself will never be a menace to India, but a great European Power dominant in Constantinople would be another matter. A railway to the Persian Gulf, under the control of a Power that might develop unfriendliness towards us, would certainly necessitate defensive measures on our part. In itself there is little danger to be apprehended from a German railway running through Turkish territory, so long as Turkey retains her independence. But Germany might sell her railway to a Power who could make more effective use of it owing to her geographical position. There is always the contingency that our rivalry with Russia, so happily laid aside for the moment, will recur; and if its recurrence were to synchronise with events in Turkey that led up to an

x

extension of Russian frontiers in Armenia, we might very well wake one morning to find that Russia had bought the Baghdad Railway and intended linking it up with her Trans-Caucasian system. A remote contingency, no doubt, but one which not so very long ago was regarded as worth discussion in political circles in Europe. The very thought of it smells of war.

Germany has much to gain from the Baghdad Railway, and much to lose. Most of the material for its construction would come from Germany, and her trade thereby would be greatly quickened; her goods would obtain a footing in markets now small, but potentially great; many educated Germans would find an outlet for their energies; and there would be huge profits on construction. I have shown at page 55 how Sections II., III., and IV., the most expensive of all to make, can be built without encroaching upon the iniquitous profit made upon Section I. Sections V. to XII. will cost, at an outside estimate, £6000 per mile. Eight sections × 125 miles × £6000 = £6,000,000. Flotation of eight loans of 54,000,000 francs each will produce in Europe £14,000,000. The difference between these two sums goes to the concessionaires. *Eight millions sterling, plus the million and a quarter already pocketed,* is the profit that the Germans stand to make out of construction of the Baghdad Railway! These are figures which there is no gainsaying. The railway may be a section shorter than I have estimated, construction might cost 10 per cent more than I have calculated, and the loans might not possibly fetch so much as I have stated. But the grand fact remains, that the railway can be built for half the money which the Convention provides. That is indisputable.

But there is another side to this pleasant financial

picture. France and ourselves have declined to participate in the project, and for reasons easily understood the financiers of neither country will care to associate themselves with an enterprise that has not the official countenance of their respective Governments. So all of the loans against the eleven sections still to be built must be floated in Berlin. Is the Berlin money market strong enough to find £20,000,000, the approximate cash equivalent, even when spread over a period of, say, fifteen years? Perhaps, for Germany is a progressive country. But will German investors care to venture so large a sum in a country whose political stability is not assured? If by any miracle Turkey could ever satisfy investors of her ability to pay the enormous guarantees involved, there would still remain the chance that a change in the *status quo* would render the security worthless. That is the salient feature of the scheme from the German point of view. Alone Germany will not find the money, not because she is unable to find it, but because the security would not be good enough. Sane people may indulge in a mild gamble in mining shares, but they put their main capital into gilt-edged securities. The place for heavy German investments is within German territory, and in regions where her military power serves as an insurance against loss; not in a country whose future lies so heavily in the lap of the Gods.

And this brings us to the crux of the situation. While Turkey is Turkey, Germany alone will never build this railway. Security for the investment is only attainable by international co-operation, by our participation in the project, in company with France. With the three Powers thus pledged to protect a mutual interest, Russia would be kept out; and Turkey would be kept intact, for all three. of us to batten upon. There would be no gain to compensate us for having involved ourselves with Germany in a course of common action, for our trade would not be benefited except in a minor degree. There is the strategic disadvantage to us of a railway penetrating to the Persian Gulf, and the obviation of that disadvantage by our obtaining control of the lower sections. But it has been postulated that Germany alone cannot build the railway, so the question of strategy will never arise if we leave the scheme severely alone.

Most important for us to realise is the fact that the Baghdad Railway must constitute a desperate handicap on Turkish finances, for which no trifling economic or strategic advantages will compensate. We ourselves have nothing to gain from the railway, for we do not want under any circumstances to share in the unfair profits which the scheme involves. We have no other wish in regard to Turkey but that she may be strong and prosperous and progressive. Her strength is an asset to us in the Mediterranean, her prosperity gives us a good market for our wares, and her development increases our opportunity for trade and gives better protection to our line of communications with the East. By participating in the Baghdad Railway project we should be taking a step leading to results exactly opposite to those we desire, for we should be weakening Turkey and strengthening Germany. If ever there was a line clearly marked for British policy it is this— to refrain from supporting the Baghdad scheme, and to do everything possible to save Turkey from further involving herself in it. Needless to say, we must make it quite clear, if we are ever to consent to an increase of the Turkish Customs duties, that the proceeds shall not be devoted to the purposes of the Baghdad Railway Company.

The Young Turks are very well aware of the character of the project, and their minds are fully made up that it must be knocked on the head. Unfortunately things have gone so far that considerable loss cannot be avoided. The first section is built, and must remain a charge on the revenue of the country. The Germans, with a keen nose for coming changes that would affect their position in Constantinople, concluded arrangements last April for the building of four more sections of the railway, involving a debt of £8,500,000, and an annual liability of £500,000. As security for the service of the loans, they procured the ear-marking of the Government's share of the surplus revenues of the Dette Publique, which, when released in 1911, will be worth nearly £400,000. All the papers in connection with this allocation of revenue have been signed, and, so far as I am aware, the money has been irrevocably alienated.[1] It is essential that this transaction should be cancelled, and while it is not quite clear how that can be done, no doubt the Turks will find a way of convincing the Germans that it would be best to forego their rights. The German idea in appearing to be intent upon building the next four sections is to convince Great Britain that Germany is able to proceed without our aid, and that when we see how splendidly she is getting along we will hurry to come in before it is too late. But we are not such fools as we look. Instead of coming in, we will stand behind the Young Turks in their entirely laudable intention to be rid of an incubus that was forced upon their country by a corrupt court. Germany will bluster. But if we are sincere in our sympathy with the new *régime*, we shall in this matter marshal our friends in

---

[1] See Appendices for the additional Convention relating to the four new sections.

Europe to the support of the Young Turks, and help them once for all to be quit of a scheme that has nothing whatever to recommend it.

In endeavouring to demonstrate the folly and iniquity of the Baghdad Railway Convention, I have doubtless laid myself open to a charge of exaggeration of the evils involved in its consummation, and of minimisation of the benefits that the carrying out of its terms would confer. But it has been impossible to study conditions in Turkey without being convinced that railway enterprise must be strictly confined if it is to be of profit to the country. The Baghdad Railway scheme, as it unfolds itself before one in the course of a journey along the route, seems with every step to become more and more disastrous, more hopeless, and more perversive of the spirit of the times. The traveller who begins his journey with an open mind, and with the intention of guarding against prejudice because the scheme is not a British one, finds himself speedily changing his attitude. Indignation turns him into an ardent enemy, and fills him with the desire to do his humble best to expose what he believes to be a ruinous project. It is not that one cannot see into the future and let the imagination rove over a land rescued from desolation, and regenerated by the civilising influences of railways and irrigation and industry. These things may very well be in the fulness of time, but they are not best attained by the indiscriminate casting of bread upon water.

There is before a Baghdad Railway a long vista of years, in each of which stands forth a heavy loss to be borne by the Turkish Government. It is perhaps a diminishing loss, each year a trifle smaller. But the reduction appears mostly among the shillings and the pence, while the pounds go on repeating themselves

year after year, twenty years, thirty, forty, fifty, and
then perhaps there will be no more loss, but at last an
entry on the credit side. That prospect, I believe,
most people who know the conditions will agree is the
most likely one. And yet it is a prospect to which
another character might easily be given. If the
Turkish Government would wipe out the Baghdad
Convention and devote some of the money they propose wasting upon its fulfilment to formulating and
executing a sound system of immigration of Moslems
from foreign countries to Turkey, they would be embarking upon enterprise that would give an almost
immediate return in the shape of rents, taxes, railway
receipts, customs dues, and increase in the population
available for military duty. If they would set up in
various districts depôts for the exhibition of agricultural machinery, if they would demonstrate its use
and encourage purchase by accepting payments by easy
instalments, they would set free from daily labour
large numbers of people who would then be available
to open up ground that is now neglected. A narrow-
gauge railway from Khanikin on the Persian border to
Baghdad, Kerbela, and Nedjef would pay its way and
more. An extension of the Adana - Mersina line to
Osmanieh would soon give a commercial return upon
the money spent. A light line from Alexandretta
to Aleppo, and from there to the right bank of the
Euphrates, would give a return before many years were
over. Perhaps before long it would pay to extend
across the river, at first to the plain of Serouj and
afterwards to Haran. That would be the limit in
that direction as things are at present. Heavy pack
transport uses all these routes, and many men and
animals would be thrown out of work if railways were
substituted. People and their beasts would then have

nothing else to do but settle on the land and develop it. There is room for a moderate annual expenditure in lower Mesopotamia on irrigation. A small dredger on the Tigris would halve the difficulties of navigation. Above all, a land settlement, fixing revenue and giving security against illegitimate exactions, would stimulate cultivation in a manner that would astonish all concerned.

All these things are possible if the Turks were prepared to put down half the money that the Baghdad Railway would cost them. The effect on the economic wealth of the country would be magnetic. It would be essential that any railway building should be on the cheapest possible scale, of no more than metre gauge, and probably mostly of a smaller gauge still. Not an inch of line should be built until there is a definite prospect of settlers upon it, or at least some justification in rear that a railway would attract settlers. The engineers who are making the Hedjaz Railway might very well undertake any enterprise of this kind. They have shown their ability with a European in charge. Perhaps they could undertake minor construction by themselves; if not, let there be employed some more of those German engineers who have done such splendid work for Turkey in the Hedjaz. But it all must be cheap, not in the sense of shoddy, but in the sense that it gives a definite prospect of return upon capital.

It is, however, rather too much to expect .that the Baghdad Railway will halt for ever at Boulgourlou. The Turks are very keen to link up Constantinople with the Hedjaz Railway, and considering what they have spent in the way of guarantees on connecting lines, it would only seem reasonable that their ambition should be realised. Unluckily the termini at Boulgourlou and

Aleppo are separated by the same difficulties that have
for so long confronted the engineers of the Baghdad
Railway, the Taurus mountains, and the Giaour and
Kurd Daghs.   A standard-gauge railway connecting
the two will cost something between four and five
million pounds to build, and there is no other route
to follow but that chosen for the Baghdad Railway.
What will inevitably happen will be that the
Baghdad Company will proceed with their line
across the mountains and will link it up at Aleppo
with the Syrian system, which farther south is continued as the Hedjaz Railway.   The Germans might
reasonably demand the right to do this on favourable
terms to themselves, if their concession for the greater
project is to be quashed.   But if Turkey is to be considered in the matter, it is quite plain that the metre
gauge of the Syrian and Hedjaz Railways should be
employed, instead of the standard gauge of the Anatolian and Baghdad Railways.   The lesser gauge line
can be built for almost half the price of the greater, and
will be equally effective for connecting with the Hedjaz
line, for the change of gauge has to take place in any
case. If the Turks cannot reconcile themselves to doing
without the sentimental gratification which the junction will afford them—there is no prospect of it paying,
though about 100 of the 220 miles involved will be
greatly benefited—they can insist, at least, that their
wishes be fulfilled as cheaply as is compatible with
efficiency.

But for a brief visit to Constantinople after the
completion of my journey to the Persian Gulf, all my
time in Turkey was spent under the old *régime,* when
the Camarilla was supreme, spying rife, and evils innumerable visible in the body politic.   The changes
that have taken place have been widely dissertated

upon in the public press, and require no discussion
in a volume devoted to travel that was finished before
the changes took place.   Nor do these changes affect
the question of the Baghdad Railway particularly,
except in so far as the old *régime* was in favour of it,
while the new *régime* declares vigorously and emphatic-
ally against it. That, however, does not obviate the
necessity for discussing the question, nor does it mean
that the Baghdad Railway is dead.   All that can
be said is that the party now in power does not
want it, and that they would quash the Convention
if they could.   But then we do not know how long
the Young Turk has come to stay.   There are re-
actionaries in Turkey, and there are bitter and powerful enemies of the movement outside.   The Moslem
people of Asiatic Turkey have no deep-rooted desire for
reform as we regard it in Europe.   Turkey, from an
Oriental point of view, has never been a badly governed
country, though a good deal of dissatisfaction has
been felt with the Hamidian *régime*, and it is perhaps
only the Christians who hope that the change will
better their lot.   That very betterment to which the
Christians look will some day, perhaps, prove to be the
cause of a revulsion in the attitude of the Moslem
population.   Greeks and Armenians are much more
intelligent than Turks, more industrious, more educated.
Let them have free institutions under which they can
expand and grow strong, and they will speedily tend
to overshadow their old - fashioned compatriots who
walk in the way of Islam.   The Turk knows this very
well, and while that minority who have absorbed
Western ideas are genuine in their profession of faith
that Christian and Moslem alike are entitled to equal
rights, the great majority do not believe it, and cannot

be convinced of it perhaps for generations. It is proposed to make the Christian liable to military service.
That is a bold project, all the more bold to those who
know something of the gulf that separates Christian
and Moslem in Turkey. The Turk now rules Turkey
by the sword, and yet he proposes to share the power
that gives him dominion. ⋅That will stick in the
throats of most Turks who are not Young Turks. If
the Turk will continue to occupy his place as the
dominant factor in the State, then the Turkish Empire,
under a constitutional *régime*, will continue to endure.
When the Christian begins to gather strength in the
land, then will the fires of revolt begin to smoulder.
The elements in Turkey are too discordant to be ruled
by anything but an autocracy, and it is only so long as
the Young Turk remains autocratic, as he is to-day,
that his rule will endure. Japan is constitutional, yet
absolutely autocratic. Turkey is the same by disposition, and the mantle of Government may alternately
lie upon the shoulders of a Committee or a Camarilla,
a Grand Vizier or a Sultan, so long as they or he are
collectively or individually sufficiently autocratic.

It is in the vigour and energy and single-mindedness
of the Young Turk that one finds hope for Turkey, not
in the Constitution. If a strong Committee of Union
and Progress sits behind the Parliament that is about
to assemble in Constantinople, then the Parliament
will do good work. If the Committee sat behind the
Sultan, without any intervening Parliament, perhaps
better work still would be done. The Young Turk
has shown marvellous discretion to date, and the
manner in which he has solved problems has been
magnificent, and typically autocratic. He has said,
Let there be no more backshish in the Custom-house,

and from that moment the passing of backshish ceased. The poor custom-house officer, however, who kept his wife and family on his backshish, and only looked to his salary for coffee and cigarettes, began to starve. He made representations, but continued to starve and abjure backshish. The Young Turks had no money with which to raise salaries, so they were compelled to say, *Let there be backshish again*, else many an unfortunate victim would have suffered upon the altar of duty. But their command was carried out literally, to the knowledge and wonder of Europeans who had believed it impossible.

The greatest difficulty with which the new order of things has to contend, is the fact that only an insignificant minority of the immense army of officials who administer the Government of the country is imbued with the spirit of the Young Turk. The great majority of them are ignorant of what he is aiming at, and many are incapable of realising his point of view. These men cannot be turned away, for they cannot be replaced. They can only be allowed to remain and to run the country on the old lines, subject to general instructions which it will be extremely difficult to have regarded. All have ridiculously small salaries, and all count for a living on what they can get by ways that in the West are called devious. There is no money in the Treasury to allow of the raising of salaries, so the old conditions must continue to rule, and backshish continue to be Lord of All. But there will be tendencies afoot, that will permeate slowly and imperceptibly and surely, for there is so much goodwill in the Young Turk, so much faith, and so much fixity of purpose, that if it is humanly possible for him to reform his Government he will do it. He has British sympathies with him, not only because the fulfilment of his aspirations accords with our own desires for Turkey, but because we believe him to be making a plucky and high-minded attempt to arrest the progress of his country in the downward path of degeneration.

APPENDICES.

CONVENTION DE LA SOCIÉTÉ IMPÉRIALE OTTOMANE DU CHEMIN DE FER DE BAGDAD.

Entre Son Excellence Zihni Pacha, Ministre du Commerce et des Travaux Publics, agissant au nom du Gouvernement Impérial Ottoman,

d'une part,

Monsieur Arthur Gwinner, Président du Conseil d'Adminis tration, Mr. le Docteur Kurt Zander, Directeur-Général, et Monsieur Edouard Huguenin, Directeur-Général-Adjoint, du Chemin de fer Ottoman d'Anatolie, agissant au nom et pour compte de la Société du Chemin de fer Ottoman d'Anatolie, à Constantinople,

d'autre part;

Il a été arrêté ce qui suit:

ARTICLE 1.—Le Gouvernement Impérial Ottoman accorde la concession de la construction et de l'exploitation du pro longement de la ligne de Konia jusqu'à Bagdad et Bassorah, en passant par ou aussi près que possible des villes de Kara man, Eregli, Kardach-Béli, Adana, Hamidié, Osmanié, Bagtsché, Kazanali, Killis, Tell-Habesch, Harran, Resulain, Nussibéin, Avniat, Mossoul, Tékrit, Sadijé, Bagdad, Kerbéla, Nédjef, Zubéir et Bassorah, ainsi que des embranchements suivants, savoir:

1) de Tell-Habesch à Alep,
2) d'un point rapproché de la ligne principale, à déter miner d'un commun accord, à Orfa.

Le Gouvernement Impérial n'accordera, sous quelque forme que ce soit, de garantie pour la construction de cet embranche-

ment d'une longueur de 30 kilom. environ, ni aucune affectation, pour frais d'exploitation, mais les recettes brutes de toute
nature de l'embranchement appartiendront exclusivement au
Concessionnaire.

    3) de Sadijé à Hanékin ;

    4) de Zubéir à un point du Golfe Persique à déterminer
d'un commun accord entre le Gouvernement Impérial
Ottoman et le Concessionnaire, ainsi que de toutes les
dépendances des dites lignes. La ligne principale et
ses embranchements devant suivre un tracé qui sera
approuvé par le Gouvernement Impérial,

à la Société du Chemin de fer Ottoman d'Anatolie aux conditions suivantes :

ARTICLE 2.—La durée de cette Concession sera de quatre-
vingt-dix-neuf ans. Cette durée s'appliquera également aux
lignes d'Angora et de Konia, et elle commencera à courir à
partir de la date de la remise du Firman et l'échange de la
présente Convention.

En ce qui concerne les nouvelles lignes, ce délai de quatre-
vingt-dix-neuf ans commencera à courir, pour chaque Section
distinctement, à partir du moment où le Gouvernement Impérial aura délivré au Concessionnaire les Titres d'Etat en
conformité de l'Art. 35 de la présente Convention.

ARTICLE 3.—Ces lignes, prises dans leur ensemble, sont
partagées en sections de 200 kilom. de longueur pour ce qui
concerne la présentation des plans et projets définitifs. Le
Concessionnaire devra, dans un délai de trois mois à partir de
la date de la remise du Firman de Concession et l'échange de la
présente Convention et du Cahier des Charges (et après l'accomplissement des stipulations de l'Art. 35) présenter au
Ministère des Travaux Publics les plans et projets complets
après études définitives et conformément aux prescriptions du
Cahier des Charges de la première section d'une longueur de
200 kilom., partant de Konia et passant par ou aussi près que
possible de Karaman et d'Eregli conformément au tracé de la
ligne de Bagdad. Quant aux autres sections, les plans et
projets y relatifs seront présentés dans un délai de huit mois à
partir de la date à laquelle commencera le délai de Concession
de chaque Section par la mise à exécution des stipulations de
l'Art. 35 afférentes à chaque section.

Ces plans et projets devront être examinés par le Ministère
et, selon le cas approuvés tels quels, ou modifiés, s'il y a lieu,
dans le délai de trois mois à partir de la date de leur présentation. Passé ce délai, si le Gouvernement Impérial n'a pas

notifié sa décision au Concessionnaire, celui-ci pourra considérer comme approuvés les projets présentés par lui et il procèdera à l'exécution de ses travaux. Si le Gouvernement Impérial apporte à ces projets des modifications de nature à entrainer des retards de plus d'un mois, dans l'approbation des plans, le délai fixé pour la construction sera prolongé d'une période égale à celle du retard causé par l'examen de ces modifications et l'approbation des plans.

Les affectations spéciales destinées à la première section de 200 kilom. partant de Konia et passant par ou aussi près que possible de Karaman et d'Eregli, sont déterminées par l'annexe I (Convention Financière) faisant partie intégrante de la présente Convention.

ARTICLE 4.—Le Concessionnaire s'engage à commencer à ses frais, risques et périls les travaux de cette première section, dans un délai de trois mois à partir de la date de l'approbation des plans et projets de ces 200 premiers kilom. et à les terminer, de même, dans un délai de deux ans au plus tard à partir de la même date.

Le Concessionnaire s'engage à commencer les travaux dans un délai de trois mois à partir de la date d'approbation des plans et projets relatifs aux autres sections, et à terminer l'ensemble de la ligne et ses embranchements, dans un délai de 8 ans à partir de la date de la remise du Firman et de l'échange de la présente Convention.   Toutefois, tous retards apportés dans la mise à exécution des stipulations de l'Art. 35 pour une section quelconque, c'est-à-dire tous retards apportés dans la remise des titres par le Gouvernement Impérial au Concessionnaire seront ajoutés au dit délai de huit années.   Les travaux devront être exécutés conformément aux règles de l'art et aux prescriptions du Cahier des Charges ci-annexé, ainsi qu'aux dispositions des plans et projets approuvés; toutefois, en cas de force majeure, les délais d'exécution seront prolongés d'une durée égale à celle de l'interruption des travaux, à la condition que le Concessionnaire avisera immédiatement les autorités locales, ainsi que le Ministère des Travaux Publics.

Seront également considérés comme cas de force majeure, une guerre entre Puissances Européennes, ainsi qu'un changement capital dans la situation financière de l'Allemagne, de l'Angleterre ou de la France.

ARTICLE 5.— Le Ministère des Travaux Publics contrôlera les travaux par l'intermédiaire d'un ou plusieurs Commissaires durant leur exécution, à l'achèvement des Travaux et avant leur réception. Ce contrôle s'appliquera, de même, à l'exploitation et au bon entretien des travaux pendant la durée de la Concession.

Le Concessionnaire déposera chaque année, à l'ordre du Ministère des Travaux Publics, et à titre de frais de contrôle, une somme de deux-cent-soixante-dix piastres or par kilom., payable mensuellement, et ce, à partir de la date fixée pour le commencement des travaux jusqu'à la fin de la Concession.

ARTICLE 6.—L'entreprise étant d'utilité publique, les terrains nécessaires à l'établissement du Chemin de fer et de ses dépendances, les carrières et les ballastières nécessaires au Chemin de fer et appartenant à des particuliers, seront pris, conformément à la loi sur l'expropriation, toutes les fois qu'une entente ne pourra pas être établie entre le Concessionnaire et les propriétaires pour l'achat de ces terrains.

Le Gouvernement fera procéder à l'expropriation et à la remise au Concessionnaire des terrains nécessaires à l'établissement de la voie et de ses dépendances, après que le tracé du Chemin de fer aura été approuvé et appliqué sur le terrain. Cette remise sera faite par le Gouvernement dans le délai de deux mois.

Les terrains nécessaires pour l'occupation temporaire pendant les travaux seront livrés au Concessionnaire par les Autorités locales à charge pour lui d'en indemniser les propriétaires.

Si dans les dits terrains nécessaires à l'établissement du Chemin de fer et de ses dépendances, il se trouve des terrains dits Arazii-Emiriéi-Halié, ceux-ci seront abandonnés gratuitement au Concessionnaire.

Si dans une zône de 15 kilom. de chaque côté du Chemin de fer, il se trouve des terrains dits Arazii-Emiriéi-Halié et que dans ceux-ci se trouve des carrières et ballastières, le Concessionnaire pourra les exploiter gratuitement pendant la période de la construction, à charge pour lui de les fermer, une fois les travaux achevés; dans le cas où le Concessionnaire désirerait faire usage de ces carrières et ballastières pendant la période d'exploitation, il devra se conformer aux règlements régissant la matière et payer la redevance fixée à cet égard.

L'occupation temporaire de ces terrains, durant les travaux de construction, lui sera également accordée à titre gratuit.

ARTICLE 7.—Les lignes seront construites à une seule voie; cependant les terrains seront acquis en vue de l'établissement d'une seconde voie. Aussitôt que les recettes brutes kilométriques atteindront annuellement le chiffre de 30,000 Frcs., le Gouvernement Impérial aura le droit de réclamer l'établissement de la seconde voie que le Concessionnaire sera tenu de construire à ses frais.

ARTICLE 8.—Le matériel de la voie et les matériaux, fers, bois, houille, machines, voitures et wagons et autres approvisionnements nécessaires au premier établissement ainsi qu'aux agrandissements et augmentations en général du Chemin de fer et de ses dépendances, que le Concessionnaire achètera dans l'Empire ou qu'il fera venir de ·l'étranger, seront exempts de tous impôts intérieurs et de tous droits de douane. La franchise des droits de douane est aussi accordée pour la houille nécessaire à l'exploitation et que le Concessionnaire ferait venir de l'étranger jusqu'à ce que les recettes brutes de la ligne et de ses embranchements atteignent 15,500 Frcs. par kilom.   De même pendant toute la durée de la Concession, le sol, fonds et revenu du .Chemin de fer et de ses dépendances ne seront passibles d'aucun impôt, et il ne sera perçu aucun droit de timbre sur la présente Convention et le Cahier des Charges annexé, sur les Conventions additionnelles et tous actes subséquents, ou pour le service des titres d'État à émettre; sur les montants encaissés par le Concessionnaire du chef du forfait d'exploitation, ni aucun droit sur ses actions, ses actions de priorité et ses obligations, comme aussi sur les Titres que le Gouvernement Impérial Ottoman délivrera au Concessionnaire.

Le Concessionnaire sera soumis aux droits de timbre pour toutes ses opérations autres que celles pour lesquelles la franchise lui est accordée dans le présent Article.

Le Concessionnaire formera une Société Anonyme Ottomane sous le nom de "Société Impériale Ottomane du Chemin de fer de Bagdad" qui remplacera la Société du Chemin de fer Ottoman d'Anatolie pour tout ce qui concerne la nouvelle ligne de Konia au Golf Persique, avec ses embranchements et qui sera régie par les statuts ci-annexés.

La Société du Chemin de fer Ottoman d'Anatolie s'engage à ne jamais céder ui transférer à une autre Société les lignes existantes de Haidar-Pacha à Angora et à Konia.

La Société Impériale Ottomane du Chemin de fer de Bagdad, qui sera formée, prend de même l'engagement de ne céder ni transférer, les lignes à construire de Konia à Bagdad et à Bassorah et ses embranchements.

ARTICLE 9.—Les matériaux de construction et autres nécessaires pour la construction et l'exploitation de cette ligne et de ses embranchements, ainsi que les agents et ouvriers seront transportés, seulement pendant la durée de la construction et sous la surveillance du Ministère de la Marine, sur le Chatt-el-

Arab, le Tigre et l'Euphrate, avec des navires à vapeur ou à voiles ou autres embarcations qui seront procurées ou louées par la Société.

Ce matériel de transport jouira de l'exemption de droits de douane, impôts et autres.

ARTICLE 10.—Les bois et charpantes nécessaires à la construction et à l'exploitation du Chemin de fer pourront être coupés dans les forêts des régions voisines appartenant à l'État, conformément au règlement y relatif.

ARTICLE 11.—Aussitôt que le Concessionnaire notifiera au Ministère des Travaux Publics l'achèvement des travaux d'une section, celui-ci fera inspecter les travaux exécutés par une Commission technique nommée à cet effet, et procédera à la réception provisoire, s'il y a lieu ; un an après la réception provisoire, une seconde inspection des travaux sera faite par une Commission technique, et dans le cas où il sera constaté que les travaux ont été exécutés conformément aux règles de l'art et aux prescriptions du Cahier des Charges, le Ministère des Travaux Publics prononcera sur le rapport de la Commission la réception définitive.

Le Concessionnaire aura le droit d'ouvrir les lignes à l'exploitation par sections successives après leur réception provisoires. Les longueurs de ces sections achevées, à partir de Konia, d'Adana, de Bagdad, de Bassorah, comme aussi des différents points intermédiaires, seront d'au moins 40 kilom. et devront aboutir à une station.

ARTICLE 12.—Dans le cas où le Gouvernement Impérial deciderait l'exécution d'embranchements reliant le Chemin de fer faisant l'objet de la présente Convention à la mer, en un point situé entre Mersine et Tripolie de Syrie, il ne pourra accorder la Concession des dits embranchements, qu'exclusivement au Concessionnaire sous réserve toutefois de sauvegarder les droits déjà accordés à la Société du Chemin de fer de Damas-Hamah et Prolongements.

Toutefois, si le Concessionnaire, dans un délai maximum d'une année compté à partir de la notification qui lui en serait faite par le Gouvernement Impérial, n'acceptait pas de construire le ou les embranchements en question aux clauses et conditions de la présente Concession, ou qu'ayant accepté, il ne les exécutait pas dans les délais arrêtés entre le Gouvernement Impérial et le Concessionnaire, ce dernier sera déchu de tout droit aux dits embranchements, et le Gouvernement Impérial pourra en accorder la concession à des tiers.

Le Concessionnaire aura en outre le droit de préférence à conditions égales, pour les embranchements suivants:

a) vers Marach;
b) vers Aintab;
c) vers Birédjik;
d) vers Mardin;
e) vers Erbil;
f) du Diala vers Salahié et Touzkourmatli;
g) de El-Badj à Hit.

Ce droit de préférence pour les sept embranchements spécifiés ci-dessus, pour être valable, est subordonné aux conditions suivantes, savoir:

Si le Gouvernement Impérial décidait d'une manière définitive d'accorder à des tiers la concession d'un de ces embranchements le Concessionnaire est obligé dans un délai de neuf mois à partir de la date de la notification qui lui en sera faite par le Ministère du Commerce et des Travaux Publics, de déclarer au Gouvernement Impérial Ottoman s'il veut assumer cette concession aux conditions acceptées par les tiers dont il vient d'être parlé.

ARTICLE 13.—Le Concessionnaire aura le droit d'établir et d'exploiter sur la ligne, avec la permission des autorités locales, des tuileries et des briqueteries. Les machines et outils destinés aux dites fabriques, jouiront des mêmes exemptions accordées au matériel et outillage de Chemin de fer. Le charbon qui sera consommé dans ces fabriques jouira de la franchise du droit de douane.

Ces fabriques feront gratuitement retour à l'État à l'expiration de la Concession.

ARTICLE 14.—Pendant toute la durée de la Concession, le Concessionnaire est obligé de tenir dans un parfait état d'entretien à ses frais, le Chemin de fer et ses dépendances, ainsi que son matériel fixe et roulant, faute de quoi, il sera procédé à son égard, conformément à l'Art., 16 du Cahier des Charges.

ARTICLE 15.—Le Concessionnaire est tenu de se conformer, quant à ce qui concerne la police et la sécurité de la voie, aux lois et règlements actuellement en vigueur et à promulguer, à l'avenir, dans l'Empire Ottoman.

Le Gouvernement Impérial prendra les mesures nécessaires pour le maintien de l'ordre le long de la ligne et sur les chantiers de construction.

Dans le cas d'interruption du service des transports sur une partie ou sur la totalité de la voie, par la faute du Concessionnaire, le Gouvernement Impérial prendra aux frais, risques et périls du Concessionnaire, les mesures nécessaires conformément à l'Art. 16 du Cahier des Charges pour assurer provisoirement l'exploitation.

ARTICLE 16.—Le Concessionnaire aura le droit de percevoir des droits de péage, conformément aux tarifs du Cahier des Charges, à partir de la réception provisoire de chaque section du Chemin de fer jusqu'à l'expiration de la Concession.

ARTICLE 17.—Le transport des militaires des Armées de terre et de mer, voyageant en corps ou isolément, tant en temps de guerre qu'en temps de paix, ainsi que du matériel et approvisionnements de guerre, des prisonniers et condamnés, des agents de l'État, des valises postales, sera effectué conformément aux prescriptions du Titre V du Cahier des Charges.

ARTICLE 18.—Comme garantie de l'exécution des présents engagements, le Concessionnaire devra, dans le délai de trois mois à partir du jour où la promulgation du Firman de Concession lui sera notifiée officiellement, déposer à une Banque de Constantinople agréée par le Gouvernement, et à titre de cautionnement une somme de Ltqs. 30,000 en numéraire ou en titres de l'État ou d'une Société Anonyme Ottomane ou garantie par l'État, au cours du jour.

Si le dépôt se fait en titres, la Banque fera prendre l'engagement de parfaire la différence en cas de baisse de prix. Aussitôt après le dépôt du cautionnement, le Firman de Concession sera remis au Concessionnaire.

Le cautionnement ne sera restitué qu'à la réception définitive des travaux et proportionnellement à la longueur des sections livrées à l'exploitation ; si dans le délai de trois mois précité, le Concessionnaire n'effectue pas le dépôt susénoncé, il sera déchu sans aucune mise en demeure préalable de tous droits à la Concession.

Dans le cas où l'exécution des stipulations de l'Art. 35 ne pourrait avoir lieu, le Concessionnaire aura le droit de toucher son cautionnement sans aucune formalité et sans qu'il ait à demander le consentement préalable du Gouvernement.

ARTICLE 19.—Le Gouvernement Impérial Ottoman conserve la faculté de reprendre la Concession à quelque époque que cela soit de la ligne de Konia à Bassorah et embranchements, moyennant le paiement au Concessionnaire jusqu'à la fin de la Concession, d'une somme annuelle équivalente aux 50% des recettes brutes moyennes des cinq années qui précèderont l'année de la reprise de la Concession, sans que la dite somme annuelle puisse être inférieure à Frcs. 12,000 par kilom. Dans ce cas le Gouvernement Impérial Ottoman devra rembourser entièrement et en une seule fois les Titres d'État qui auront été accordés au Concessionnaire et qui n'auraient pas été amortis antérieurement, et la somme annuelle à laquelle le Concessionnaire a droit en vertu du présent Article, sera diminuée de l'annuité des dits Emprunts, à savoir de Frcs. 11,000 par kilom. Le Gouvernement assurera au- Concessionnaire le paiement régulier aux époques determinées, du solde lui revenant du chef de la reprise de Concession qui fera l'objet d'une Convention spéciale.

Il sera procédé à la remise des lignes et de toutes leurs dépendances au Gouvernement, ainsi qu'à l'achat par ce dernier du matériel, matériaux et approvisionnements existants conformément à l'Art. 19 du Cahier des Charges.

En cas de reprise de la Concession de la ligne, si le Gouvernement Impérial ne juge pas convenable d'exploiter par ses propres agents, il n'en cèdera pas l'exploitation à une autre Société, mais il promet de la faire exploiter par le Concessionnaire par voie de bail.

ARTICLE 20.—A l'expiration de la Concession de chaque section le Gouvernement Impérial sera substitué à tous les droits du Concessionnaire sur le Chemin de fer et ses dépendances, ainsi que sur le matériel et matériaux et entrera en jouissance des produits y afférents.

Il sera procédé à la remise des lignes et de leurs dépendances libres de toute dette et engagement, au Gouvernement Impérial et à l'achat par ce dernier du matériel et approvisionnements conformément à l'Art. 20 du Cahier des Charges.

ARTICLE 21.—Les employés et agents du Chemin de fer porteront la tenue qui sera fixée et adoptée par le Gouvernement Impérial ; ils porteront tous le fez et ils seront, autant que possible choisis parmi les sujets ottomans.

Cinq ans après la date de l'ouverture à l'exploitation de chaque section tout le personnel exécutif de l'exploitation de chaque section, sauf les fonctionnaires supérieurs, devra être exclusivement composé de sujets ottomans.

ARTICLE 22.—Le Concessionnaire pourra exploiter les mines qu'il aura découvertes dans une zône de 20 kilom. de chaque côté de l'axe de la voie, en se conformant aux lois et règlements y relatifs, et sans que cela constitue pour lui un privilège ou un monopole.

Il pourra de même opérer des coupes dans les forêts avoisinant la ligne, soit pour faire du bois de charpente, soit pour faire du charbon, après recours à l'Administration compétente et en se conformant aux règlements régissant la matière.

ARTICLE 23.—Le Concessionnaire aura la faculté de construire à ses frais à Bagdad, Bassorah et au point terminus de l'embranchement partant de Zubéir, des ports avec toutes les installations nécessaires pour l'accostage à quai, des navires, et l'embarquement, le débarquement et le magasinage des marchandises.

Le projet de ces ports devra être présenté dans un délai maximum de huit ans, à partir de l'échange de la présente Convention, et les travaux de chaque port devront être achevés au plus tard dans douze ans à partir de la date du commencement des travaux de chaque section où se trouve le port respectif.

Aux projets seront joints les tarifs à appliquer.

Ces trois ports feront partie intégrante du Chemin de fer, et les recettes nettes en seront versées au compte des recettes brutes du Chemin de fer.

A l'expiration de la Concession, ces ports et leurs dépendances feront gratuitement retour à l'État.

Dans le cas où le Concessionnaire n'exécuterait pas l'un ou l'autre de ces ports dans le délai ci-dessus, le Gouvernement Impérial pourra en accorder la concession à des tiers.

En tous cas le Concessionnaire pourra pendant la période de construction du Chemin de fer, établir en ces trois points, ainsi que dans le port de Castaboul, des installations provisoires pour le débarquement des matériaux destinés au Chemin de fer.

Ces installations devront, si le Gouvernement Impérial en fait la demande, être supprimées après l'achèvement des travaux.

ARTICLE 24.—Le Concessionnaire pourra, également, établir et exploiter, là où le besoin s'en fera sentir et sur les terrains faisant partie du domaine du Chemin de fer, des dépôts et magasins dont l'usage sera facultatif pour le public.

Ces dépôts, magasins et autres installations fixes deviendront propriété du Gouvernement à l'expiration de la Concession, en conformité de l'Art. 20 du Cahier des Charges.

Le Gouvernement aura une participation de 25% dans les recettes nettes de ces dépôts et magasins.

ARTICLE 25.—Le Concessionnaire est autorisé à utiliser gratuitement le long des lignes, les forces hydrauliques naturelles dont le droit de jouissance n'appartient à personne, ou à créer, destinées à produire l'énergie électrique pour la traction des trains, leur éclairage et pour l'usage des differents services de l'exploitation.   Les plans et projets des travaux à exécuter dans ce but seront soumis à l'approbation du Ministère du Commerce et des Travaux Publics.

Dans le cas où on ferait usage de cette énergie électrique, les 50% de l'économie résultant de ce chef dans les frais d'exploitation seront portés au crédit du Gouvernement Impérial Ottoman.

Toutes ces installations feront gratuitement retour à l'État, à l'expiration de la Concession.

ARTICLE 26.—Le Gouvernement pourra faire élever, à ses frais, des retranchements et travaux de défense sur les points de la ligne principale ou de ses embranchements et où il le jugera nécessaire.

ARTICLE 27.—Les objets d'art et antiquités découverts pendant les travaux, seront soumis aux règlements régissant la matière.

Toutefois, le Concessionnaire sera dispensé de la formalité de présenter une demande et d'obtenir une autorisation pour les recherches.

ARTICLE 28.—Le Concessionnaire est tenu de présenter au Ministère des Travaux Publics un état mensuel de toutes les recettes ; ces états seront dressés conformément aux indications de l'Art. 17 du Cahier des Charges.

ARTICLE 29.—Le Chemin de fer étant considéré comme divisé en sections de 200 kilom. de longueur, si le Concessionnaire, à moins d'un cas de force majeure dûment constaté, n'avait pas commencé les travaux dans les délais fixés, ou s'il ne terminait pas les travaux d'une section dans les délais fixés, ou s'il interrompait le service des transports, ou enfin s'il n'exécutait pas, pour une section quelconque, les autres principaux engagements découlant de la présente Convention, le Gouvernement Impérial fera au Concessionnaire une mise en demeure indiquant lesquelles des susdites obligations restent à remplir par le Concessionnaire, et si ce dernier, dans l'espace de 18 mois à partir de la date de cette mise en demeure, ne lui a pas donné la suite qu'elle comporte, il sera déchu de ses droits concessionnels pour toute section de ligne pour laquelle il aura été dûment constaté en défaut et il sera procédé à son égard en conformité de l'Art. 18 du Cahier des Charges.

Il est entendu que tant que la ligne principale entre Konia et Bagdad ne sera pas achevée en son entier, le Concessionnaire ne pourra pas mettre en exploitation les parties de la ligne de Bagdad à Bassorah qu'il aurait construites.

Pendant cette période de non exploitation des sections comprises entre Bagdad et Bassorah, le Concessionnaire remboursera au Gouvernement Impérial à l'échéance des annuités, l'annuité de 11,000 Frcs. par kilom. payée pour intérêts et amortissement des Titres que le Gouvernement Impérial lui aura remis pour les dites sections, et il ne touchera naturellement pas les frais d'exploitation; mais ces clauses n'infirment en rien les autres droits du Concessionnaire sur la ligne de Bagdad à Bassorah.

La déchéance prononcée sur une ou plusieurs sections du Chemin de fer ne portera aucune atteinte aux droits du Concessionnaire, quant au reste des sections des nouvelles lignes, non plus que quant à l'ensemble des anciennes lignes.

ARTICLE 30.—Le Concessionnaire établira gratuitement sur les points désignés par le Gouvernement, les locaux nécessaires aux bureaux des Commissaires Impériaux du Chemin de fer et des employés de la Douane, des Postes et de la Police.

Le Concessionnaire établira dans les stations importantes, après entente avec le Ministère du Commerce et des Travaux Publics, deux chambres avec Water-Closet pour le service postal.

ARTICLE 31.—Le Concessionnaire pourra établir, à ses frais, sur tout le parcours de la voie, des poteaux et des fils télégraphiques; cette ligne ne pourra pas servir aux correspondances privées n'ayant pas trait à l'exploitation du Chemin de fer.

Le Gouvernement Impérial se réserve le droit de faire contrôler à tout moment par des inspecteurs délégués par le Ministère des Postes et Télégraphes, toute la correspondance télégraphique effectuée par les fils de la Société.

Le Gouvernement pourra faire usage des poteaux du Chemin de fer pour l'établissement d'un et au besoin de deux fils télégraphiques, et les poteaux du Chemin de fer seront établis de façon à pouvoir supporter ces deux fils supplémentaires ainsi que ceux de la Société. En cas de besoin le Gouvernement aura le droit de faire établir à ses frais d'autres poteaux sur le parcours de la voie, ou d'installer, en cas de rupture et de dérangement de ses lignes, des télégraphistes dans les stations pour la transmission par les lignes télégraphiques du Chemin de fer des dépêches officielles importantes et urgentes, à la condition toutefois, de n'apporter aucune entrave au service du Chemin de fer.

ARTICLE 32.—Le Concessionnaire aura le droit de faire transporter, avec ses propres moyens de transport et sans payer aucune taxe à l'Administration des Postes de l'Empire, les correspondances et valises concernant exclusivement le service du Chemin de fer; mais à la condition de les soumettre, suivant la règle, au contrôle des agents de l'Administration des Postes. Les lettres privées du personnel seront soumises aux taxes postales. Le Concessionnaire ne pourra effectuer le transport de lettres de cette nature qu'en se soumettant aux prescriptions du Règlement intérieur des Postes en vigueur dans l'Empire. Il aura également le droit de faire transporter et, sans leur appliquer aucune taxe, les objets et matières de consommation, tels que houille, graisses, les matériaux et le matériel nécessaires à la construction, à l'entretien et à l'exploitation du Chemin de fer, tant sur les lignes existantes que sur les lignes faisant l'objet de la présente Convention.

ARTICLE 33.—Le Gouvernement Impérial s'engage à faire desservir par l'Administration de la Mahsoussé la ligne de Haidar-Pacha à Sirkedji et au pont de Karakeuy par trois bateaux neufs ayant, en service, une vitesse moyenne à l'heure d'au moins 14 milles de 1855 mètres.

Si dans un délai de un an compté à partir de la date de l'échange de la présente Convention, l'Administration de la Mahsoussé n'organisait pas le service dans les conditions indiquées ci-dessus, le Concessionnaire aura le droit de faire le transport des voyageurs et des marchandises entre les dits points, à la condition de choisir les équipages de ces bateaux, parmi les anciens officiers et marins de la Flotte Impériale ou parmi les élèves diplômés de l'Ecole Navale Impériale.

Les bateaux du Concessionnaire feront leur service au lieu et place de ceux de l'Administration de la Mahsoussé, tout en restant exclusivement affectés au susdit service de transport, et le Concessionnaire versera annuellement à cette Administration, une somme égale aux 5% des recettes brutes afférentes aux transports de voyageurs et de marchandises effectués par lui entre les points susmentionnés.

De l'excédant des recettes brutes, on déduira:

1. les frais d'exploitation;

2. une annuité de 8,30% du capital de premier établissement affecté à l'acquisition des bateaux; après avoir défalqué

les dites sommes, le restant sera porté au compte des recettes brutes des nouvelles lignes garanties.

Le montant du capital de premier établissement sera arrêté après l'achat des bateaux.

Il est bien entendu que si les recettes brutes d'une année ne permettent pas de faire face aux frais précités, la Société n'aura rien à réclamer du Gouvernement Impérial.

Par contre, elle pourra prélever le déficit sur les recettes des années suivantes.

Les bateaux du Concessionnaire étant considérés comme une section de la Mahsoussé, ils jouiront des mêmes droits que celle-ci.

ARTICLE 34.—La Société Concessionnaire, et celle que cette dernière constituera étant anonymes Ottomanes, toutes contestations et différends qui surviendraient, soit entre le Gouvernement Impérial et le Concessionnaire ou la Société, soit entre le Concessionnaire ou la Société et les particuliers, par suite de l'exécution ou de l'interprétation de la présente Convention et du Cahier des Charges y annexé, seront déférés aux Tribunaux compétents Ottomans.

La nouvelle Société étant Ottomane, elle devra correspondre avec les Départements de l'État en langue turque, qui est la langue officielle du Gouvernement Impérial Ottoman.

ARTICLE 35.—Le Gouvernement Impérial garantit au Concessionnaire, par kilom. construit et exploité, une annuité de 11,000 Frcs. ainsi qu'une somme forfaitaire de 4,500 Frcs. par année et par kilom. exploité pour frais d'exploitation.

Cette annuité de 11,000 Frcs. sera représentée par un Emprunt de l'État Ottoman, portant 4% d'intérêt et 0,087,538% d'amortissement, amortissable pendant la durée de la Concession. Le Concessionnaire aura donc droit à un montant nominal de Frcs. 269,110,65 de cet Emprunt d'État, pour chaque kilom. construit et exploité, sans que le Concessionnaire puisse demander d'autres sommes de ce chef au Gouvernement Impérial Ottoman.

Le montant total nominal de Titres de l'État revenant au Concessionnaire en conformité de ce qui précède, lui sera remis par le Gouvernement Impérial Ottoman, à la signature de chaque Convention spéciale pour chaque section, mais le Concessionnaire devra bonifier au Gouvernement Impérial Ottoman, les sommes que celui-ci aura payées pendant la période de construction, pour le service des Titres remis au Concessionaire, c'est-à-dire jusqu'à la date de la réception provisoire de chaque section du Chemin de fer. Ces sommes seront remises par le Concessionnaire entre les mains de la Dette Publique, pour le compte du Gouvernement Impérial Ottoman.

Le Gouvernement Impérial se réserve le droit de modifier à tout moment le système de paiement de l'annuité kilométrique de Frcs. 11,000 fixée au 1er alinéa du présent Article, après remboursement des Titres d'État émis en représentation de la dite annuité.

Aussitôt que le développement du trafic et des recettes et la situation financière, permettront l'émission de titres privés par le Concessionnaire lui-même, destinés à remplacer les titres d'État qui lui auront été délivrés par le Gouvernement Impérial, le Concessionnaire se mettra d'accord avec le Gouvernement Impérial pour procéder à cet effet.

Pour la première section de 200 kilomètres au delà de Konia, le montant nominal des Titres à remettre par le Gouvernement Impérial Ottoman au Concessionnaire, est fixé à 54,000,000 de Frcs. Mais lors de la réception définitive de cette section, et aussitôt que la longueur de la ligne exécutée sera arrêtée, on établira le montant nominal exact des Titres à raison de Frcs. 269,110,65 par kilom. qui sera acquis au Concessionnaire pour cette section. Le surplus du montant nominal, sera calculé au cours d'émission, plus les intérêts 4% courus jusqu'au jour du paiement, et sera versé en effectif, par le Concessionnaire, au Trésor Impérial. Il est bien entendu que ce calcul sera fait au minimum à 81½%.

La Société du Chemin de fer Ottoman d'Anatolie se porte garante vis-à-vis du Gouvernement Impérial Ottoman pour la construction de la dite première section de 200 kilom. jusqu'à l'achèvement des travaux de cette section.

Dans le cas où le Gouvernement Impérial Ottoman le jugera nécessaire, il pourra aussi demander à la Société du Chemin de fer Ottoman d'Anatolie de se porter garante pour d'autres sections et la Société du Chemin de fer Ottoman d'Anatolie aura le droit de le faire.

La somme forfaitaire pour frais d'exploitation, de Frcs. 4,500 par an et par kilom. exploité, sera garantie au Concessionnaire par une Convention spéciale pour chaque section, simultanément avec la Convention qui règlera l'annuité de 11,000 Frcs.

En ce qui concerne la rem ère section de 200 kilom. au delà de Konia, cette somme fprfaitaire de 4,500 Frcs. par kilom. et par an, est garantie au Concessionnaire par les excédents des garanties actuellement affectées aux lignes de la Société du Chemin de fer Ottoman d'Anatolie.

Le service des Titres de l'État à émettre pour la dite annuité kilométrique de 11,000, Frcs. sera assuré par les affectations spéciales, déterminées d'un commun accord avec le Gouvernement Impérial avant la mise à exécution de chaque section.

En outre, la Société Impériale Ottomane du Chemin de fer

de Bagdad, de son côté, affecte en gage d'une façon irrévocable et inaliénable, aux porteurs de ces mêmes titres, la ligne de Konia au Golfe Persique et ses embranchements, avec leur matériel roulant. Elle affecte pareillement et pour le même objet, sa part dans les recettes de cette ligne, après paiement des frais d'exploitation, mais les porteurs des Titres n'auront aucun droit de s'immiscer dans l'Administration de la Société.

La dite part des recettes, déduction faite des frais d'exploitation, tels que cette part et ces frais seront établis par les comptes de la Société, sera, en cas de besoin, versée annuellement par celle-ci à l'Administration de la Dette Publique Ottomane, pour le compte du service des Titres. Le Gouvernement Impérial Ottoman remboursera à la Société les sommes que celle-ci pourrait avoir fournies de ce chef, pour compte du service des Titres émis. Le Gouvernement Impérial Ottoman affecte encore d'une façon irrévocable et inaliénable, aux porteurs des Titres d'État précités, la part lui revenant dans les recettes brutes de la dite ligne.

Si la recette kilométrique brute de la ligne, dépasse 4,500 Frcs. mais sans dépasser 10,000 Frcs., l'excédent au delà de 4,500 Frcs. reviendra entièrement au Gouvernement.

Si la recette kilométrique brute dépasse 10,000 Frcs., la partie jusqu'à 10,000 Frcs. devant toujours être partagée comme il est dit plus haut, les 60% de l'excédent au delà de ces 10,000 Frcs. reviendront au Gouvernement Impérial et les 40% à la Société.

Il est bien entendu que si la recette kilométrique brute n'atteint pas 4,500 Frcs., la somme nécessaire pour parfaire la différence de ce chiffre sera payée au Concessionnaire par le Gouvernement en même temps que l'annuité de Frcs. 11,000 sur les affectations spéciales à déterminer d'un commun accord entre le Gouvernement Impérial et le Concessionnaire, avant la mise à exécution par le Concessionnaire des clauses de la présente Convention afférente à chaque section.

Les dites affectations seront encaissées et payées par les soins de l'Administration de la Dette Publique Ottomane.

Pour les Titres d'État à émettre pour l'exécution des différentes sections du Chemin de fer, masse commune sera faite des recettes revenant au Gouvernement Impérial, de façon à ce que le montant disponible reste affecté à la communauté de ces mêmes Titres dans la proportion du montant primitif nominal de chaque émission.

Aussitôt après le paiement des coupons et de l'amortissement des Titres d'État émis, le surplus des recettes appartenant au Gouvernement Impérial Ottoman, sera versé à celui-ci chaque année, après accomplissement des formalités prévues à l'Art. 40 de la présente Convention.

ARTICLE 36. — Pour pouvoir déterminer la moyenne des recettes kilométriques des nouvelles lignes de Bagdad, il sera fait masse, au fur et à mesure de la mise en exploitation des sections des nouvelles lignes, de toutes les recettes afférentes à toutes les parties des nouvelles lignes, ainsi que des recettes nettes prévues aux Articles 23 et 33 de la présente Convention.

La moyenne des recettes brutes kilométriques ainsi obtenue servira de base pour déterminer le montant des sommes à payer en conformité de l'Art. 35.

ARTICLE 37. — Le Concessionnaire prend l'engagement d'exécuter à ses frais, sur les anciennes lignes de Haidar-Pacha à Angora et Eski-Chehir à Konia, toutes les améliorations exigées par l'introduction d'un service de trains express et ce jusqu'à concurrence d'une dépense de huit millions de francs.

En compensation de ces frais et des nouvelles charges extraordinaires qu'entraînera pour l'exploitation, l'introduction du service des trains express, le Gouvernement Impérial reconnaît au Concessionnaire :

1) une annuité de 350,000 Frcs. pendant trente ans pour le service de l'intérêt et de l'amortissement du capital de huit millions de Frcs. ci-dessus.

Cette annuité commencera à courir à partir du commencement des travaux d'amélioration.

2) une annuité de 350,000 Frcs. pour l'établissement des trains express.

Cette dernière annuité ne sera exigible qu'à partir du moment où la ligne principale aboutira à Alep.

Les annuités prévues au présent Article, seront payées à la Société du Chemin de fer Ottoman d'Anatolie sur les affectations actuelles aux garanties de l'ancien réseau, et de la même manière que celles-ci.

ARTICLE 38. — Le Concessionnaire s'engage à construire et à exploiter, aussitôt que le Gouvernement Impérial lui en fera la demande, aux conditions de la présente Convention, un embranchement partant de la ligne Konia-Bassorah, et aboutissant à Diarbékir et à Karpout.

ARTICLE 39. — Le raccordement éventuel de la ligne de Damas-Hamah et Prolongements, avec le réseau faisant l'objet de la présente Convention, aura lieu à Alep.

ARTICLE 40. — Le Concessionnaire remettra au Ministère des Travaux Publics, dans le courant du mois de Janvier de chaque année, les comptes des recettes préalablement vérifiés et approuvés par le Commissaire Impérial sur la base desquels les sommes revenant au Gouvernement Impérial et à la Société seront déterminées en conformité de l'Art. 35 de la présente Convention.

Aussitôt que le montant de la part du Gouvernement dans ces recettes sera établi, la Société Impériale Ottomane du Chemin de fer de Bagdad en fera le versement pour le compte du service des Titres d'État à l'Administration de la Dette Publique Ottomane et celle-ci remettra en effectif au Gouvernement Impérial tout surplus qui restera disponible au delà des sommes exigées pour le paiement du coupon échéant le 1er Juillet[1] de l'exercice en cours.

Le Gouvernement Impérial s'engage de son côté à faire connaître à l'Administration de la Dette Publique dans les deux mois qui suivront la présentation des comptes de recettes d'un exercice, le montant des sommes reconnus dues à la Société pour son paiement immédiat.

ARTICLE 41.—Le Concessionnaire aura la faculté d'établir entre Hamidié et le port de Castaboul, un embranchement provisoire pour transporter le matériel et les matériaux nécessaires au Chemin de fer. Il est toutefois entendu qu'après l'achèvement des travaux faisant l'objet de la présente Convention le Concessionnaire devra, si le Gouvernement Impérial lui en notifie la demande, enlever les rails de cet embranchement provisoire.

Il est bien entendu que durant cette exploitation provisoire le Gouvernement Impérial ne payera pour le dit embranchement, ui annuité, ni frais d'exploitation.

ARTICLE 42.—Les terrains et carrières qui seront expropriés conformément à l'Art. 6 de la Convention, seront de l'étendue strictement nécessaire pour les travaux du Chemin de fer et de toutes ses dépendances, et ne pourront pas être d'une étendue plus grande. Les expropriations se feront sous la surveillance du Ministère des Travaux Publics.

ARTICLE 43.—Tous les matériaux et le matériel nécessaires pour la construction des nouvelles lignes et de toutes leurs dépendances, dont il est question dans l'Art. 8 de la Convention, étant exempts de tous impôts et droits de douane, seront à

---

[1] En vertu d'un bouyroultou Gr. Véziriel en date du 24 Juillet 1319 communiquant l'Iradé Impérial du 20 Juil. 1319, le mot "Juillet" figurant dans l'alinéa 3 (du texte turc et l'alinéa 2 du texte français) de l'Art. 40 de la présente Convention est remplacé par le mot "Septembre."

En foi de quoi cette rectification est faite et signée, Constantinople, le 17 Chaban 1321 25/7 Novembre 1903 (1319).

l'arrivée, inspectées conformément à l'usage, par les employés de la douane.

ARTICLE 44.—Les dépôts et les magasins à construire sur les terrains des stations, conformément à l'Article 24 de la Convention, ne serviront qu'à l'emmagasinement des marchandises à transporter.

Ces dépôts et magasins seront construits conformément aux plans qui seront présentés par le Concessionnaire et approuvés par le Ministère des Travaux Publics.

ARTICLE 45.—Le Concessionnaire devra établir à ses frais, et jusqu'à concurrence d'une dépense totale de quatre millions de Francs les stations militaires qui seraient reconnues nécessaires par le Ministère de la Guerre.   Le nombre, l'emplacement et les dispositions de ces stations militaires et leurs dépendances seront arrêtés après entente entre le Concessionnaire et le Ministère de la Guerre.

ARTICLE 46.—Le Concessionnaire s'engage à verser annuellement à l'Asile des Pauvres, à partir de l'ouverture à l'exploitation de la ligne principale, une somme de 500 Livres Turques.

La présente Convention a été, conformèment à l'Iradé promulgué par Sa Majesté Impériale le Sultan, faite en double, signée et échangée à Constantinople.

La présente Convention, Cahier des Charges[1] et le Firman Impérial seront échangés avec la Convention et Cahier des Charges du 8/21 Janvier 1317 (1902) 11 Chewal 1319 et le Firman Impérial en date du 8 Zilhidjé 1319.

Fait le 20 Février 1318, 5 Mars 1903.

Certifié conforme à l'original.
Le Directeur du Bureau de Traduction
du Ministère du Commerce et des Travaux Publics.

(s.) MOUHIB.

(s) ARTHUR GWINNER.

(s) KURT ZANDER.   (s.) ZIHNI.

(s) HUGUENIN.

[1] The *Cahier des Charges* bears the same signatures and date as the Convention.

CAHIER DES CHARGES.

TITRE I.

PROJETS ET PLANS, TRAVAUX ET MATÉRIEL.

ARTICLE 1.—Le Concessionnaire s'engage à exécuter, à ses frais, risques et périls, et à terminer dans les délais fixés dans la Convention, tous les travaux du Chemin de fer, de manière qu'il soit praticable et exploité dans toutes ses parties.

ARTICLE 2.—Le Concessionnaire devra, conformément à l'Article 3 de la Convention, soumettre au Ministère des Travaux Publics, rapporté sur un plan général à l'échélle de 1/5.000, le tracé du Chemin de fer, les emplacements des stations, les voies de garage, de chargement et de déchargement.

A ce plan seront joints : un profil en long suivant l'axe du Chemin de fer, un certain nombre de profils types de la voie, un tableau des pentes et rampes et les types relatifs aux travaux d'art les plus importants.

Le profil en long sera dressé à l'échelle de 1/5.000 pour les longueurs et de 1/500 pour les hauteurs, dont les côtes seront rapportées au niveau moyen de la mer pris pour plan de comparaison, au-dessous de ce profil, on indiquera au moyen de trois lignes horizontales disposées à cet effet, savoir :—

(a) les distances par mille mètres de longueur du Chemin de fer, comptées à partir de son origine ;

(b) la longueur et l'inclinaison des pentes et rampes ;

(c) la longueur des parties droites et le développement des parties courbes du tracé, en faisant connaître le rayon correspondant à chacune de ces dernières.

Le Concessionnaire présentera en outre un plan général à l'échelle de 1/100.000 et un profil en long à l'échelle de 1/100.000 pour les longueurs et de 1/2.000 pour les hauteurs.

ARTICLE 3.—Les travaux de la ligne seront exécutés pour une seule voie.

ARTICLE 4.—La largeur de la voie entre les bords intérieurs des rails devra être de 1ᵐ 435 à 1ᵐ 455.

La largeur des accotements, c'est-à-dire des parties comprises de chaque côté, entre le bord extérieur du rail et l'arête supérieure du ballast sera de 1 mètre pour une voie ; s'il y a deux voies, l'entrevoie aura deux mètres.

ARTICLE 5.—Le Concessionnaire établira le long du Chemin de fer les fossés, les rigoles et banquettes qui seront jugés nécessaires pour l'écoulement des eaux, l'assainissement de la voie et des chambres d'emprunt, et le maintien des ouvrages.

Le ballast aura une épaisseur de 0^m 40, et les traverses seront métalliques.

La largeur en couronne du terrassement sous le ballast aura 5^m 50. Cette largeur pourra être réduite à 5^m 10 dans les parties difficiles de la ligne. Elle pourra même être réduite à 4^m 50, lorsque les murettes soutenant le ballast reposent sur la maçonnerie ou sur le rocher compact.

ARTICLE 6.—Les alignements seront raccordés entre eux par des courbes dont le rayon ne pourra être inférieur à cinq cents mètres ; une partie droite de 100 m. devra être ménagée entre deux courbes consécutives, lorsqu'elles seront dirigées en sens contraire.

En outre, les courbes devront être raccordées avec les alignements au moyen d'une courbe parabolique dont la moitié sera prise sur l'alignement. La partie droite restant entre les origines des paraboles de raccordements pourra alors être réduite à 10 m., à condition que la rayon de courbure soit augmenté autant que possible.

ARTICLE 7.—Le maximum normal de l'inclinaison des pentes et rampes est fixé à dix-huit millimètres par mètre.

Les raccordements des pentes se feront au moyen de courbes verticales d'un rayon égal à 1000 m.

Les déclivités correspondant aux courbes de faibles rayons devront être réduites autant que faire se pourra.

Le Concessionnaire aura la faculté de proposer aux dispositions de cet Article et à celles de l'Article précédent les modifications qui lui paraîtraient utiles, c'est-à-dire une réduction des rayons de courbure jusqu'à 300 mètres et une augmentation des rampes jusqu'à 25 $8/_{00}$ dans les parties présentant des difficultés spéciales. Mais ces modifications ne pourront être exécutées qu'après avoir été approuvées par la Gouvernement Impérial, et que pour autant qu'elles n'empêcheront pas, en cas de nécessité, de pratiquer une vitesse moyenne de 75 kilomètres à l'heure, arrêts compris, sur l'ensemble de le ligne.

ARTICLE 8.—Les voies d'évitement, de stationnement, de

chargement et de déchargement, devront être en nombre suffisant et seront déterminées par le Gouvernement, sur la proposition du Concessionnaire. Il est stipulé, dès à présent, que la distance moyenne des stations sera d'environ 20 kilomètres. La longueur de la voie d'évitement ne sera pas moindre de 300 m., mesurée entre les poteaux d'arrêt de garage. Dans l'établissement du profil en long, on aura soin de ménager des paliers d'une longueur convenable aux endroits où l'établissement ultérieur de stations nouvelles sera probable.

ARTICLE 9.—Lorsque le Chemin de fer devra traverser des Chemins ou routes qu'il sera nécessaire de conserver pour la communication du pays, on établira des passages en dessus, en dessous ou à niveau, suivant la configuration du terrain.

Lorsque le Chemin de fer devra passer au-dessus d'une route, l'ouverture du viaduc sera fixé, en tenant compte des circonstances locales, par le Gouvernement sur la proposition du Concessionnaire, et pourra varier de 3 à 10 mètres.

Pour les viaducs de forme cintrée, la hauteur sous clef, à partir du sol de la route, sera de 5 mètres au moins (5ᵐ 00) pour ceux qui seront formés de poutres horizontales, en bois ou en fer, la hauteur sous-poutre sera d'au moins 4ᵐ 30.

La largeur entre les parapets des viaducs sera au moins de 4ᵐ 50 pour une voie et de 8ᵐ pour deux voies.

Lorsque le Chemin de fer devra passer au-dessous d'une route, la largeur entre les parapets du pont qui supporte la route, sera fixée par le Gouvernement en tenant compte des circonstances locales et variera de 3 m. à 10 m. suivant l'importance de la route.

L'ouverture du pont entre les culées sera au moins de 4ᵐ 50 pour une voie et 8 m. au moins pour deux voies; la distance verticale ménagée au-dessus des rails extérieurs jusqu'à la clef de la voûte, pour le passage des trains, ne sera pas inférieure à 4ᵐ 80.

Dans le cas où les routes seraient traversées à leur niveau par le Chemin de fer, les rails devront être posés sans aucune saillie ni dépression sur la surface de ces routes, et de télle sorte qu'il n'en résulte aucune gêne pour la circulation des voitures.

Les passages à niveau ne seront pourvus de barrières que sur les points où l'utilité de gardiennage, démontrés par la fréquentation de la route, sera reconnue par le Gouvernement.

Pendant la construction du Chemin de fer, s'il devient nécessaire de détourner ou de modifier l'emplacement ou les profils des routes préexistantes, l'inclinaison des pentes et rampes sur les parties modifiées ne devra pas, dans tous les cas dépasser le maximum de l'inclinaison des anciennes routes.

Dans tous les cas, les passages à niveau devront, dans le sens de l'écoulement des eaux, se raccorder avec les routes par des inclinaisons de 0ᵐ, 02 par mètre au maximum sur 10 mètres au moins de longueur.

ARTICLE 10. — Le Concessionnaire sera tenu de rétablir et d'assurer, à ses frais l'écoulement de toutes les eaux dont le cours serait arrêté, suspendu ou modifié par les travaux ; les débouchés, d'après les règles de l'art, des ponts à construire à la rencontre des rivières, des canaux et des cours d'eau quelconques, seront fixés par le Ministère des Travaux Publics sur la proposition du Concessionnaire.

ARTICLE 11.—Le Concessionnaire n'emploiera, dans l'exécution des travaux, que des matériaux de bonne qualité pris dans la contrée, et il devra se conformer à toutes les règles de l'art, de manière à obtenir une construction parfaitement solide tant des ouvrages que du matériel.

Les ponts et ponceaux à construire sur les cours d'eau ou sur les voies publiques et privées, ainsi que les aqueducs, seront construits en pierre et en fer ou en acier ; le bois ne sera employé que dans les fondations, les tabliers et les longrines à placer sous les rails. Les ponts métalliques de 10 m. de portés et au-delà, seront, avant la réception, soumis à l'épreuve conformément au programme qui sera présenté à l'approbation du Ministère des Travaux Publics, en même temps que les projets de ces ouvrages.

Les ponts métalliques, seront calculés suivant la dernière circulaire du Ministère des Travaux Publics, soit de Prusse, soit de France.

Quelles que soient les déclivités, la longueur des rails en acier sera de 12 mètres, et le poids en sera de 37 kilogrammes 240 par mètre. Les rails reposeront sur quinze traverses en acier de 58 kilogrammes 300.

Les rails seront posés sur des selles sur chaque traverse.

Les rails, traverses, &c. . . . seront du type adopté par les Chemins de fer de l'État Prussien.

En ce qui concerne les dispositions et la construction des bâtiments, des stations et des guérites, il est convenu que les règles de la plus stricte nécessité seront maintenues tout en n'ayant en vue que la commodité et les usages ordinaires du pays.

Les stations seront construites en pierre ou en briques ; elles pourront avoir des toits plats, des planchers en pierre, briques ou béton.

Les talus des remblais, déblais et emprunts, auront une

inclinaison variable déterminée par la nature des terrains. Ces inclinaisons seront, sur la demande du Concessionnaire, déterminées en cours d'exécution par le Ministère des Travaux Publics ou ses délégués.

ARTICLE 12.—Au plan général qui sera présenté, le Concessionaire joindra un tableau faisant connaître la nomenclature détaillée et les principales dispositions des gares d'évitement et de stationnement, des passages à niveau, des ponts et aqueducs, des viaducs par dessus et par dessous le Chemin de fer, et de tous les travaux qu'il se propose de construire.

Les plans des stations et des ouvrages d'art seront dressés à l'échelle de 1/200.

ARTICLE 13.—A la traversée des villes, villages, et aux stations, la voie sera, s'il est jugé nécessaire, séparée des propriétés et des bâtiments riverains par des clôtures.

ARTICLE 14.—Les plans à présenter pour l'expropriation des terrains seront dressés à l'échelle de 1/2000.

ARTICLE 15.—Au fur et à mesure de l'exécution des diverses sections le Concessionnaire fera faire, à ses frais, un bornage contradictoire et un plan cadastral de toutes les parties du Chemin de fer et de ses dépendances.

Il fera également, au fur et à mesure de l'exécution des diverses sections, dresser à ses frais et contradictoirement avec le Gouvernement, un état descriptif des ponts, aqueducs et autres ouvrages d'art exécutés : une expédition authentique des proces-verbaux du bornage, du plan cadastral et de l'état descriptif, sera déposé dans les archives du Ministère des Travaux Publics.

Tous terrains expropriés après ce bornage général, pour travaux complémentaires, seront soumis à la formalité du bornage au fur et à mesure de leur expropriation, et il en sera fait mention dans l'état plus haut indiqué : de même tout ouvrage d'art construit après la remise au Ministère des Travaux Publics de l'état descriptif, y sera indiqué à son achèvement.

TITRE II.

ENTRETIEN ET EXPLOITATION.

ARTICLE 16.—Le Concessionnaire entretiendra toujours en bon état la ligne et ses dépendances, ainsi que le matériel fixe et roulant, de manière que la circulation sur toute son étendue soit toujours facile et sùre, il aura soin d'écarter constamment toute cause qui poùrrait donner lieu à des accidents.

Si le Concessionnaire fait preuve de négligence ou apporte des retards dans l'exécution des présents engagements, il lui sera fait une mise en demeure, et si, dans l'espace d'un mois à partir de la date de la mise en demeure; il ne s'est pas conformé à cette mise 'en demeure, le Gouvernement Impérial y pourvoira d'office, aux frais du Concessionnaire, et procédera aux travaux de réparations nécessaires; les frais de ces travaux seront pris sur les frais d'exploitation et sur certaines recettes revenant au Concessionnaire, et en cas d'insuffisance, le Concessionnaire sera tenu de les parfaire.

ARTICLE 17.—Le Concessionnaire dressera mensuellement et remettra au Ministère des Travaux Publics un état indiquant les recettes de toute nature des lignes et de leurs dépendances.

Dans l'état indiquant les recettes brutes, il sera fait mention des recettes brutes provenant de transports des voyageurs et march andises, ainsi que de tous les autres produits et recettes des lignes proprement dites.   Les taxes afférentes aux transports militaires qui, pourraient être effectués à crédit feront l'objet d'un relevé mensuel séparé.   Leur montant sera porté dans les recettes brutes, après encaissement.

TITRE III.

REPRISE ET DÉCHÉANCE DE LA CONCESSION, FORMALITÉS À REMPLIR À L'EXPIRATION DE LA CONCESSION.

ARTICLE 18.—En cas de déchéance prononcée contre le Concessionnaire, conformément aux dispositions de l'Article 29 de la Convention, il sera pourvu à l'exécution des engagements contractés par le Concessionnaire au moyen d'une adjudication, après mise à prix des ouvrages déjà construits, des objets et du matériel fixe et roulant, qui lui appartiennent, et enfin de tous les matériaux et des terrains achetés par lui; le dernier enchérisseur assumera ainsi l'exécution de tous les engagements incombant au Concessionnaire évincé.

Le Concessionnaire évincé recevra du nouveau Concessionnaire la valeur que l'adjudication aura ainsi déterminée pour les dits objets, après toutefois déduction des frais.   Le reste sera versé pour compte du Gouvernement Impérial, à l'Administration de la Dette Publique, pour être assigné à l'affectation de l'amortissement et intérêts des titres d'État émis pour la section déchue. Si la susdite adjudication n'amène aucun résultat, une seconde adjudication sera tentée après un délai de six mois, et avec une réduction convenable de prix; et si cette seconde tentative reste également sans résultat, le Concessionnaire sera définitivement déchu de ses droits à la présente Concession, et les objets mis en adjudication deviendront, sans aucun paiement, la propriété de l'État.

Le cautionnement non encore restitué sera acquis au Gouvernement.

Article 19.—En cas de reprise de la Concession de la ligne par le Gouvernement Impérial, conformément à l'Article 19 de la Convention, le matériel fixe ainsi que le matériel roulant, tels que locomotives, wagons et chariots, servant à l'exploitation, seront remis gratuitement au Gouvernement Impérial.

Tous les approvisionnements, combustibles et tous objets mobiliers servant à l'exploitation et existant à l'époque de la reprise de la Concession, seront achetés, à dire d'experts, par le Gouvernement Impérial.

Article 20.—A l'expiration de la durée de la Concession de chaque Section, le Concessionnaire devra, sans aucun paiement, livrer en bon état et libres de toute dette et engagement, au Gouvernement Impérial, les stations et voies de chargement et de déchargement ainsi que les batiments d'exploitation, tels que baraques et maisons destinées aux agents chargés du contrôle d'inspection et de la perception, les machines fixes et enfin tous les objets immobiliers et ne servant pas au transport. Le matériel fixe et le matériel roulant, tels que machines, wagons et chariots servant à l'exploitation seront remis gratuitement au Gouvernement Impérial. Le matériel de construction et de réparation, combustibles, approvisionnements, et enfin tous les objets mobiliers servant à l'exploitation existant à l'époque de la reprise de la Concession seront achetés, à dire d'experts, par le Gouvernement Impérial. Toutefois, le Gouvernement Impérial ne sera tenu de prendre que les approvisionnements nécessaires à l'exploitation pendant six mois.

Dans le cas où, cinq années avant l'expiration de la Concession, le Gouvernement Impérial constaterait que la Chemin de fer ne se trouve pas dans un état de bon entretien, il sera fait une mise en demeure au Concessionnaire, et un délai lui sera accordé pour mettre la voie en bon état d'entretien. Si cette mise en demeure n'amène pas de résultat, le Gouvernement prendra en main l'exploitation de la ligne et de ses dépendances et fera exécuter d'office, aux frais du Concessionnaire, les réparations nécessaires pour mettre la voie en bon état. Les frais de réparations seront pris sur les frais d'exploitation et sur certaines recettes revenant au Concessionnaire ; en cas d'insuffisance des recettes, le Concessionnaire sera tenu d'y suppléer.

TITRE IV.

TARIFS ET CONDITIONS RELATIFS AU TRANSPORT DES VOYAGEURS ET DES MARCHANDISES.

ARTICLE 21.—Les droits de transport que le Concessionnaire, en vertu de l'Article 16 de la Convention est autorisé à percevoir, sont déterminés par les tarifs maximum ci-dessous qui ne seront dépassés en aucun cas sans l'autorisation du Gouvernement Impérial. Ces tarifs une fois abaissés ne pourront être relevés dans la limite du maximum qu'après un avis préalable d'un mois. De même, en cas d'abaissement de ces tarifs, il en sera donné avis trois jours à l'avance. Tous les tarifs sont perçus par kilomètre de par cours. Les taxes minima sont comptées pour 8 kilomètres au moins.

Les sommes qui grèvent les envois à titre de remboursement ne sont payées qu'après encaissement, et le Concessionnaire percevra une commission de 2%.

TARIF I.

Voyageurs.

Par tête et par kilomètre (trains mixtes et de Voyageurs) :

1re Classe	Ps. 27 paras
2me Classe	20 paras
3me Classe	13 paras

Les voyageurs transportés par trains de grande vitesse composés de wagons de 1re et de 2me Classe, paieront une surtaxe de 30%. Les enfants jusqu'à l'âge de trois ans, portés sur les genoux des personnes qui les accompagnent, seront transportés gratuitement ; à partir de trois ans jusqu'à sept ans, ils paieront la demi-taxe et occuperont place entière ; toutefois deux enfants ne pourront, dans un compartiment, occuper plus d'une place entière.

TARIF II.

Bagages.

Tout voyageur muni de son billet a droit au transport gratuit de 30 klg. de bagages ; les enfants payant demi-place n'auront droit à la gratuité que pour 20 klg. Prix de transport par fraction indivisible de 10 klg. d'excédants et par kilomètre, 1 para.

Les objets encombrants qui, sous une capacité de 30 décimètres cubes, pèseraient moins de 7 klg. seront assujettis au paiement du double de la taxe indiquée au tarif.

Frais accessoires.

En outre de la taxe du tarif, il sera perçu: 1° par Bulletin de bagage délivré, un droit d'enregistrement de 20 paras, que le poids excède ou non le poids règlementaire de 30 klg.; 2° un droit d'entreposage de 5 paras par jour pour tout colis non enlevé par le destinataire après l'arrivée des trains; 3° un droit de 20 paras par fraction indivisible de 100 klg. pour tout pesage supplémentaire effectué sur la demande de l'expéditeur ou du destinataire, si ce pesage est conforme à la déclaration de la Compagnie.

Tarif III.

Chiens.

Les chiens transportés dans les trains de voyageurs ou les trains mixtes, paieront 4 paras par kilomètre.

Frais accessoires.

En outre de la taxe du tarif, il sera perçu par tête: 1° un droit d'enregistrement de 20 paras; 2° un droit de 5 piastres par jour pour tout chien non réclamé par le destinataire et mis en fourrière par les soins du Concessionnaire, aux risques et périls de qui de droit.

Tarif IV.

Objets expédiés par grande vitesse.

Il sera perçu:

1 para par kilomètre et par fraction indivisible de 10 klg. Tout objet qui, sous un volumede 30 décim. cubes, pèserait moins de 7 klg. sera assujetti au paiement de la double taxe du tarif.

Frais accessoires.

En dehors des tarifs, il sera perçu: 1° un droit d'enregistrement de 20 paras pour chaque expédition; 2° un droit de manutention de 4 paras par fraction indivisible de 10 klg.; 3° un droit d'entreposage de 10 paras par jour, par fraction indivisible de 50 klg. pour tout objet qui, pour quelque cause que ce soit, ne serait pas enlevé dans les 24 heures après l'envoi de la lettre d'avis, par le destinataire, s'il demeure dans la localité d'arrivée, et dans les 36 heures, s'il demeure dans une autre localité; 4° un droit de 20 paras par fraction indivisible de 100 klg. pour tout pesage supplémentaire fait sur la demande de l'expéditeur ou du destinataire, et dont le résultat serait conforme à la déclaration de la Compagnie.

TARIF V.

Paquets, Colis et objets pesant moins de 25 klg. expédiés par grande vitesse.

Pour chaque paquet ou colis, il sera perçu, pour les premiers 30 kilomètres, une taxe de 3 piastres, y compris les droits d'enregistrement et de manutation, et 20 paras pour chaque 15 kilomètres en sus.

Frais accessoires.

En dehors de cette taxe, il sera perçu : 1° un droit d'entrepôt de 10 paras pour les paquets et colis qui, pour quelque cause que ce soit, ne seraient pas enlevés dans les 24 heures suivant l'expédition de l'avis au destinataire, s'il demeure dans la localité d'arrivée, et dans les 36 heures s'il demeure dans une autre localité ; 2° un droit de 20 paras pour tout pesage supplémentaire effectué sur la demande de l'expéditeur ou du destinataire, s'il a pour résultat de justifier la déclaration de la Compagnie.

TARIF VI.

Titres, espèces et objets de valeur.

L'or et l'argent, soit en lingots, soit en monnaies ou travaillés, le mercure, le platine, les bijoux, les pierres précieuses et autres valeurs, ne sont admis à l'expédition que comme marchandises de grande vitesse. La taxe à percevoir est le double de la taxe normale de grande vitesse appliquée au poids effectif, mais au minimum à 25 klg. Le Concessionnaire n'est pas tenu d'assurer les transports de l'espèce. La responsabilité du Concessionnaire, pour les envois non assurés par lui, n'est engagés que dans les limites des dispositions qui règlent les conditions de transport des marchandises de grande vitesse.

TARIF VII.

Voitures et matériel roulant.

Par kilomètre.	Vitesse.	
	Grande.	Petite.
Voitures à deux ou à quatre roues à une banquette	94 Paras	47 Paras
Voitures à quatre roues à deux banquettes	134 Paras	67 Paras

Frais accessoires.

En dehors de la taxe du tarif, il sera pour toute expédition perçu : 1° un droit d'enregistrement de 20 paras ; 2° ses frais de manutention de 10 piastres par véhicule ; 3° un droit de magasinage de 5 piastres par jour et par voiture, ces droits de magasinage ne seront perçus que pour les voitures non réclamées par les destinataires 48 heures après l'arrivée du train. En outre, si les objets se trouvant dans la voiture pèsent plus de 50 klg. il sera perçu pour l'excédent de ces 50 klg. la taxe prévue pour les marchandises de 2me classe transportées à petite vitesse, et ce par fraction indivisible de 50 klg.

TARIF VIII.

Bestiaux.

Par tête et par kilomètre.	Vitesse.	
	Grande.	Petite.
1° Boeufs, Vaches, Taureaux, Buffles, Chameaux, Chevaux et Bêtes de trait .	54 Paras	27 Paras
2° Veaux, ânes et porcs	18 Paras	9 Paras
3° Moutons, brebis et chèvres . . .	8 Paras	4 Paras

Frais accessoires.

En outre du tarif, il sera perçu pour chaque expédition : 1° un droit d'enregistrement de 20 paras ; 2° un droit de manutention de 100 paras par tête de 1re catégorie ; un droit de manutention de 40 paras par tête de 2me catégorie ; 3° un droit de fourrière de 5 piastres par jour pour chaque tête de bétail non enlevé par le destinataire dans les 24 heures et parqué à ses risques et périls, et ce, sans préjudice des frais de fourrage à réclamer en outre.

TARIF IX.

Marchandises transportées à petite vitesse, par tonne et par kilomètre.

1re Classe.

Armes, bois de menuiserie et de teinture et autres bois de valeur, chandelles, boissons spiritueuses, cuivre, cotons, café, colle de poisson, matériel de carrosserie, cuirs, drogues, denrées coloniales, duvet, étoffes, épiceries, fers ouvrés, faïences, fruits, fontes, métaux bruts, ou travaillés, garance, miroiteries, huiles d'olive et autres, herbes, instruments de musique, meubles, objets de librairie, plombs ouvrés, plumes en fer, porcelaines, plantes, fourrures, suifs, soieries, sucre, verres à glace, stéarine, vinaigre, vins, verres de table, carreaux, lainages, livres, thé, tabacs, graines de pavot, tinctoriales, sésames, anis, etc.

35 paras.

2me Classe.

Ardoise, charpentes, bitume, coke, charbon de bois, chanvre, fer brut et fondu, fers en barres et en plaques, toiles, minerais, planches, marbres bruts, madriers, pierres de taille, poissons salés, plomb en saumon, viandes salées, légumes conservés.

27 paras.

3me Classe.

Terre glaise, briques, tuiles, paille, son, bois à brûler, cailloux, riz, céréales, chaux, charbon de terre, cendres, farines, fumiers, pierres de maçonnerie, argile, plâtre, terres à chaux, pavés et autres, sel, sable et légumes frais.

22 paras.

Toutefois, les céréales à transporter par wagons complets sur des distances non inférieures à 900 kilomètres, ne paieront pas plus de 6 paras par tonne et par kilomètre.

La taxe à percevoir sera calculée par fraction indivisible de 50 klg. et pour un parcours qui ne sera pas inférieur à 8 kilomètres.

Frais accessoires.

En dehors du tarif, il sera perçu pour chaque expédition · 1° un droit d'enregistrement de 20 paras; 2° 9 piastres par tonne, c'est-à-dire 18 paras par fraction indivisible de 50 klg. si la manutation est opérée par les soins du Concessionnaire; 3° un droit de magasinage de 10 paras, par jour et par fraction indivisible de 50 klg. pour les marchandises non enlevées dans les 48 heures qui suivront la mise à la poste de la lettre d'avis au destinataire; 4° un droit de 20 paras par fraction indivisible de 100 klg. pour tout pesage supplémentaire opéré sur la demande de l'expéditeur et du destinataire et dont le résultat serait reconnu conforme au premier pesage.

Observations.

Les taxes du présent tarif ne sont pas applicables aux masses indivisibles pesant plus de 3000 klg.; pour toute masse indivisible pesant de 3000 à 5000 klg. le présent tarif sera augmenté de moitié; la Compagnie ne pourra être tenue de

transporter des masses indivisibles pesant plus de 5000 klg.
et nécessitant l'emploi d'un matériel spécial ; si elle prend sur
elle le transport et le factage de masses de ce poids, les frais et
conditions de transport et de factage seront déterminés de gré
à gré par les deux parties.

TARIF X.

Assurances.

Les marchandises assurées paieront les frais supplémentaires
d'assurance suivants :

Marchandises d'une valeur de 500 piastres transportées
à petite vitesse . . . Ps. 1,20.
Marchandises d'une valeur de 500 piastres transportées
à grande vitesse . . Ps. 4
Bagages de voyageurs, voitures, chevaux et autres,
d'une valeur de 1000 Ps. Ps. 2

TARIF XI.

Trains spéciaux ; taxe à percevoir par kilomètre.

Locomotives avec wagons de sûreté	Ps. 15
Wagon salon	Ps. 10
Wagon voyageur	. Ps. 5
Wagon ordinaire .	Ps. 2,20
Pour tout essieu en plus de 2 essieux par wagon	Ps. 2,30
Pour chaque demi-heure d'attente en plus du temps indiqué dans l'itinéraire .	Ps. 460
Minimum à percevoir par kilomètre pour un train spécial . .	Ps. 35
Minimum à percevoir pour tout train spécial	. Ps. 700

Les taxes ci-dessus ne sont pas susceptibles des réductions
prévues au Titre V.

Si la taxe à percevoir des voyageurs, bêtes et bagages transportés ar train spécial est inférieure à la taxe qu'aurait produit
le tarifppar train ordinaire, le Concessionnaire pourra appliquer
le tarif ordinaire. La demande d'un train spécial doit être
faite au moins 24 heures à l'avance.

ARTICLE 22.—Pour les évaluations à faire conformément aux
tarifs spécifiés plus haut et à ceux à intervenir, le para est
considéré comme la quarantième partie de la piastre, et la
piastre comme la centième partie de la Livre Turque.

Toutefois, le Concessionnaire sera tenu d'accepter toutes les
monnaies avant cours dans l'Empire, au change fixé par le
Trésor.

ARTICLE 23.—Tous bestiaux, marchandises, objets et céréales non spécifés dans les articles précédents seront assimilés, pour la perception de la taxe, à la classe avec laquelle ils ont le plus de rapport.

ARTICLE 24.—Tous les tarifs, qu'ils soient généraux, spéciaux ou proportionnels ou différentiels, sont applicables à tous les voyageurs et expéditeurs sans distinction. En outre, ces tarifs, avant d'être appliqués, seront soumis à l'approbation du Gouvernement Impérial. En cas d'urgence, ces tarifs pourront être appliqués, en les notifiant au Commissaire Impérial, avant l'approbation par le Gouvernement.

ARTICLE 25.—Il est formellement interdit au Concessionnaire de passer tout traité particulier ayant pour objet d'accorder des réductions des prix indiqués dans les tarifs. Toutefois, cette interdiction ne s'applique pas aux traités à passer avec le Gouvernement Impérial. Les pauvres et indigents seront, sur pièces justificatives délivrées par les Autorités locales, transportés à moitié du Tarif en vigueur.

TITRE V.

STIPULATIONS RELATIVES À DIVERS SERVICES.

ARTICLE 26.—En temps de paix comme en temps de guerre, le Concessionnaire mettra à la disposition du Gouvernement Impérial, sur la réquisition écrite des Autorités militaires, toutes les voitures et autres matériels et moyens de transports toutes les fois que le Gouvernement aura à expédier par le Chemin de fer, soit isolément soit en corps, des militaires appartenant à l'armée de terre, à la flotte, à la police et à la gendarmerie, ainsi que des zaptiés et volontaires, leurs bagages et leurs bêtes, toute sorte de matériel, munitions de guerre et approvisionnements; au besoin le Gouvernement pourra même, alors, prendre en main la direction de la ligne avec son matériel et son personnel. Ces expéditions seront faites, tant en temps de paix qu'en temps de guerre, qu'elles soient effectuées par le Concessionnaire ou par le Gouvernement occupant la ligne, au tiers du tarif sauf en ce qui concerne les officiers et les soldats, qui seront transportés au quart du tarif; de même, le matériel et autres objets expédiés par le Gouvernement, par les trains de voyageurs, seront également transportés au tiers du tarif, les officiers et soldats au quart du tarif. Il est entendu que pour les transports militaires les soldats, en dehors des objets qu'ils porteront avec aux et dans le wagon ou ils se trouverent, auront droit au transport gratuit de 30 kilogrammes de bagages par homme. Ces bagages pourront être composés des articles suivants.

Fusils, havresacs, gibernes sacs à pain, bidons, vêtements, chaussures, batterie de cuisine, matériel d'ambulance, matériel d'armurier, de maréchal ferrant, de pansement pour les chevaux, instruments de chirurgie, médicaments, tentes, pelles, pioches, haches, instruments de musique, ainsi que les vivres nécessaires aux hommes pendant leur voyage en chemin de fer.

Toutefois, dans le cas où le Gouvernement Impérial en ferait la demande, le Concessionnaire sera tenu de passer avec le Ministère de la guerre une Convention spéciale pour les transports et expéditions militaires, conformément aux règles établies à cet égard dans les autres pays.

ARTICLE 27.—Le Gouvernement jouira aussi d'une réduction au tiers du tarif pour le transport des détenus et condamnés, ainsi que de leurs gardiens; à cet effet, le Concessionnaire sera tenu de mettre à sa disposition lorsqu'il le requerra, le nombre de compartiments nécessaires dans les voitures de deuxième ou troisième classe, des trains ordinaires.

ARTICLE 28.—Les fonctionnaires ou agents du Gouvernement chargés de l'inspection ou contrôle et de la surveillance de la construction et de l'exploitation du chemin de fer, ainsi que les employés de l'Administration des Télégraphes et des Contributions Indirectes seront transportés gratuitement dans les voitures de la Compagnie. Le matériel télégraphique des lignes de l'État sera transporté avec une réduction de 20% sur le tarif.

ARTICLE 29.—La Compagnie est tenue d'effectuer gratuitement, dans les trains ordinaires des voyageurs, le transport des valises postales plombées accompagnées des agents nécessaires au service; à cet effet, elle réservera, dans chaque train de voyageurs, un ou plusieurs compartiments de voitures de 2me classe, jusqu'à concurrence d'une voiture entière, suivant qu'elle en sera requise par le Gouvernement.

Dans le cas où l'Administration Impériale des Postes ferait construire un wagon spécial approprié au transport de la poste et le livrerait à la Compagnie, la Compagnie sera tenue de l'atteler à ses trains et de le transporter gratuitement.

Le Concessionnaire ne pourra accepter aucun service postal étranger sans une autorisation préalable du Gouvernement.

ARTICLE 30.—Le Concessionnaire est obligé de faire circuler, journellement, au moins un train mixte dans chaque sens.

En dehors de ce train mixte, la Société établira entre Haidar-Pacha et Alep et vice-versa, au moins un train express direct par semaine.

-- Au moins toutes les deux semaines, ce train express direct sera prolongé jusqu'au Golfe Persique et vice-versa.

La vitesse moyenne de ce train sur le réseau faisant l'objet de la présente convention, ne sera pas inférieure à 45 kilomètres à l'heure, arrêts compris, et ce pendant les cinq premières années comptées à partir de la mise en exploitation de la ligne principale toute entière.

Après l'expiration des dites cinq années, la vitesse moyenne, arrêts compris, de ce train direct, ne sera pas inférieure à 60 kilomètres.

La Société établira en autre, si l'importance du trafic en démontre la nécessité, des trains directs comprenant des voitures de I. et II. Classes, dont la vitesse moyenne entre Haidar-Pacha et le Golfe Persique et vice-versa, ne sera pas inférieure à 40 kilomètres à l'heure.

Le présent Cahier des Charges a été conformément à l'Iradé promulgué par Sa Majesté Impériale le Sultan fait en double, signé et échangé à

Constantinople, le $\dfrac{\text{20 Février 1318.}}{\text{5 Mars 1903.}}$

Certifié conforme à l'original.
Le Directeur du Bureau de Traduction
du Ministère du Commerce et des Travaux Publics.

(s.) MOUHIB.

(s.) ARTHUR GWINNER.
(s.) KURT ZANDER.　　　　(s.) ZIHNI.
(s.) HUGUENIN.

2 A

STATUTS.

La soussignée Société du Chemin de fer Ottoman d'Anatolie à Constantinople:

En vue de réaliser la Concession accordée à la Société du Chemin de fer Ottoman d'Anatolie susnommée, par Convention en date du 20 Février/5 Mars 1903 (1318) pour la construction et l'exploitation de la ligne de Koniah à Bassorah et embranchements, ainsi que toutes les dépendances dudit Chemin de fer accordé par le Gouvernement Impérial Ottoman et des engagements qu'elle comporte, forme une Société Anonyme Ottomane qui sera soumise aux clauses et conditions suivantes:

TITRE I.

FORMATION ET OBJET DE LA SOCIÉTÉ, DÉNOMINATION, SIÈGE.

ARTICLE 1.—Il est formé entre la soussignée et tous les propriétaires des actions ci-après créées, une Société Anonyme Ottomane ayant pour objet de construire, administrer et exploiter les lignes du chemin de fer indiquées dans la Convention et Cahier des Charges échangés en date du 20 Février/ 5 Mars 1903 (1318) entre le Gouvernement Impérial Ottoman et la Société du Chemin de fer Ottoman d'Anatolie, conformément aux stipulations de la dite Convention et Cahier des Charges. La Société pourra aussi s'intéresser par achat de titres à des Sociétés nouvelles ou déjà existantes de construction et d'exploitation de chemins de fer dans l'Empire Ottoman.

ARTICLE 2.—La Société prend la dénomination de:

Société Impériale Ottomane du Chemin de fer de Bagdad et sera soumise aux lois et règlements de l'Empire en qualité de Société Ottomane.

ARTICLE 3.—La Société a son siège à Constantinople, et pourra établir des succursales dans toute autre ville de l'Empire Ottoman ou à l'étranger.

ARTICLE 4.—La durée de la Société est fixée à 99 années, sauf le cas de dissolution anticipée ou de prorogation. Cette durée sera prolongée conformément à l'Art. 2 de la Convention en date du 20 Février/5 Mars 1903 (1318).

TITRE II.

APPORT ET TRANSFERT DE LA CONCESSION À LA SOCIÉTÉ.

ARTICLE 5.—La Société du Chemin de fer Ottoman d'Anatolie apporte à la nouvelle Société, la concession qui lui a été octroyée par le Gouvernement Impérial Ottoman, avec tous les droits, privilèges t avantages y attachés ou en dérivant, et la nouvelle Société devient titulaire et propriétaire de la dite Concession et se trouve substituée à tous les droits et obligations du Concessionnaire. Toutefois, la Société du Chemin de fer Ottoman d'Anatolie garde pour son propre compte exclusif les droits et obligations qui ne regardent que les anciennes lignes et notamment ceux de ces droits et obligations qui découlent des Articles 2, 33 et 37 de la Convention du 20 Février/ 5 Mars 1903 (1318). Remise sera faite par la Société du Chemin de fer Ottoman d'Anatolie à la nouvelle Société des Firman, Conventions, actes et documents quelconques concernant la Concession.

ARTICLE 6.—Le fonds social se compose du capital-actions et des obligations qui seront émises ultérieurement selon les besoins résultant de l'application des clauses et conditions des actes de concession. Le capital-actions initial de la Société est de Francs: 15,000,000.—, soit Mark: 12,240,000.—, soit Livres Sterling: 600,000.— divisé en 30,000 Actions au montant nominal de Francs: 500.—, soit Mark: 408.—, soit Livres Sterling: 20.—, chacune. Le capital-actions pourra être augmenté de 50% par l'Assemblée Générale.

La Société du Chemin de fer Ottoman d'Anatolie souscrira 10% du capital-actions; ces actions seront inaliénables et la Société du Chemin de fer Ottoman d'Anatolie ne pourra pas s'en dessaisir sans le consentement du Gouvernement Impérial Ottoman.

Le Gouvernement Impérial Ottoman aura aussi le droit de souscrire jusqu'à concurrence de 10% du capital-actions.

ARTICLE 7.—La Société ne sera définitivement constituée qu'après la souscription de la totalité du capital et le versement du premier dixième de ce capital.

Des certificats provisoires constatant les versements seront remis aux souscripteurs pour être échangés contre des titres définitifs après le versement de la moitié du capital. Toutefois les actions souscrites par la Société du Chemin de fer Ottoman d'Anatolie, resteront inscrites au nom de cette Société.

Les actions seront libellées d'une part en turc et de l'autre en allemand, en français et en anglais.

Les 90% restants seront appelés au fur et à mesure des besoins de la Société, conformément aux décisions du Conseil d'Administration et après avis inséré, trente jours d'avance au moins, dans plusieurs journaux officiels ou non, se publiant à Constantinople ou dans d'autres pays.

Article 8.—Les titres sont nominatifs jusqu'au paiement de la moitié du montant des actions; leur négociation ne peut avoir lieu avant le versement du premier dixième. La négociation s'opère par un transfert sur les registres de la Société, signé par le Concessionnaire et le cédant et l'un des administrateurs; mention de ce transfert est faite sur le titre.

Après leur libération de moitié les actions seront au porteur.

Article 9.—Toute action est indivisible à l'égard de la Société qui n'en reconnaît aucun fractionnement.

Les héritiérs ou ayants cause d'un actionnaire ne peuvent, pour quelque motif que ce soit, provoquer l'apposition des scellés sur les biens et valeurs de la Société, ui s'immiscer en aucune manière dans son administration; ils doivent, pour l'exercice de leurs droits, s'en rapporter aux inventaires sociaux et aux délibérations de l'Assemblée Générale.

Article 10.—Tout versement en retard porte intérêt de plein droit en faveur de la Société à raison de 6% per an, à compter du jour de l'exigibilité et sans aucune mise en demeure.

Article 11.—A défaut de paiement des versements à leurs échéances la Société poursuit les débiteurs et peut faire vendre les actions en retard.

A cet effet, les numéros de ces actions sont publiés comme défaillants par voie des journaux, et quinze jours après cette publication, il est procédé à la vente des actions pour le compte et aux risques et périls du retardataire, sans aucune mise en demeure ni formalité judiciaire; cette vente a lieu dans les bourses de Constantinople et de Berlin et dans d'autres bourses, si les actions sont cotées, et dans le cas contraire aux enchères publiques.

Les titres ainsi vendus deviennent nuls de plein droit; il en est délivré aux acquéreurs de nouveaux sous les mêmes numéros.

Le prix la de vente s'impute dans les termes de droit sur ce qui est dû à la Société par l'actionnaire exproprié, qui reste passible, de la différence ou profite de l'excédent.

TITRE III.

ADMINISTRATION DE LA SOCIÉTÉ.

ARTICLE 12.—La Société est administrée par un Conseil d'Administration composé d'au moins 11 Membres. Au moins trois Membres du Conseil d'Administration seront nommés par la Société du Chemin de fer Ottoman d'Anatolie qui exercera ce droit par son Conseil d'Administration. Les autres Administrateurs seront nommés par l'Assemblée Générale. Trois Membres du Conseil d'Administration seront sujets Ottomans.

Le Conseil d'Administration se réunit à Constantinople.

ARTICLE 13.—La durée des fonctions des membres du Conseil d'Administration est de trois ans; la première année sera calculée à partir de la constitution de la Société jusqu'à la clôture de l'Assemblée Générale Ordinaire qui suivra l'expiration du premier exercice, et les années suivantes seront calculées jusqu'à la clôture de l'Assemblée Générale Ordinaire subséquente à l'expiration de l'exercice correspondant. Le Conseil se renouvelle chaque année par la sortie d'un tiers de ses membres. Les membres sortants sont désignés par le sort pour les deux premières années et ensuite par voie d'ancienneté. Dans le cas où parmi les membres sortants il se trouverait des personnes nommées par la Société du Chemin de fer Ottoman d'Anatolie celle-ci aura à nommer leurs remplaçants.

Les membres sortants peuvent toujours être réélus.

ARTICLE 14.—Le Conseil d'Administration se réunit aussi souvent que l'intérêt de la Société l'exige et au moins une fois par mois. La présence de plus de la moitié des membres au moins est nécessaire pour la validité des délibérations.

Les délibérations sont prises à la majorité des voix des membres présents. En cas de partage la proposition est renvoyée au Conseil suivant et alors, en cas de nouveau partage, elle est rejetée.

ARTICLE 15.—Les délibérations sont constatées par des procesverbaux transcrits sur un registre spécial et signés par les Administrateurs qui y ont pris part. Les copies ou extraits de ces délibérations pour faire foi, doivent être signés par le Président du Conseil ou celui qui le remplace.

ARTICLE 16.—Chaque Administrateur doit être propriétaire de dix actions inaliénables pendant la durée de ses fonctions;

elles seront frappées d'un timbre indiquant l'inaliénabilité et déposées dans la Caisse Sociale.

ARTICLE 17.—En cas de vacance par décès, démission ou autre cause, le Conseil pourvoit provisoirement au remplacement jusqu'à la prochaine Assemblée Générale qui procède à l'élection définitive.

ARTICLE 18.—Chaque année le Conseil nomme parmi ses membres un Président et un ou plusieurs Vice-Présidents.

En cas d'absence du Président et des Vice-Présidents, le Conseil désigne celui de ses Membres qui doit remplir les fonctions de Président.

ARTICLE 19.—Les Administrateurs qui résident à l'Étranger et ceux qui seront accidentellement absents, peuvent se faire représenter dans les délibérations par un de leurs Collègues, sans que celui-ci puisse réunir plus de trois votes y compris le sien.

ARTICLE 20.—Le Conseil a les pouvoirs les plus étendus pour l'administration des biens et affaires de la Société ; il peut même transiger et compromettre, il arrête les comptes qui doivent être soumis à l'Assemblée Générale et propose les répartitions de dividendes.

Le Président du Conseil d'Administration représente, soit personnellement, soit par un mandataire, la Société en justice tant en demandant qu'en défendant.

ARTICLE 21.—Le Conseil peut déléguer tout ou partie de ses pouvoirs à un ou plusieurs de ses membres, par un mandat spécial, pour les objets déterminés ou pour un temps déterminé.

Il peut aussi les déléguer, pour l'expédition des affaires courantes, à une ou plusieurs personnes prises en dehors de son sein.

ARTICLE 22.—Les Administrateurs reçoivent des jetons de présence dont la valeur est fixée par l'Assemblée Générale, indépendamment de la quote-part qui leur est allouée dans les bénéfices nets.

TITRE IV.

ASSEMBLÉE GÉNÉRALE.

ARTICLE 23.—L'Assemblée Générale régulièrement constituée représente l'universalité des actionnaires.

ARTICLE 24.—Il est tenu une Assemblée Générale Ordinaire chaque année dans le courant des six premiers mois. Le lieu de la réunion est fixé par le Conseil d'Administration.

En outre l'Assemblée Générale peut être convoquée extraordinairement en cas de besoin par le Conseil d'Administration.

ARTICLE 25.—L'Assemblée Générale se compose des actionnaires qui possèdent, soit à titre de propriétaire, soit à titre de mandataire, trente actions au moins.

Tout Membre de l'Assemblée Générale a droit à autant de votes qu'il possède comme propriétaire ou mandataire, de fois trente actions, mais sans qu'il puisse jamais réunir plus de cent voix.

ARTICLE 26.—Les convocations doivent être faites par un avis annoncé par la voie de la presse, un mois au moins avant l'époque de la réunion, ainsi qu'il est indiqué à l'Art. 7.

ARTICLE 27.—L'Assemblée est régulièrement constituée lorsque les membres présents ou représentés réunissent le quart du fonds social.

Pour vérifier si le quart du fonds social est représenté, tous les actionnaires ayant droit de prendre part à l'Assemblée sont invités par les avis de convocation à déposer leurs titres dans les dix jours aux lieux indiqués par le Conseil.

Si à la première réunion le nombre d'actions représentées n'est pas suffisant, une nouvelle Assemblée est convoquée, et elle délibère valablament quelle que soit la portion du capital représentée par les actionnaires présents, mais seulement sur l'ordre du jour de la première convocation.

Cette nouvelle réunion doit avoir lieu à quinze jours au moins et un mois au plus d'intervalle et les convocations peuvent n'être faites que vingt jours à l'avance.

ARTICLE 28.—L'Assemblée Générale est présidée par le Président du Conseil ou à son défaut par un Administrateur désigné par le Conseil.

Deux des plus forts actionnaires présents remplissent les functions de scrutateurs.

Le Bureau désigne le secrétaire.

ARTICLE 29.—Les délibérations sont prises à la majorité des voix.

L'ordre du jour est arrêté par le Conseil.

Il n'y est porté que les propositions émanant du Conseil et celles qui lui auront été communiquées vingt jours au moins avant la réunion avec la signature d'actionnaires représentant au moins 10% du capital.

Il ne peut être mis en délibération que les objets portés à l'ordre du jour.

ARTICLE 30.—L'Assemblée Générale désignera, soit parmi les actionnaires, soit parmi les personnes étrangères à la Société, un ou plusieurs commissaires chargés de la vérification des comptes.

ARTICLE 31.—L'Assemblée Générale annuelle entend le rapport que le Conseil doit lui représenter chaque année sur la situation des affaires de la Société, et celui des commissaires sur les comptes.

Elle discute, approuve ou rejette les comptes.

Elle fixe le Dividende.

Elle nomme les Administrateurs à remplacer.

Elle délibère et statue souverainement sur tous les intérêts de la Société et confère au Conseil d'Administration tous les pouvoirs supplémentaires qui seraient reconnus utiles.

L'Assemblée ne peut décider l'augmentation du capital qu'avec une majorité réunissant les deux tiers au moins des actionnaires présents ou représentés.

ARTICLE 32.—Les délibérations de l'Assemblée Générale sont constatées par des procès-verbaux inscrits sur un registre spécial et signés par les membres du Bureau.

Une feuille de présence contenant les noms et domiciles des actionnaires membres de l'Assemblée et le nombre d'actions dont chacun est porteur, est signée par les membres présents et annexée au procès-verbal pour être communiquée à tout ayant droit.

ARTICLE 33.—Les copies ou extraits des délibérations, pour faire foi, doivent être signés par le Président du Conseil ou celui qui le remplace.

ARTICLE 34.—Les décisions de l'Assemblée Générale, prises en conformité des présents Statuts, sont obligatoires même pour les actionnaires absents ou dissidents.

TITRE V.

INVENTAIRES ET COMPTES ANNUELS.

ARTICLE 35.—L'année sociale commence le 1ᵉʳ Janvier et finit le 31 Décembre.

Par exception le 1ᵉʳ Exercice comprendra le temps écoulé entre la constitution définitive de la Société et le 31 Décembre suivant.

A la fin de chaque année sociale il est dressé par les soins du Conseil un inventaire général de l'actif et du passif.

Cet inventaire ainsi que le bilan et les comptes sont mis à la disposition des commissaires 40 jours avant l'Assemblée Générale annuelle. Ils sont ensuite présentés à l'Assemblée.

Tout actionnaire ayant droit de prendre part à l'Assemblée peut en prendre communication.

TITRE VI.

PARTAGE DES BÉNÉFICES ET AMORTISSEMENT.

ARTICLE 36.—Sur les bénéfices nets disponibles de chaque exercice ainsi qu'ils résulteront des bilans établis par le Conseil d'Administration, on prélèvera :

1°) 10% pour le Fonds de Réserve, jusqu'à ce que celui-ci ait atteint le quart du capital nominal de la Société.

2°) le surplus sera employé pour payer aux Actionnaires un premier dividende jusqu'à concurrence de 5% d'intérêts sur le montant versé des actions.

3°) de l'excédent éventuel les Administrateurs recevront 10% à titre de tantième et les Actionnaires auront droit au solde de 90% qui sera réparti à titre de dividende à moins que l'Assemblée Générale, sur la proposition du Conseil d'Administration, ne décide l'emploi d'une part de la somme disponible à la création de réserves extraordinaires.

ARTICLE 37.—L'Assemblée Générale pourra prélever chaque année un tant pour cent sur les bénéfices nets pour amortir un nombre déterminé d'actions à échoir par voie de tirage au sort. Les actions amorties continueront à jouir du dividende, mais n'auront pas droit à l'intérêt.

TITRE VII.

FONDS DE RÉSERVE.

ARTICLE 38.—Le Fonds de réserve se compose de l'accumulation des sommes prélevées sur les bénéfices annuels, en conformité de l'Article 36.

Il est destiné à faire face aux dépenses extraordinaires ou imprévues.

ARTICLE 39.—En cas d'insuffisance des produits d'une année pour donner un intérêt ou dividende de 5% par action, la différence peut être prélevée sur le fonds de réserve.

ARTICLE 40.—A l'expiration de la Société et après la liquidation de ses engagements le fonds de réserve sera partagé entre toutes les actions.

TITRE VIII.

PROROGATION, DISSOLUTION, LIQUIDATION.

ARTICLE 41.—Le Conseil d'Administration peut, à toute époque et pour quelque cause que ce soit, proposer à l'Assemblée Générale convoquée à cet effet, la prorogation, la dissolution et la liquidation de la Société, ainsi que tout projet de fusion avec d'autres Sociétés. Toutefois la prorogation ou la fusion, s'il y à lieu, ne pourra se faire qu'avec l'autorisation du Gouvernement Impérial.

ARTICLE 42.—En cas de perte des trois quarts du fonds social, les Administrateurs convoquent l'Assemblée Générale à l'effet de statuer sur la question de savoir s'il y à lieu de prononcer la dissolution de la Société ou de continuer ses opérations.

ARTICLE 43.—A l'expiration de la Société ou en cas de dissolution anticipée, l'Assemblée Générale convoquée règle le mode de liquidation et nomme un ou plusieurs liquidateurs.

Pendant la liquidation, les pouvoirs de l'Assemblée Générale continuent comme pendant l'existence de la Société.

Les liquidateurs peuvent, en vertu d'une délibération de cette Assemblée et avec l'autorisation du Gouvernement Impérial, faire le transfert à toute Société ou à tout particulier des droits, actions et obligations de la Société dissoute.

ARTICLE 44. — Les Assemblées Générales extraordinaires, appelées à statuer sur les objets indiqués au présent titre, ne seront valablement constituées que si elles réunissent un nombre d'actions représentant la moitié au moins du capital social.

Les présents Statuts ont été dressés en conformité de l'Iradé Impérial transmis par Tezkéré Grand-Véziriel en date du 5 Zilhadjé 1320 et 19 Février 1318.

Constantinople, le $\dfrac{20 \text{ Février } 1318.}{5 \text{ Mars } 1903.}$

Certifié conforme à l'original.
Le Directeur du Bureau de Traduction
du Ministère du Commerce et des Travaux Publics.

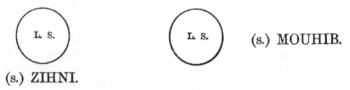

(s.) ZIHNI.

(s.) MOUHIB.

(s.) ARTHUR GWINNER.
(s.) KURT ZANDER.
(s.) HUGUENIN.

(s.) ZIHNI.

CONVENTION ADDITIONNELLE

FAISANT SUITE À LA CONVENTION DU 20 FÉVRIER 1318/ 5 MARS 1903 DU CHEMIN DE FER DE BAGDAD POUR LA CONSTRUCTION DE LA LIGNE DE BAGDAD, À PARTIR DE LA STATION DE BOULGOURLOU JUSQU'À LA LOCALITÉ DITE HÉLIF, PRÈS DE MARDINE, ET D'UN EMBRANCHEMENT DE TEL-HABESCH À ALEP.

Le Gouvernement Impérial a décidé de prolonger la ligne de Bagdad depuis Boulgourlou jusqu'à la localité dite Hélif, située aux abords de Mardine, et de construire un embranchement de Tel-Habesch à Alep. La ' longueur de cette ligne et de l'embranchement est d'environ 840 kilomètres.

L'excédent des revenus concédés à la Dette Publique ayant

été affecté au prolongement de la ligne de Bagdad, la garantie pour ces 840 kilomètres de ligne sera payée sur les excédents des Revenus Concédés à la Dette Publique, à raison de 11,000 Frs. par kilomètre, en conformité de l'Art. 35 de la Convention de Bagdad. Etant entendu que si l'excédent en question n'est pas suffisant pour la garantie de ces 840 kilomètres, l'insuffisance qui serait constatée à la fin d'une année sera comblée par les premières recettes des aghnams des vilayets de Koniah et d'Adana afférentes à l'année suivante, ainsi que par les premières recettes des aghnams du vilayet d'Alep, après déduction de la part affectée au paiement de l'indemnité de guerre.

Quant aux frais d'exploitation, ils seront garantis en premier lieu par les recettes brutes de ces 840 kilomètres, étant entendu que si les recettes brutes de cette ligne étaient inférieures au chiffre de 4500 Frs. par kilomètre stipulé à l'Art. 35 de la Convention de Bagdad, la différence qui serait constatée à la fin de l'année sera réglée, elle aussi, sur l'excédent des revenus concédés à la Dette Publique affecté à la garantie de la ligne, si ledit excédent y suffit ; et, dans le cas contraire, la différence sera, de même que l'insuffisance de la garantie, comblée par les premières recettes des aghnams des trois vilayets en question de l'année suivante.

Bien que, suivant les stipulations de l'Article 3 de la Convention du 20 Février 1318/5 Mars 1903, les plans et projets des sections à construire doivent être présentés au Ministère du Commerce et des Travaux Publics dans un délai de huit mois à partir de la date à laquelle commencera le délai de concession de chaque section, après mise à exécution des stipulations de l'article 35 afférentes à ladite section, et que les plans et projets en question doivent être examinés et approuvés par ledit Ministère dans un délai de trois mois à partir de leur présentation, comme il ne serait pas possible de compléter les études dans le délai de huit mois prévu à l'article 3, il a été décidé que les plans et projets de la partie comprise entre Boulgourlou-Tel-Habesch et Alep seront présentés au Ministère du Commerce et des Travaux Publics dans un délai d'un an, compté à partir de la date de l'échange de la présente Convention Additionnelle, que les plans et projets de la partie comprise entre Tel-Habesch et Hélif seront présentés dans un délai de trois ans, toujours compté à partir de la même date; que le délai pour l'approbation des plans et projets par ledit Ministère sera porté à quatre mois ; et que la construction de ces 840 kilomètres de ligne sera achevée dans un délai de huit ans compté à partir de la date de l'échange de la présente Convention Additionnelle.

Le service des Obligations à émettre en conformité de l'Art. 35 de la Convention du chemin de fer de Bagdad pour l'exécution des 840 kilomètres de ligne susmentionnés, sera réglé par une Convention spéciale simultanément avec la présente Convention Additionnelle.

La présente Convention additionnelle a, conformément à l'Iradé Impérial promulgué par Sa Majesté Impériale le Sultan, été faite en double, signée et échangée à Constantinople

le 3 Djémazi-ul-Ewel 1326.
le 20 Mai 1324 (2 Juin 1908).

Certifié conforme à l'original.
Le Chef du Bureau de Traduction
du Ministère du Commerce et des Travaux Publics.

(s.) BOGHOS.

Société Impériale Ottomane du chemin
de fer de Bagdad,

(s.) ED. HUGUENIN,
Administrateur-Délégué.

Sceau du Ministère du Commerce
et des Travaux Publics,

(s.) ZIHNI.

(s.) HELFFERICH,
Administrateur.

PRINTED BY WILLIAM BLACKWOOD AND SONS

THE

MARCHES OF HINDUSTAN.

The Record of a Journey in Thibet, Trans-Himalayan India, Chinese Turkestan, Russian Turkestan, and Persia.

Published by Messrs Wm. Blackwood & Sons at 21s. net.

Japan Chronicle.—".......the book is written in a style that will captivate the attention of all, both old and young. Mr Fraser is gifted with an easy style, coupled with a pawky Scotch humour, which enables him to clothe the varied incidents abounding in his book with that personal interest excited by the *vivâ voce* narration of a friend, and the reader almost imagines that he is accompanying the writer through all his vicissitudes and experiencing his compensations, so vivid is the series of pictures conjured up in the mind."

Liverpool Courier.—".......emphasises very entertainingly and shrewdly the human aspect......a very valuable and sprightly record of travel."

Liverpool Daily Post.—"Mr Fraser describes vividly and with charming unconventionality what he saw. Indeed, for a combination of amusing observation, graphic description, and useful information, this charming book of travel has few, if any, rivals."

Manchester Courier.—".......this book is a striking contribution to public knowledge. Mr Fraser's general style of writing is cheery and breezy—at times too expressively breezy—while here and there it assumes a poetry and dignity not unsuitable to the sublimity of those magnificent natural features through which his wanderings led him."

Manchester Guardian.—".......able, observant, well-informed, and humorous."

Newcastle Chronicle.—Mr Fraser, in this bulky volume, places the general reader under a debt of gratitude for the lucidity and conciseness with which he has laid bare the weakness and strength of our military position in India."

Pall Mall Gazette.—"This interesting work throws valuable light upon problems of particular interest at the present moment."

Pioneer.—"Mr Fraser writes modestly, and though we may not agree with all his conclusions, there is every justification for congratulating him on the production of a very readable volume."

Scotsman.—"One of the best books of travel that have appeared for a long time....... Mr Fraser is a delightful narrator, and his book is rich in amusing incidents and shrewd observations, and is enlivened by an increasing flow of genial and humorous comment. The romance and adventure of mountaineering and exploration and lonely wandering among half-civilised peoples have rarely been better illustrated."

Standard.—".......an imposing as well as a readable volume."

Somerset Guardian.—"The author is frankly personal, and tells of what he himself saw, not a technical report of the country, and the result is eminently satisfactory."

Sydney Morning Herald.—".......a simple and effective style, with shrewd and keen observation of economic and political problems."

The Spectator.—".......an uncommonly entertaining book of travels. Mr Fraser...... has the true traveller's spirit. We recommend Mr Fraser's account of his sixty-three hours' task recrossing the Himalaya to those who wish a spirited narrative of mountain adventure. Near the summit of the pass (Karakorum) a murder was committed some years ago, and the story of how the criminal was hunted down over all Central Asia is as good a piece of detective romance as we have read for some time. Not every good expedition produces a good book, but in this case letters are justified of their son. Let us add that the book is printed in a way that is a credit to English publishing."

The Times.—".......a fine journey, and its incidents are admirably recounted. Mr Fraser has a good natural turn for vivid description, and writes without effort and often with considerable grace."

Times of India.—"Mr Fraser writes with freshness, vigour, and humour. It is precisely the every-day incidents of travel, when set forth with so much charm and vividness, which shed the clearest light upon the conditions of countries which some of us may never see."

Tribune.—"Mr Fraser, who writes with lively humour, but observes and thinks to serious purpose, is a witness of considerable value with regard to matters on India's borders."

Westminster Gazette.—"Mr Fraser always writes with spirit and confidence, and there is no doubt about his gifts as a resolute traveller and journalist. How well he can describe scenery that appeals to him is shown in the chapter, vivid and even beautiful, in a glacier near the Saser Pass, by the old road to Yarkand. The glacier has been described by masters of English and men of powerful intellect as well as imagination—such as Tyndall; but we do not know any writer who brings out the personality of the glacier as Mr Fraser does in this chapter. Mr Fraser's is the common-sense view (of the Anglo-Russian Agreement), but it also happens to be the view of an expert and acute and bold observer."

Yorkshire Post.—".......a most attractive book. Mr Fraser has humour and keen observation, and the subjects of a number of his photographs suggest that they were not averse from laughing with the genial alien who levelled his camera at them."

Lightning Source UK Ltd.
Milton Keynes UK
UKOW06f1946061215

264237UK00005B/93/P